ECCLESIAL IDENTITIES IN
A MULTI-FAITH CONTEXT

American Society of Missiology Monograph Series

Series Editor, James R. Krabill

THE ASM MONOGRAPH SERIES provides a forum for publishing quality dissertations and studies in the field of missiology. Collaborating with Pickwick Publications—a division of Wipf and Stock Publishers of Eugene, Oregon—the American Society of Missiology selects high quality dissertations and other monographic studies that offer research materials in mission studies for scholars, mission and church leaders, and the academic community at large. The ASM seeks scholarly work for publication in the Series that throws light on issues confronting Christian world mission in its cultural, social, historical, biblical, and theological dimensions.

Missiology is an academic field that brings together scholars whose professional training ranges from doctoral-level preparation in areas such as scripture, history and sociology of religions, anthropology, theology, international relations, interreligious interchange, mission history, inculturation, and church law. The American Society of Missiology, which sponsors this series, is an ecumenical body drawing members from Independent and Ecumenical Protestant, Catholic, Orthodox, and other traditions. Members of the ASM are united by their commitment to reflect on and do scholarly work relating to both mission history and the present-day mission of the church. The ASM Monograph Series aims to publish works of exceptional merit on specialized topics, with particular attention given to work by younger scholars, the dissemination and publication of which is difficult under the economic pressures of standard publishing models.

Persons seeking information about the ASM or the guidelines for having their dissertations considered for publication in the ASM Monograph Series should consult the Society's website—www.asmweb.org.

Members of the ASM Monograph Committe who approved this book are:
Craig Ott, Trinity Evangelical Divinity School
Roger Schroeder, Catholic Theological Union
Gary Simpson, Luther Seminary

RECENTLY PUBLISHED IN THE ASM MONOGRAPH SERIES

Kim Marie Lamberty, *Eyes from the Outside: Christian Mission in Zones of Violent Conflict*

Runchana P. Suksod-Barger, *Religious Influences in Thai Female Education (1889–1931)*

Ecclesial Identities
in a Multi-faith Context

Jesus Truth-Gatherings (Yeshu Satsangs)
among Hindus and Sikhs in Northwest India

DARREN TODD DUERKSEN

Foreword by
WILLIAM A. DYRNESS

American Society of Missiology Monograph
Series vol. 22

☙PICKWICK *Publications* · Eugene, Oregon

ECCLESIAL INDENTITIES IN A MULTI-FAITH CONTEXT
Jesus Truth-Gatherings (*Yeshu Satsangs*) among Hindus and Sikhs in Northwest India

America Society of Missiology Monograph Series 22

Pickwick Publications
An Imprint of Wipf and Stock Publishers
199 W. 8th Ave., Suite 3
Eugene, OR 97401

www.wipfandstock.com

ISBN 13: 978–1–62564–655–2

Cataloging-in-Publication data:

Duerksen, Darren Todd

    Ecclesial identities in a multi-faith context : Jesus truth-gatherings (*Yeshu satsangs*) among Hindus and Sikhs in northwest India / Darren Todd Duerksen.

    xxiv + 292 p. ; 23 cm. —Includes bibliographical references and index.

    America Society of Missiology Monograph Series 22

    ISBN 13: 978–1–62564–655–2

1. India, Northwest—Religion. 2. Christianity—India, Northwest. 3. Hindus—India, Northwest. 4. Sikhs—India, Northwest. I. Title. II. Series.

BR1155 D89 2015

Manufactured in the U.S.A.   01/12/2015

To Shahna

Contents

PART I: FOUNDATIONS OF THE STUDY

PART II: THE FORMATION AND MARKERS OF ECCLESIAL IDENTITIES OF *YESHU SATSANGS*

Tables

Figures

Maps

Foreword

WILLIAM A. DYRNESS

ONE OF THE MAJOR challenges facing the Christian Church, especially in Asia, is the inescapable presence of multiple religious traditions. While this situation is not new, recent developments have given it a fresh urgency. On the one hand newly aroused strains of radical Hinduism and Islam (and, most recently, even Buddhism), throughout Asia, have begun to pose an existential threat to Christians. On the other hand various insider movements and notions of multi-religious belonging have forced a rethinking of relationships between Christianity and these faith traditions.

Among the questions this situation poses, theologically, is the nature of the Church. This question has recently become especially contentious—partisans range from those insisting on traditional structures and institutional forms on the one hand, to those seeking to dispose of such structures and forms in favor of indigenous practices on the other. While both sides are anxious to claim the biblical high ground for their views, practices of church in the New Testament are not as definitive as we would like: early believers, and even the Apostles, wrestled with issues of circumcision and food offered to idols. What are Christians to make of indigenous religious traditions and the cultural structures these have influenced? More crucially are cultural patterns, often with their religious overtones, to be used only as means of outreach, or are they critical to an emerging Christian identity? Finally, how is 'church' to be understood in such a setting?

These vital questions provide the substance of Darren Duerksen's important research among the *Yeshu satsangs* (or Jesus truth-gatherings) in Northwest India. Darren shows how Christianity planted in this region came to be seen as a threat to indigenous religious traditions and cultural structures and was perceived as un-Indian and therefore unattractive, with the result that only a tiny percentage of the population became Christian—the chapter on this history is one of the most interesting of the book. His work studies the small but growing insider movement among the Hindu/Sikh population there, who follow Christ while refusing to identify as "Christian." Making use of an emergentist theory of identity formation, he shows how these believers have inscribed new Christ centered properties on traditional Hindu/Sikh practices. Darren argues that this process is forming unique markers of ecclesial identity featuring a devotion to Jesus, experiences of power and healing, discernment of evil and vibrant witness. Finally he rereads the book of Acts with the same emergent categories and discovers deep resonance with the experience of these Indian believers.

No one can predict where these movements will lead and how they will find their place in the long history of Christianity. But seeing these groups in the light of that long history is one of the strengths of Darren's argument. He notes that ecclesial identities are not fixed, but "emerge over the course of time as people, cultures and structures interact." And his narrative makes a strong case for believing the Spirit of God is at work in this exciting process.

Preface

THERE ARE, IN MY opinion, few issues as important within missiological circles these days as theological understanding, clarity, and creativity regarding the nature of the church. The need for this kind of ecclesiological discussion is multiplied with the growth of non-Western Christianity, and the explosion of new forms of church that challenge and stretch the ecclesiological traditions of the West.

Such theological reflection can and is, of course, done by the academies of various contexts, using a variety of hermeneutical and theological tools developed at that level. However, the theological community has for some time recognized the legitimacy and importance of "vernacular," or implicit theologies, particularly those expressed through the prayers, liturgies and practices of churches. The regular articulations of followers of Christ at local levels represent an important nexus between the lived-faith of the people and the contexts in which they are required to negotiate and articulate that faith. Though not framed in systematic, consistent ways, it is the lived theologies of people and their churches that provide resources for deeper reflection on the ways in which God is revealing himself and shaping church communities that are, as Andrew Walls has stated, both "indigenous" and "pilgrim" to their contexts and communities.[1]

This study is a theological exploration of six "churches" in northwest India who are in various ways seeking to be Jesus-following communities within their wider Hindu and Sikh communities. The strategies and degrees of identification vary, but the ecclesiologies they are forming generally seek for ways to be a community-within-a-community. Of course, every church is a community of people who exist within a wider social community or, more accurately, within multiple social communities.

1. Walls, *The Missionary Movement in Christian History.*

What makes the *Yeshu satsangs* (Jesus truth-gatherings) unique, however, is their attempt to negotiate this same type of relationship within the context of *religious* communities. As they negotiate how to be followers of Jesus in their Hindu and Sikh contexts, I find that these *Yeshu satsangs* display certain ecclesiological markers or themes that, should they be further developed, could lead to a new and exciting Indian ecclesiology that is both "evangelical" and deeply authentic to their socio-religious identities. A critical correlation of these themes with the Book of Acts begins to chart some of the ways in which these can be developed in relation to Scripture.

To trace these ecclesiological themes requires, I argue, attention to current practices as well as the histories and processes by which leaders developed these practices. Understanding the cultural and theological influences that helped shape present practices gives us insight not only into the practices themselves, but also the factors that influence the development of vernacular, or local theologies such as these. As such, in this study I use the tools of Sociology and Cultural Anthropology to more accurately understand the ecclesial identities that these groups are shaping.

Though I use sociological and anthropological themes and tools, this study is not primarily about the extension of such theories. Rather, my focus is squarely on analyzing the theological themes as expressed through the lived practices of these groups and their leaders. In addition, though this is primarily a theological study, it has important implications both for evangelism and missions. The ecclesiological themes, and the ways in which these are emerging among the groups, give insight into the processes that shape such groups, and offer instruction and suggestions regarding not only the development of vernacular theologies in general, but also the mission and development of *Yeshu satsangs* among Hindus and Sikhs in India.

Acknowledgments

WRITING A BOOK IS similar, I have found, to preparing and performing a good piece of ensemble music. The director is of course integral to the rehearsal and production, but is very dependent on a whole host of others who work with him in the effort to present a piece of art. I am very grateful to the many people who have added their encouragement and voices to help bring the present piece into the light of day.

To the *Yeshu satsang* leaders of northwest India, and particularly Gaurav, to whom I am grateful for the chance to be a part of their communities, sit at their feet, and learn from their incredible journeys of faith and experience. Some of them ventured into the unknown by allowing me, a person outside their communities, to come and be a part of them. They also bravely set aside the risk of yet again being misunderstood by other Christians, and opened up their lives and stories to me. I hope that this analysis and discussion will honor their generosity by enhancing further ministry among Hindu and Sikh communities.

To William Dyrness and Dan Shaw at Fuller Theological Seminary: thank you for your encouragement, wisdom and guidance as my doctoral committee. I also greatly appreciated the help and advice provided by Sherwood Lingenfelter in the early stages of my research, and the encouragement provided by numerous friends in the PhD program at Fuller.

Finally, my family has been a tremendous support. Though my children, Ethan and Asha, only vaguely understood what this thing called a "PhD" was, they provided cheers and encouragement each step of the way. My amazing wife, Shahna, was all-too-aware of what this thing called a PhD was about but encouraged me anyways, selflessly giving up various comforts and time with me so as to allow this dream to come to fruition. I love and appreciate you.

Abbreviations

BSP	Bahujan Samaj Party
CEP	Cultural Emergent Property
CS	Cultural System
IIIC	Indigenous Independent Indian Churches
OBC	Other Backward Caste
S-C	Socio-Cultural Community
SEP	Structural Emergent Property
SS	Structural System

Introduction

IN RECENT YEARS, MANY missiological discussions have ensued regarding religious and cultural "insider movements" of various types and in various places. Within the Muslim context, for example, some followers of Jesus Christ have continued to identify themselves as "Muslim" and retain certain cultural practices. In the West, some "Emergent" churches have reshaped themselves to more closely identify with the contemporary younger-generation culture, with some rejecting the identity label "Christian" in favor of "Christ-follower." In India, the regional focus of this present study, some followers of Jesus seek for ways to remain associated with their Hindu and Sikh families and communities. Though each context is unique, these people share a common tendency to distance themselves from some of the ways Christianity has been characterized and practiced in their culture, yet still seek ways to follow and worship Christ. If and when they pursue this with others, they form new church or ecclesial identities that, they hope, authentically express their faith identities in a culturally relevant way.

In this study I focus on the leaders and members of several churches or *Yeshu satsangs* (Jesus truth-gatherings) in northwest India. Over the last ten years an increasing number of studies have addressed people and groups in India who profess and practice a faith in Jesus outside of institutional churches. In this there have been two interrelated but distinct foci of study. The first and most discussed involves individuals whom Herbert Hoefer in his seminal study called "Non-Baptized Believers in Christ," and who have since occasionally been called *Yeshu Bhakta* (Jesus devotees). These people, as Hoefer highlighted, are followers of Jesus who are sometimes unassociated with each other and who have chosen to remain unbaptized and unaffiliated with an institutional church. Hoefer's qualitative research indicated that these people generally have an orthodox understanding of Jesus and the Bible while also maintaining a social relationship with their Hindu families and communities. His quantitative data suggested that a large number of such believers may exist throughout India.[1] Both premises have prompted further discussion and study.[2]

A second focus involves leaders who have recently begun evangelizing and discipling people toward the type of *Yeshu Bhakta* faith and identity that Hoefer's respondents displayed, but without the isolation factor. These leaders are developing *Yeshu satsangs* to provide fellowship and nurture, and that counter the teaching and identities promoted by Christian churches of their areas. To date only one such study, with a focus on a group in Chennai, has been conducted.[3]

Thus, whereas one prong of these studies regards the spontaneous movements of individual *Yeshu Bhakta*, the second regards leaders that are creating *satsangs* whose identities and practices reflect the member's religious culture as well as their faith in Jesus. Because of my interest in ecclesiology and effective ministry among Hindus and Sikhs, I became particularly intrigued with the second of these: the existing *Yeshu satsangs* and their *Yeshu satsangis* (members).

My interest in *Yeshu satsangs* reflects an overall conviction regarding the importance of the local church, and causes me to consider what "church" would look like for the type of believers that Hoefer highlighted. As I indicated, however, there have been few studies that have critically or extensively engaged questions of what "church" community may look like for such people. Because of this I have determined a need for a qualitative study that investigates the ways in which existing *Yeshu satsangs* form new ecclesial identities.

RESEARCH DESIGN

The purpose of this study is to understand the ecclesial identities of *Yeshu satsangs* in northwest India[4] and how these emerge from and are shaped

1. Hoefer, *Churchless Christianity*.

2. See for example Jeyaraj, *Followers of Christ*; Richard, "Community Dynamics"; Richard, "A Response to Timothy C. Tennent"; Tennent, "A Response to H. L. Richard's Community Dynamics"; Tennent, "The Challenge of Churchless Christianity."

3. Jorgensen, *Jesus Imandars and Christ Bhaktas*.

4. In this study I focus on a particular region—northwest India—rather than a specific religious community. Though the study includes *Yeshu satsangs* from Hindu and Sikh religious communities, I find many similarities in the ways the various *Yeshu*

by their practices. My goal in this is to articulate a social theory and a biblical theology of ecclesial identity formation appropriate for Hindu and Sikh insider movements in particular, and contextual church movements in general. To achieve this I narrow the research to particular identity theories and formulate what I call Emergentist theory of identity formation. From a biblical theological perspective I investigate the ways in which the Book of Acts provides markers and themes for ecclesiological identity. In light of this the central research issue of this study is to analyze the ecclesial identity and markers of six *Yeshu satsangs* in northwest India through an Emergentist theory of identity formation and the Book of Acts.

Several research questions help guide this study. First, how does Emergentist and related social theories help us understand the formation of social identities? In particular, how does a composite Emergentist theory of identity help describe and analyze the ecclesial identities of *Yeshu satsangs*? Second, since practices are an important part of an Emergentist theory of identity, how do the leaders of six *Yeshu satsangs* in northwest India use, modify and resist various practices? Third, how do these practices shape and mark these *Yeshu satsang*'s ecclesial identities? Fourth, in what ways did the *Yeshu satsang* leaders' Hindu and Sikh backgrounds and their interaction with Christian churches impact and shape the marks and practices of ecclesial identity evident in their *Yeshu satsangs*? Finally, and as I turn to a discussion of biblical theology, what are some of the practices and markers of ecclesial identity evident from the Book of Acts? How do these critically correlate with the ecclesial identities of the *Yeshu satsangs*? The research questions thus begin by identifying the choices, practices and contexts of the *Yeshu satsangs* and to then critically correlate scripture in light of these practices and identities.

OVERVIEW

In Part I, I provide the theoretical and contextual foundations for this study. In Chapter 1, I present the precedent literature regarding Hindu

---

satsangs are influenced by and seek to influence their respective communities. In addition, though the Hindu and Sikh communities often have many distinct beliefs and practices, in northwest India they also have many characteristics in common and share similar regional influences. For this reason I include both the Hindu and Sikh communities and their influence on the regional *Yeshu satsangs* in the same study. For further description of the relationship of Hindu and Sikh communities in northwest India see Appendix A.

followers of Christ (or *Yeshu Bhakta*). Through this brief review I argue that, though recent scholarship has provided helpful perspectives on the theoretical issues facing Hindu and Sikh followers of Christ, there still exists a gap in knowledge regarding the nature and theology of "church" for these believers. In addition, there is a need for theory that focuses on the formation process of ecclesial identities. In Chapter 2, I introduce my integrated theoretical framework based on an Emergentist theory of identity formation. This addresses my first research question: How does an Emergentist theory of identity formation help describe and analyze the ecclesial identities of *Yeshu satsangs*? In Chapter 3, I outline the research methodology that I used in this study, including that which I used for data collection and analysis. In Chapter 4 I then give a brief introduction to the *Yeshu satsangs* and their leaders, describing these according to the particular religious communities with which they relate. In addition, because all of these leaders have interacted with the Christian church in the area, I briefly discuss the characteristics of the Christian church and their emergence through an Emergentist theory of identity formation

In Part II, I describe the findings from my ethnography regarding the ecclesial identities of the six *Yeshu satsangs*. In Chapters 5 through 7, I address my second research question: How do *Yeshu satsang* leaders in northwest India use, modify and resist various practices to shape their ecclesial identities? To answer this, in Chapter 5, I analyze the ways in which certain practices relate to Hindu and Sikh social structures, and in Chapter 6 the way in which *Yeshu satsang* leaders seek to inscribe new cultural meanings into these practices. In Chapter 7, I then examine the Christian practices that the *Yeshu satsang* leaders employ, and how they do and do not modify these for their purposes. In Chapter 8, I summarize the theological markers suggested by these practices. In so doing I address my third research question: What are the ecclesial identity markers of six Hindu and Sikh *Yeshu satsangs* in northwest India? To conclude this section, in Chapter 9, I look backward and analyze, or "retroduce," the processes and interactions that occurred over time to help shape the present ecclesial identities of the *Yeshu satsangs*. This chapter thus addresses my fourth research question; How did the *Yeshu satsang* leaders' Hindu and Sikh backgrounds and interaction with Christian churches help shape the ecclesial identity markers of their *Yeshu satsangs*?

In Part III, I address the final research question: How does a theological understanding of ecclesial identities based on the Book of Acts critically correlate with the ecclesial identities of the *Yeshu satsangs*? To answer this, in Chapter 10, I analyze the *Yeshu satsangs'* ecclesial identity markers through the Book of Acts and further clarify and discuss the theological implications of the *Yeshu satsangs'* ecclesial identity markers. Finally, in my Conclusion, I discuss the contributions of this study to academic knowledge and theoretical conversations, and make recommendations regarding the ministry and formation of Hindu and Sikh *Yeshu satsangs.*

In summary, the purpose of this study is to understand the nature and emergence of the ecclesial identities of *Yeshu satsangs* in northwest India, and my central argument is that an Emergentist theory of identity formation and an analysis based on the Book of Acts will help me to identify the ecclesial identities of six *Yeshu satsangs* in northwest India. I now turn to the study of the ecclesial identities of *Yeshu satsangs*, beginning with the theoretical and contextual background for this study.

PART I

Foundations of the Study

CHAPTER 1

Precedent Literature

Early Pioneers and Present Scholars of Contemporary *Yeshu Satsangs*

IN THIS CHAPTER I will locate my research within the growing number of studies regarding Hindu Christ-followers, Hindu "insider movements," and *Yeshu satsangs*. Much of this extends from debates regarding baptism and ecclesiology that originated in the 1960s and 1970s. Prior to this, however, several important and influential "non-conformist" Indian leaders critiqued and raised questions regarding the ways in which Christian churches related to Indian religious communities.[1] I will thus briefly discuss two important leaders, Brahmabandhav Upadhyay and Kalagara Subba Rao, and their ecclesial perspectives. I will then follow this with a more extensive analysis of recent scholars that have advanced concepts and studies that are pertinent to my focus on *Yeshu satsangs* and their ecclesial identity.

EARLY PIONEERS: BRAHMABANDHAV UPADHYAY AND KALAGARA SUBBA RAO

Since the nineteenth century followers of Jesus in various parts of India have critiqued the forms and theologies of established Christian churches

1. In their account of Indian church history Fernando and Gispert-Sauch speak about the protestant "non-conformist tradition" of the nineteenth century, consisting of various leaders who reacted to missionary Protestant forms of church with their own faith articulations and ecclesial forms (Fernando and Gispert-Sauch, *Christianity in India*, 163). Though I do not agree that the various leaders form a unified "tradition," I find the general label of "non-conformist" a helpful descriptor.

and offered their own variations. Though few of the ecclesial groups and institutions that these leaders founded actually outlasted them, several of these reflected on and wrote about their critiques and theologies of church. In this section I will briefly discuss two prominent leaders, Brahmabandhav Upadhyay and Kalagara Subba Rao.

Brahmabandhav Upadhyay

Brahmabandhav Upadhyay (1861–1907) was a pioneering leader in non-conformist ecclesiology.[2] Born into a high-caste Hindu Brahmin family in Bengal, Upadhyay was influenced by family members and friends involved in the nationalist movement. As a result, he joined the Brahmo Samaj and became the disciple of its then-leader, Keshub Chundar Sen.

Upadhyay was influenced by Sen's openness to Christ and the rationalism with which he and the samaj approached religion. In 1890, through interaction with Church Missionary Society missionaries, Upadhyay became convinced of the divinity and supremacy of Christ and was subsequently baptized in 1891.[3] Later that year he investigated and joined the Catholic Church, drawn in part through the Catholic's respect and regard for Hinduism, as well as their understandings of natural theology. Though he became a member of the Church, Upadhyay retained a strong desire to "clothe" Christianity in the garments of Hindu vedantic thought.[4] In 1894 he literally clothed himself in the light red garments of a *sannyasi* (Hindu monk) and adopted a traveling itinerary and lifestyle, for a time, to more closely identify with the Hindu community, while remaining a part of the Catholic Church.[5] An active writer and journal editor, Upadhyay regularly articulated his developing ideas regarding the

---

2. Upadhyay's contribution to Indian theology goes well beyond ecclesiology, particularly in his explorations of intersections between Christian theology and Hinduism. See Boyd, *An Introduction to Indian Christian Theology*; Tennent, *Building Christianity on Indian foundations*. Felix Wilfred summarizes Upadhyay's overall contribution, saying he was "a pioneer in exploring creative ways of relating Christian faith with the culture, tradition, philosophy and genius of India" (Wilfred, *Beyond Settled Foundations*, 19–20).

3. Though he was baptized by an Anglican bishop, Upadhyay insisted on being baptized outside of a church so as not to be identified with the church of the colonizers. Jeyaraj, *Followers of Christ Outside the Church*, 59.

4. Boyd, *An Introduction to Indian Christian Theology*, 64.

5. Upadhyay later left the Catholic Church towards the end of his life over disagreements regarding his openness to Hindu philosophy, his *sannyasi* identity, and his growing criticism of British rule in India.

Christian faith, Hindu philosophy, and politics. Though he did not begin an organization or ecclesial structure, he developed several important ecclesiological ideas and critiques.

First, Upadhyay was convinced of the integrity of the Christian faith, and that God had clearly given this to the Catholic Church. Though he increasingly conflicted with the Catholic Church, he retained a strong core faith in Christ and considered himself a member of the universal Church.[6]

Second, particularly in his earlier years, Upadhyay believed that the Indian culture, and Hindu religion, was "humid soil" in which the revelation of Christ could be planted and cultivated. Because of this he became convinced of the need to convert the whole of India to the Catholic Church.[7] In this he had no misgivings about calling Hindus to become followers of Jesus as it was articulated through the historic teachings of the Catholic Church.

Third, though Upadhyay was firm in his Christology and affirmed the idea that God had "deposited" the truth of His revelation in the Catholic Church, he had serious misgivings about the way in which Christian churches, including Catholic churches, expressed their faith. If India was to be converted, Upadhyay felt, the Catholic faith needed to rid itself of its European practices and culture and adopt the "clothes" of the Hindu religion.[8] As part of this Upadhyay regarded himself a "Hindu Catholic," and never insisted that converts to Christ renounce their Hindu identity.

In order to hold these three points together, Upadhyay gradually refined and clarified his understanding of both "Church" and "Hinduism." In line with Catholic doctrine, the "Church" for Upadhyay was ultimately a universal gathering of those committed to Christ Jesus, capable of incorporating a variety of Christological and ecclesiological expressions.

6. Boyd, *An Introduction to Indian Christian Theology*, 83.

7. Upadhyay states, "(India) is sure to be converted. Was not the blood of the incarnate God shed for India, the fair land of the Aryans? Do not the prayers of St. Thomas and St. Xavier, the patron saints of India, rise incessantly to the throne of God for her conversions? India is sure to be, in the long run, brought over as an inheritance of Jesus Christ" (Upadhyay, "Conversion of India," 15).

8. As one of Upadhyay's disciples, B. R. Animananda states, "It is the foreign clothes of the Catholic Faith that have chiefly prevented our countrymen from perceiving its universal nature. Catholicism has donned the European garb in India . . . When the Catholic Church in India will be dressed . . . in Hindu garments then will our countrymen perceive that she elevates man to the Universal Kingdom of Truth by stooping down to adapt herself to his racial peculiarities" (Animananda, *The Blade,* 74).

Regarding Hinduism, Upadhyay distinguished between two *dharmas*, or duties, of the Hindu. The *samaj dharma* are comprised of social duties, including customs, eating and dressing. The *sadhana dharma*, on the other hand, are the individual duties that focus on personal devotion and, ultimately, on personal salvation.

Both duties, asserted Upadhyay, are present in Hinduism and Christianity. However, in Hinduism it is the *samaj dharma*, or social duties, that are most important, while in Christianity it is the personal duties of devotion to Christ that supersede social rules and duties.[9] Thus, Hindus could remain Hindu in their social duties and identities while following a personal devotion to Christ and expressing this devotion using Hindu terminology and philosophical categories.[10] Upadhyay did not explicitly state the ecclesiological implications of this formulation. I will, however, suggest two. First, though Upadhyay affirmed the importance of receiving the sacraments during mass for personal devotion, he did not place high emphasis on the local gathered community of faith as an expression of Church. Rather, he begins to indicate that the "Church" could be manifest through a Hindu society committed to Jesus. Second, Upadhyay did not see a tension between a Hindu religious identity and a Christian identity. New Christians thus did not need to renounce their Hindu identity as a pre-requisite for becoming members of a Church.

Upadhyay's theological formulations of a Hindu-Christian synthesis are recognized as important contributions to an early Indian Christian theology. However, the particular articulations were rarely adopted or developed by ecclesial communities. Indeed, as Jeyaraj has pointed out, the high philosophical nature of Upadhyay's arguments rarely appeal to most Hindus, the vast majority of whom do not engage in deeply philosophical considerations of the Hindu faith.[11] However, though Upadhyay's philosophy may have only appealed to a small number of elite Hindus, he identified and grappled with the commonly felt tension between the identity of the Hindu family and the identity of the individual Christian and the Christian community. One way of dealing with this, as I have described, was to divide the Hindu dharma between social and personal devotion and duties. Though many Hindus do not make

9. See Animananda's summary of this teaching, ibid., 200–201.

10. As well, for Upadhyay the Hindu identity was closely linked with Indian nationalism. To affirm the Hindu identity was to affirm an integral aspect of India's identity and character.

11. Jeyaraj, *Followers of Christ Outside the Church*, 76.

such formal divisions, Upadhyay nonetheless posited that, in theory, they could be divided and that a disciple community could thus retain a Hindu identity. Unfortunately, the Catholic Church could ultimately not accept this proposition and distanced itself from Upadhyay. Over one hundred years following Upadhyay's death, a new group of scholars continue to debate similar tensions and suggest similar ways in which the Hindu and Christian faiths can be understood.

Subba Rao

Kalagara Subba Rao (1912–1981)[12] is unique among many leaders and thinkers of non-conformist ecclesiologies in that whereas most non-conformist leaders often began their work in the midst of Christian institutions and churches and gradually moved to the periphery, Subba Rao remained distant and critical of Christian churches from the outset.[13] Born into a higher landowning caste (kamma) in Andhra Pradesh, Subba Rao gained a good education and became a teacher. He was familiar with but hated Christian priests and their teachings. However, one evening, while suffering from bad health, he had a spectacular vision of a being he later identified as Jesus. A line in a song that Subba Rao later wrote reflects on that experience and anticipates aspects of his ecclesiology.

> Yes, I heard that you were the God of a religion. I also saw several churches beautifully built for you. I also heard that very many worship you there. Then what made you come here to me without gladly receiving their services? Have the very fanatics that destroyed you in the name of religion now made you an article of merchandise? Unable to tolerate them bartering you in the market of religion for their livelihood, have you come to me,

---

12. The principal early studies of Subba Rao were conducted by C. D. Airan and Kaj Baago in 1965 and 1968 respectively, based primarily on interviews with Rao and analyses of his songs. See Airan, *Kalagara Subba Rao*; Baago, *The Movement Around Subba Rao*. More recently K. P. Aleaz and H. L. Richard have contributed more extensive analyses of Rao, based primarily on his songs and biographies but, in Richard, supplemented with interviews with some of Subba Rao's followers and his widow. See Aleaz, *Christian Thought through Advaita Vedanta*; Richard, *Exploring the Depths of the Mystery of Christ*. In addition, Dasan Jeyaraj contributes further analysis via this material and further interviews with Subba Rao's followers. See Jeyaraj, *Followers of Christ Outside the Church*.

13. Jeyaraj, *Followers of Christ Outside the Church*, 152.

this fallen atheist, as your refuge? Above all, how could you slip out of that impregnable fortress of religion?[14]

After later experiencing further miraculous events, Subba Rao began to preach about Jesus and to heal people in Jesus' name. Subba Rao soon began to travel around the region, preaching and healing people, eventually establishing prayer meetings in numerous places, including a main center in Vijayawada. As news spread about the effectiveness of Subba Rao's prayers, people began to come from long distances. His proclamations about Jesus also raised the interest of local churches and priests, who invited him to come to the churches and talk with them. However, he disliked the local churches and soon stopped going to them. As he told Kaj Baago, "Had I continued going (to the churches), I would have forgotten Christ long ago, for the churches won't tell us anything about Christ. They tell us about a religion called Christianity."[15]

This quote and the lines from the above song give indications regarding Subba Rao's developing ecclesiology. He remained intensely critical of local churches. In one of his more scathing works Subba Rao in particular criticizes various rituals, including baptism, which Christian leaders use as a form of power and exclusion.[16] Instead, Subba Rao advocated an internal, personal experience of Christ that united Christ-followers with others in a universal church.[17]

---

14. Baago, *The Movement Around Subba Rao*, 11–12.

15. Ibid., 15.

16. In one section Rao says, "Dear Padri, we are at our wits' end to understand the curious lives of your tribe. You have made religion a fashionable thing. Change of names, taking of oaths, daily prayers, Sunday gatherings, putting on attractive garb, observing festivals and several such things you do, except what the Lord preached and practiced. What the Lord said and did is made into a religion and transformed into a department. Decrying other religions is your religion. If all your books, your grand religions, your long laborious prayers, your thunderous sermons, your showy baptisms and all your customary gymnastics can't uplift your soul and can only be millstones round your neck, don't you realize that all of them are quite useless and even harmful?" (Subba Rao, *Retreat, Padri!*, 17).

17. There is no consensus among scholars reagarding Subba Rao's Christology due to spurious evidence from his teachings and songs (Richard, *Exploring the Depths of the Mystery of Christ*, 146). However, Richard and Jeyaraj concur that one of Subba Rao's major weaknesses was that his teaching and theology were guided primarily by his experiences and visions, and only marginally by the Bible (Jeyaraj, *Followers of Christ Outside the Church*, 169; Richard, *Exploring the Depths of the Mystery of Christ*, 152–53).

In addition, Subba Rao's critique of the church mirrored an overall disdain for "religion." Though Subba Rao clearly used Hindu vocabulary to express his faith in Christ, he consistently preached against all religions whose leaders and rituals, he felt, kept people bound and alienated from true freedom.[18] In like manner, Subba Rao critiqued the church for improperly making Christ into a religion through which people could only enter by way of rituals and the acceptance of a hierarchical leadership structure.

Subba Rao was particularly critical of Cyprian's claim that "there is no salvation outside the church." In response Subba Rao articulated an ecclesiology that was not limited by physical or institutional structures and instead emphasized the universal connection of all true followers of Christ. Such a church could not be properly characterized or identified by religious terms, including the term "Christian."

Summary of Upadhyay and Subba Rao

Upadhyay and Subba Rao are two important examples of leaders who formed ecclesiologies contrasting those of surrounding churches in their regions. Though from different regions, time periods and castes, each share some common features. First, both leaders criticized the European rituals and forms of church in their contexts. Upadhyay, more so than Subba Rao, attempted to operate from within ecclesial structures and frameworks, but shared with Subba Rao a disdain for the manner in which the churches distanced themselves from the Hindu masses through their unfamiliar rituals and language.

Relatedly, both leaders were generally clearer in their ecclesiological critiques than they were in their suggestions of what ecclesiology should consist of. However, neither leader advocated a strong separation between followers of Jesus and the Hindu community. Upadhyay was most clear in this through his adoption of the role of *sannyasi* (wandering renunciant) and his identification as a Hindu-Catholic. Subba Rao tended to avoid religious labels altogether but clearly advocated—even if somewhat unconsciously—the appropriation of Hindu vocabulary, poetry, song-forms, and mystical experiences common in popular Hinduism. For neither leader was there a discrepancy between Hinduism as a culture and a Christ-centered ecclesiology. The need for ecclesiology to more critically

---

18. Jeyaraj, *Followers of Christ Outside the Church*, 167.

engage and identify with the Hindu social community is a theme that has remained important and crucial to various leaders since then.

PRESENT SCHOLARS: RECENT SCHOLARSHIP REGARDING YESHU SATSANGS

Upadhyay, Subba Rao, and several other Indian Christian leaders pioneered and laid the groundwork for non-conformist expressions of ecclesiology. However, though the communities begun by Subba Rao and others[19] continue in various states to the present day, none have grown significantly nor have fostered continued dialogue on alternative forms of ecclesial communities. Very recently, however, interest and dialogue regarding non-conformist ecclesiologies has been renewed among missiologists and practitioners interested in "insider movements" and "New Christian Movements," or "indigenous independent Indian Churches." It is to this present discussion that I now turn.

Herbert Hoefer

Herbert Hoefer is a missionary scholar whose seminal study, *Churchless Christianity*,[20] has inspired and informed much of the current discussion regarding Hindu insider movements. Hoefer's book is based on a qualitative and quantitative study that he conducted in 1980–1981 on people who professed a faith in Christ but had not taken baptism or joined a local church. Hoefer called these people "Non-baptized believers in Christ," and later *Yeshu Bhakta* (devotees of Jesus).[21] For qualitative data, Hoefer

---

19. Another important set of examples is the various Christian *ashrams* (spiritual hermitages) that were begun by Protestant and Catholic missionaries and leaders in the early twentieth century. Many of these were begun with a desire to shape new ecclesial communities that reflected Hindu culture. As one leader expressed it, "The Ashramas are the small circles which will reflect fullness of Christian life. Unless we discover the church in this sense, it would be impossible for the group life of Christians to permeate, regenerate the existing society and furnish it with ideals of a social order nearer to the heart of man and God. Ashramas reproduced in the *grahastha* (family) life will be the new church in the world" (Richard, *The Theology of Dr. Savarirayan Jesudasan*, 24). Unfortunately, except for a select few (such as Sat Tal ashram near Nanital or Matri Dham ashram near Varanasi) most have dwindled in size or have closed. Though these initiatives in themselves are important case studies in non-conformist ecclesiologies, a full discussion of these falls outside of the scope of this study.

20. Hoefer, *Churchless Christianity*.

21. Hoefer later uses the phrase *"Jesu bhakta."* Because *"Jesu"* and *"Yeshu"* are alternative transliterations of the same Hindi word, I will use *"Yeshu bhakta"* to be

and his colleagues conducted interviews with eighty-four *Yeshu Bhakta*s known to local pastors and determined that, though these people lacked knowledge in certain areas, they generally had "a wonderful clarity on the essentials of the Christian faith."[22] Hoefer then conducted a quantitative survey of 810 people to gather wider statistics regarding *Yeshu Bhaktas*. From the quantitative study Hoefer determined that perhaps five percent of Hindus and Muslims in Chennai were *Yeshu Bhakta*s and sixty percent of these women.

As indicated above, data from Hoefer's book has helped to catalyze the current debate on Hindu insider movements. Of particular interest and importance to this study, however, are Hoefer's ecclesiology and reflections regarding the ecclesial identity of the *Yeshu Bhakta*s. To understand this I will briefly review the background to, and context of, Hoefer's study.

Hoefer's interest in *Yeshu Bhakta*s began in the mid-1970s with his work with Gurukul Lutheran Theological College and Research Institute in Madras (Chennai). During that time theologians at Gurukul were discussing recent articles and debates by Kaj Baago, M. M. Thomas and Leslie Newbigin regarding the identity of the Indian Christian church, and how baptism and conversion helped or hindered this identity. Kaj Baago, in his 1966 article "The Post-colonial Crisis in Missions," asked several provocative questions, including:

> Must Buddhists, Hindus and Muslims become Christians in order to belong to Christ? Do they have to be incorporated into church organizations which are utterly alien to their religious traditions? Do they have to call themselves Christians—a word which to them signifies a follower of the Western religion? Should they necessarily adopt the Christian traditions, customs and rites which often have their root in Western culture more than in the Gospel? Are all these things conditions for belonging to Christ?[23]

---

consistent in this study.

22. Hoefer, *Churchless Christianity*: 61.

23. Baago goes on to answer his own questions, saying, "The answer is obviously 'No.' The Christian religion, to a large extent a product of the West, cannot and shall not become the religion of all nations and races. The resurgence and revival of Hinduism, Buddhism and Islam has made that clear. The missionary task of today cannot, therefore, be to draw men out of their religions into another religion, but rather to leave Christianity (the organized religion) and go inside Hinduism and Buddhism, accepting these religions as one's own, in so far as they do not conflict with Christ,

A few years later M. M. Thomas published a landmark study that also critiqued the Indian church and proposed the need for a "Christ-centred secular fellowship outside the Church."[24] Lesslie Newbigin entered the discussion, first responding to Baago[25] and then to Thomas. When Thomas responded to Newbigin's critique a subsequent correspondence developed into the so-called "Thomas-Newbigin debates."[26] A significant issue in these debates regarded the practice of baptism and the importance of an institution identifiable as a "church." Both agreed that the social identity of the existing Christian church was problematic and that "radical questions need to be asked regarding the form of the Church."[27] However, each had different answers for the radical questions they posed. For his part, Newbigin desired to uphold the visible and distinctive nature of the church.[28] Thomas, on the other hand, argued that Christians should recognize and encourage the presence of Christ-followers outside of the empirical church as what he called the "new humanity of Christ" or "Christ-centered fellowships."[29] Such followers and any fellowships they may form should be distinct from the existing church and should not be constrained by the church's institutions, rituals or doctrines. Thomas asserted, however, that these followers and fellowships are related to the church through their common focus on Christ.

Of particular interest in this discussion is Thomas's articulation of a version of the classic visible/invisible doctrine of the Church. On the one hand, he affirms the historic and institutional Church and its various rituals as a visible expression of God's kingdom. On the other, however, he

---

and regarding them as the presupposition, the background and the framework of the Christian gospel in Asia. Such a mission will not lead to the progress of Christianity or the organized Church, but it might lead to the creation of Hindu Christianity or Buddhist Christianity." Baago, "The Post-Colonial Crisis of Missions," 331–32.

24. Thomas, *Salvation and Humanisation*, 13.

25. Newbigin, "The Finality of Christ."

26. See Newbigin, "Review of Salvation and Humanisation"; Thomas, *Salvation and Humanisation*; Thomas, Newbigin, and Krass, "Baptism, the Church, and Koinonia"; Thomas, *Some Theological Dialogues*. For an overview, see Hunsberger, "Conversion and Community"; Richard, "Community Dynamics in India and the Praxis of 'Church.'

27. Newbigin, "Review of Salvation and Humanisation," 76.

28. Newbigin summarizes his viewpoint, saying, "The New Testament knows nothing of a relationship with Christ which is purely mental and spiritual, unembodied in any of the structures of human relationships." Newbigin, "The Finality of Christ," 96.

29. Thomas, "Baptism, the Church, and Koinonia," 73.

advocates for fellowships that exist outside of, and may not be as visible as, the institutional church, but are nonetheless part of God's kingdom.

As Hoefer and Gurukul's research institute engaged this debate, they conducted a series of conferences to discuss the issues of baptism and how it hindered "the expression of our solidarity to the new humanity in Christ which transcends all communal or caste solidarities."[30] In particular, Gurukul scholars considered the phenomenon of *Yeshu Bhakta*s as an example of Thomas's "new humanity." The church, they contended, should accept these *bhaktas* as Christ followers, even though they have not taken baptism in the existing church.[31] Hoefer's subsequent *Churchless Christianity* further developed this theme, encouraging the Christian Church to recognize and accept *Yeshu Bhakta*s as a part of "Jesus' flock who are not in our fold."[32]

As this background shows, Hoefer in *Churchless Christianity* engages relatively recent theological questions and debates regarding the identity of the church in India, and Hoefer's solution to these questions, in part, draws from and builds on aspects of Thomas's ecclesiology. Like Thomas (and Newbigin), Hoefer recognizes that *Yeshu Bhakta*s find it socially difficult to take baptism and join the institutional church. However, and also similar to Thomas, Hoefer believes that *Yeshu Bhakta*s are somehow a part of God's kingdom. Thomas's "Christ-centered fellowships," asserts Hoefer, provide a possible model, articulating that "fellowships" or various individuals can remain separate from the church sociologically and theologically, but have membership in the wider kingdom of God. As Hoefer states,

> The (*Yeshu Bhakta*) cannot be considered members of the church (nor, I feel, can they be called "Christians," for that is a title ascribed to any who take baptism). Yet, they certainly are part of our fellowship in Christ through faith. They are the sheep of Jesus' flock who are not in our fold, but they are fellow-sheep responding to the voice of the same Master and entering in by the same gate (Jn. 10:9ff).[33]

Thus, similar to Thomas, Hoefer asserts that God's kingdom has both visible and invisible "churches," and that *Yeshu Bhakta* should be

---

30. Philip, "A History of Baptismal Practices and Theologies," 321.

31. Rajashekar, "The Question of Unbaptized Believers," 323.

32. Hoefer, *Churchless Christianity*, 164.

33. Ibid., 164.

considered a part of a wider "faith community" that is related to but distinct from a visible "church community."

Though many of the *Yeshu Bhakta*s that Hoefer has in view are individuals, he at times suggests that such individuals could meet together in local gatherings, such as a Bible study or new "Hindu" forms.[34] Such visible gatherings, however, are still not, in Hoefer's view, the sociological or theological equivalent of the church. He says:

> We also must distinguish between church communities and faith communities. The church is a faith community, but not all faith communities are churches. One can be a part of a Bible Study group or a prayer group quite separate from one's congregation. A faith community may be a group with whom one relates face-to-face, or one may participate at a distance . . . The faith community is the classical "invisible Church," with a capital "C." One can be a part of the Church and never part of the visible church.[35]

I find it important to note that though Hoefer is concerned to maintain a sociological and theological distinction between the *Yeshu Bhakta*s and the church, he makes a strong plea for the church to be open to and serve the *Yeshu Bhakta*s. In this he continues to articulate the original overall hope that he and his Gurukul colleagues voiced in the mid-1970s. Since churches and *Yeshu Bhakta*s are all a part of the same "fellowship," Hoefer asserts, churches should seek to serve *Yeshu Bhakta* within the context of Hindu communities where they can remain influential, and not insist that they take baptism and thus leave those communities and thus lose their influence.[36]

In summary, how helpful is Hoefer's (and Thomas') ecclesiology of the visible/invisible church for understanding the ecclesial identities of *Yeshu satsangs*? Though I recognize and appreciate Hoefer's intent to create an ecclesial and eschatological space for the *Yeshu Bhakta*s and *satsangs*, his application of an ecclesiology that differentiates between a visible "church" and an invisible "fellowship" has, I believe, led Hoefer's critics to misunderstand his "churchless Christianity," and to dismiss people and groups such as the *Yeshu satsangs* as unbiblical.[37] Relat-

34. Hoefer, *Churchless Christianity*, 219.

35. Ibid., 225.

36. Ibid., 167.

37. For example, see Hedlund, "Present-day Independent Christian Movements," 56–57.

edly, Hoefer's ecclesiology makes unclear the way groups such as *Yeshu satsangs* should read and apply biblical and theological resources that would be applied to visible "churches."

In light of the difficulties raised by an ecclesiology of the visible/ invisible church, and particularly by a narrow and sacramental under-standing of "church," I suggest that a better theological approach recog-nizes any gathering of committed Christ-followers as a church that are in turn related to each other as part of the universal church. Thus, in this study I proceed by affirming that, if and when *Yeshu satsangs* and the Indian Christian churches display a commitment to Christ and each other, they are both "church" in the theological sense.[38] Such an affirma-tion, I believe, allows me to affirm that there exists a plurality of ecclesial identities and expressions of "church" in India. Also, the conviction that a group committed to Christ and each other theologically forms a "church" allows me to look closely at the ecclesial identity of the *Yeshu satsangs* in and through a closer reading of their social and cultural context. This basis also then allows me to be more precise in analyzing the way the *Ye-shu satsangs* are seeking ecclesial identities that contrast with the Chris-tian church. I will further demonstrate the importance of and need for ecclesiological clarity below, particularly in reference to Dasan Jeyaraj. First, however, I will turn to a scholar who has championed and advanced aspects of Hoefer's work.

H. L. Richard

H. L. Richard is a missionary scholar who has published numerous stud-ies related to Hindu followers of Christ, including books on the life of N. V. Tilak and K. Subba Rao.[39] Along with other insider movement advocates, Richard believes that movements of Christ-followers can and should spread "inside" religious communities.[40] Though Richard writes

38. This in part reflects my Anabaptist perspective of church, which theologically affirms as "church" any local gathering of believers who share a commitment to Christ and each other and express this through common practices. See Snyder, *From Anabap-tist Seed*. However, though practices such as baptism are integral to this, I (and other Anabaptists) would place less emphasis on the actual form of the practice and more emphasis on the meaning ascribed by the community.

39. Richard, *Following Jesus in the Hindu Context*; Richard, *Exploring the Depths of the Mystery of Christ*.

40. As the reference to insider movements suggests, many of its advocates, includ-ing Richard, have been influenced by and expand upon the teachings of Donald Mc-Gavran, and particularly the concepts of the homogenous unit principle and people

on various issues related to this, I will focus on two issues that have particular bearing on how to understand the ecclesial identity of *Yeshu satsangs*.

The first issue regards the nature of the Hindu religion. Richard asserts that Hinduism should not be viewed as a single "religion" but as a cultural community with a wide range of beliefs and cultural practices. As Richard says, "'Hinduism' is a complex amalgamation of phenomena that cannot possibly be sensibly understood as 'a religion.' At the very least, various 'religions' need to be recognized within the complexity of 'Hinduism.'"[41] Richard is particularly interested in contrasting many of the traditional, Christian views that portray Hinduism as a monolithic set of beliefs.[42] Such views do not allow Christians, in Richard's view, to appreciate and address the wide variety of beliefs that exist under the banner of "Hinduism." Such views also lead Christians to misunderstand how they should interact with, evangelize, and conduct Christian worship among and for Hindus.

In addition, however, and of particular importance to my study, Richard's nuanced view of Hinduism is important for understanding Hindu insider movements such as the *Yeshu satsangs*. In particular, Richard emphasizes the possibility that many peoples' "Hindu" identity is as much based on cultural practices and family/community relationships as it is on commitments to religious doctrines. If such is the case, at least for some Hindus, then it is possible for such Hindus to be wholly devoted to a deity such as Jesus while retaining a "Hindu" identity. Though I would caution (as perhaps Richard would) against minimizing the importance of religious doctrine in Hindu identity, Richard's assessment has support from a growing literature in the sociology of Indian religions that point

---

movements. See McGavran, *Understanding Church Growth*. Though a discussion of McGavran's concepts are beyond the scope of this study, it is important to note that one area of his teachings that insider movement advocates expand upon is the assertion that the Gospel can spread within a religious community, and not just ethnic/language/class communities. Kevin Higgins summarizes this by saying, "As I use it, the phrase 'Insider Movements' encompasses not only (McGavran's) earlier descriptions of people movements but adds 'religion' to the . . . list of aspects of 'togetherness' or unity. In other words, I suggest that followers of Jesus can continue to embrace at least some of their people's religious life, history, and practice without compromising the gospel or falling into syncretism." Higgins, "The Key to Insider Movements," 156. See also Lewis, "Insider Movements."

41. Richard, "Religious Movements in Hindu Social Contexts," 145n1.

42. Richard, *Hinduism*.

to the fluid and multi-centered nature of religious communities.[43] I thus build this study on Richard's assertion that people with a "Hindu" identity often select from a variety of religious, structural and cultural practices and meanings when expressing that identity. Because of this, a group of Jesus-followers can authentically claim and express a Hindu identity that does not conflict with their devotion to Jesus.

A second issue that Richard discusses regards the form and identity that would best facilitate a Christ-centered movement within the Hindu community. Though it is theoretically possible for Hindus to follow Jesus without leaving their Hindu community, what social or ecclesial form might this take? In 2007 Richard engaged Timothy Tennent in a discussion regarding Hindu followers of Jesus and ecclesiology.[44] The discussion was spurred in part by a 2005 article written by Tennent in which he critiques aspects of Hoefer's book (which also included an appendix by Richard). In his article Tennent raises several questions concerning ecclesiology, asking:

> For example, can a Hindu or a Muslim or a postmodern American disillusioned with the institutional church come to Jesus Christ, accept him as Lord and Savior, and not unite with the visible church? Does someone have to use or accept the name "Christian" in order to belong to Christ? What is the meaning of baptism? Is it a public profession of one's personal faith in Christ, or does it also require incorporation into a visible community of believers?[45]

To answer his own questions, Tennent reviews various theological traditions, as well as the Thomas-Newbigin debate and concludes that the "invisible" Christianity that Hoefer and M. M. Thomas advocate is contrary to biblical and traditional understandings of church. Further, Tennent states that such an invisible Christianity is not the only way for "Indian" forms of Christianity to develop, since there are many visible

---

43. For discussions regarding the constructed and multiple identities of historic and contemporary Hinduism see Pernau, "Multiple Identities"; Hedge, Bloch and Keppens, *Rethinking Religion in India*; Ludden, "Introduction"; Inden, *Imagining India*; Oberoi, *The Construction of Religious Boundaries*; Fuller, *The Camphor Flame*. For a contrasting view asserting that the beliefs and communities of Hinduism have long been distinct from others see Lorenzen, *Who Invented Hinduism?*

44. Richard, "Community Dynamics"; Tennent, "A Response to H. L. Richard's Community Dynamics"; Richard, "A Response to Timothy C. Tennent."

45. Tennent, "The Challenge of Churchless Christianity," 171.

Christian churches in India that practice Indian traditions. He summarizes, "The churchless Christians should, in my view, be baptized and then, as members of a global movement (even if they continue to reject Westernized forms of worship), find creative ways to express their catholicity with the global church."[46]

In 2007 Richard responded in an article that, among other things, reevaluated the Thomas-Newbigin debate. In this he clarified that though Newbigin was more committed than Thomas to a group or institution that could be identified as a "church," Newbigin was nonetheless aware of some of the unhelpful sociological meanings attached to the church in India. In addition, Newbigin was open to Christ-centered fellowships that could exist outside of the existing Christian church and within Hindu society. However, as Richard shows, Newbigin and Thomas's debate became complicated in part because of differing but not well-defined ideas of what was meant by "Hinduism." In conclusion Richard states, "The complex nature of 'Hinduism,' the complex nature of Indian society, the variety of expressions of existing 'church' in India, and the nature of the New Testament *ekklesia* cannot be brought together in any simplistically agreed manner."[47] Nonetheless, Richard claims that Newbigin and Thomas were closer in their overall agreement for "new patterns of corporate discipleship within Hindu cultures and communities."[48]

In his discussion with Tennent, Richard helpfully clarifies aspects of his understanding regarding the corporate nature of Christ-centered movements in the Hindu community. In response to Tennent's charge that Richard and Hoefer encourage individual Christ-followers to remain isolated, Richard contends that he agrees with Newbigin and opposes "the concept of individualistic discipleship to Jesus within the Hindu community."[49] In addition, he indicates that a corporate identity or gathering is an important aspect of Christianity. He says, "I expect all followers of Jesus who take the New Testament seriously will agree with this. That there is a corporate aspect to discipleship is everywhere in the Bible."[50]

---

46. Ibid., 174.
47. Richard, "Community Dynamics," 193.
48. Ibid., 193.
49. Ibid., 192.
50. Ibid., 192.

However, though Richard clarifies that he does not advocate an individualistic discipleship, in other writings Richard is clearly wary of establishing firm corporate identities. For example, in his discussion of the Newbigin/Thomas debate he highlights, and resonates with, Newbigin's distaste for what the latter calls "sectarianism" that hinders ecumenical relationships. In another article, Richard examines the Lingayat movement, the Vārkari Vaishnavite sect, and the Kabirpanthis for possible patterns and forms for "church" among Hindus.[51] Of these, the Christian church in India has most resembled the Lingayat sect, which has separated completely from Hindu caste society. In so doing, however, it has created a new caste and community and has become isolated from and uninfluential among other communities. Richard summarizes, "It is almost inconceivable that such an approach could result in anything but the birth of another, actually many, new castes and communities. Is this really a viable model for new Christ-centered movements?"[52] More preferable, argues Richard, is the example of the Vaishnavites, a collection of sects who are broad, diverse and united by some core similarities. Using this as a possible model Richard asks:

> Might it be preferable for Christ-focused people to become comfortable within their sociological communities, as seen in the Vārkari Panth and other Vaishnava *sampradāyas* (sects)? Is it possible that the future shape of Christ movements in India will be less separated from Indian society, more incarnational, yet still opposed to hierarchical caste ideologically and (as far as is viable) in practice?[53]

In the end, Richard concedes, "There are no simple answers to such questions, and history often takes turns that no one anticipates or plans."[54] He remains somewhat skeptical, however, of the ability of corporately identifiable followers of Christ to remain in close relationship with their own communities and castes.

One response to Richard, which I will build on, comes from one of the *Yeshu satsang* leaders of this study. Gaurav[55] has discussed the issue

51. Richard, "Religious Movements."

52. Ibid., 144.

53. Ibid., 144.

54. Ibid., 144.

55. The names of all *Yeshu satsang* members and leaders have been changed to pseudonyms in this study for confidentiality purposes.

of separate groups or "sects" with Richard and presented his own un-published paper on the subject. Though short and undeveloped, Gaurav points to other, more recent *bhakti* sects in northwest India, such as the Radha Soami, who have developed a distinct identity, but have contin-ued to attract people from a variety of religious and caste communities.[56] Some members of Radha Soami communities maintain dual identities with the Radha Soamis and their Hindu and Sikh communities. Further research is needed regarding the reasons for and means by which sects such as the Radha Soami continue to grow and form such identities. However, Gaurav's thesis opens up the possibility that groups such as the *Yeshu satsangs* may be able to develop ecclesial identities that are iden-tifiably unified and distinct in their devotion to Jesus while also closely identified with their Hindu and Sikh communities.

In summary, I find Richard's discussion regarding the various so-ciological and religious aspects of Hindu identity important for a study of *Yeshu satsang* ecclesial identities. In this, Richard helpfully argues for the need to nuance and distinguish between the various meanings that people themselves give to a Hindu identity. In his discussion of corporate forms of identity, however, I find Richard theologically unclear. Whereas he agrees that a corporate element to discipleship is integral to biblical Christianity, he does not explain this theologically. Relatedly, though Richard helpfully and clearly discusses the dangers of associating a faith with one particular group or community, he stops short of placing this critique in conversation with an ecclesiology. He affirms a visible nature to discipleship, but is skeptical about how such a visible and corporate identity may impact the *Yeshu Bhaktas'* ability to create a widespread movement. I appreciate these cautions, but theologically contend that a corporate identity is an integral aspect of ecclesiology. Further, and as Gaurav has suggested, I base this study on the belief that groups such as the *Yeshu satsangs* can provide a helpful model for how to be distinct from, yet sociologically related to, their Hindu and Sikh communities.

Dasan Jeyaraj

Dasan Jeyaraj is the Director for Training for Operation Mobilization, India. His doctoral research, conducted in 2001–2002 and published in 2010, followed a similar path as Hoefer's quantitative study in *Churchless Christianity*, investigating the presence and beliefs of what Jeyaraj calls

56. See also Juergensmeyer, "The Social Significance of Radha Soami."

"followers of Christ outside of the church" in Chennai. An important part of Jeyaraj's contributions are the analyses of a quantitative survey conducted with 12,166 respondents, of whom 390 respondents (3.20%) declared that they "follow Jesus Christ as their religious leader and that they do not associate with the Christian religion."[57] He also collected interviews with pastors, first-generation Christians, and "mission leaders" regarding their views of followers of Christ outside the church.

Similar to Hoefer's study, Jeyaraj's research is helpful in providing data through which to better understand the numbers and profiles of people (in Chennai) that may be followers of Christ outside the church, the influences which led them to follow Jesus, and the common perceptions among Christian leaders about these people. Of particular importance to my research, however, are Jeyaraj's ecclesiological reflections regarding this data. In this regard, the study suffers from a crucial lack of precision in two areas. The first is what Jeyaraj considers and labels a "movement." There has been and continues to be, he asserts, a large "non-church movement" that goes back to the "early part of the nineteenth century."[58] The thesis is striking and highly intriguing for those interested in insider movements. However, his only evidence for this are seven "non-church theologians" and one current "movement" whose lives and work span from the late nineteenth century to the present. Several of these leaders started groups and began or inspired the formation of *ashrams* (devotional centers). However, of these, only one group outlasted the founder, Subba Rao. Thus, though the leaders that Jeyaraj surveys provide important historical case studies of people who followed Christ in a Hindu context, they do not represent a "movement" in any sociological sense.

The second area of imprecision, and the one most relevant to my study, is Jeyaraj's understanding of and use of the word "church." Jeyaraj gives a definition of this at the beginning of his study, explaining that "church" refers to "the universal body of Christian believers and to local churches, and is here applied to the universal church and to all local churches in general."[59] This definition emphasizes a theological understanding of church and highlights both its local and universal nature. However, he goes on to explain that those "outside the church" refers to

57. Jeyaraj, *Followers of Christ Outside the Church*, 241.

58. Ibid., 42.

59. Ibid., 31.

those who "remain outside the organized church for various reasons."[60] Jeyaraj acknowledges both the theological nature of the church, including its local manifestation, as well as the sociological, communal form that this has taken in India, and he seems to have in mind the latter when he speaks about a "non-church movement" and "followers of Christ outside of the church."

Unfortunately, however, Jeyaraj's distinctions are not always clear. For example, at one point Jeyaraj describes a well-known group of followers of Christ in the northern Indian city of Allahabad called the *Yeshu dabar*. This gathering began several years ago on the campus of a Christian agricultural university and has at times attracted thousands of people to worship, receive prayer for healing and hear the leader's preaching about Jesus. Because the movement was not started through an existing church denomination, and because the leader uses some contextual forms for worship, Jeyaraj calls this an example of a current "movement outside of the church." However, aside from its independent origins, it is unclear if or how its leader considers it "outside the church," or how it differs from the many other churches that have started independent of any denominational affiliation. In such cases Jeyaraj blurs the distinctions between such groups and other "churches," and further obscures the way these supposedly relate to the individual followers of Christ in Chennai.

In the conclusion of his study Jeyaraj more clearly defines his understanding of "church," this time emphasizing historic and theological practices. The church, he says, is marked by baptism which, for him, is "the decisive step for joining the Christian community" and through which people "enroll themselves as members of the church."[61] In addition, a church is marked by regular worship, the verbal and non-verbal proclamation the gospel, and the acknowledgement of its "hierarchy" or "church order" which people are meant to obey.[62] Here Jeyaraj displays his own training and ordination in the Anglican Church and asserts that the 390 respondents, and many others like them, are staying out of this type of church. However, whereas Jeyaraj's understanding of church is certainly valid, such a definition would exclude any number of believers, gatherings and "churches," not just those who desire to in some ways remain in their Hindu communities.

60. Ibid., 33.
61. Ibid., 417.
62. Ibid., 418.

In summary, whereas Jeyaraj's study contributes helpful data regarding *Yeshu Bhakta* in Chennai, and other Christians' views of them, I find that his lack of sociological and ecclesiological clarity in the area of "movements" and "church" hinders helpful discussion regarding such groups' ecclesial identity. Similar to what I stated above in regards to Hoefer, in this study I thus seek to give greater theological and sociological clarity regarding the theological "church" identity of the *Yeshu satsangs*, as well as how these seek to be sociologically distinct from the Christian churches in their area.[63]

Roger Hedlund

Roger Hedlund has taught and researched in India since 1974, and many of his recent projects and publications have focused on what he calls "indigenous independent Indian churches."[64] Though Hedlund discusses many examples of such churches and offers various reflections based on these, I will focus on two particular contributions that he makes and how these relate to understanding ecclesial identities of *Yeshu satsangs*.

The first of Hedlund's related contributions is his focus on New Christian Movements,[65] or the indigenous independent Indian churches (IIICs).[66] Such churches, Hedlund shows, have been under-valued and under-researched because of their lack of association with historic, western-originated mission organizations and churches. The IIICs, however, are examples of exciting and new Christian movements that in many ways are more "indigenous" to their historic counterparts. To help theorize and conceptualize the way the IIICs relate to other Indian churches Hedlund adapts and uses the concept of "great" and "little" traditions.[67] In

---

63. A convention I use, in contrast to Jeyaraj, is to avoid phrases such as "outside of the church." As my research will show, even though the *Yeshu satsangs* contrast themselves from local churches, their theological and sociological relationships to the church make labels such as "inside" and "outside" problematic.

64. Hedlund, *Quest for Identity*; Hedlund, "Introduction: Indigenous Christianity as a Field for Academic Research."; Hedlund, "The Witness of New Christian Movements in India"; Hedlund, "Present-day Independent Christian Movements: A South Asian Perspective."

65. Hedlund draws on the research and theories of Harold Turner on New Religious Movements. Turner, "Religious Movements in Primal (or Tribal) Societies."

66. I am introducing and using the acronym IIIC based on Hedlund's "Independent indigenous Indian churches," though Hedlund himself does not use an acronym.

67. Hedlund adapts the concept of the great and little traditions as first developed by Robert Redfield. Redfield, *Peasant Society and Culture*.

the context of Indian Christianity, major denominational churches with foreign origins, such as the Orthodox, Roman Catholic, Church of South India and Church of North India, represent the great tradition. In contrast, the little tradition "consists of lesser known small denominations, evangelical and Pentecostal movements, a host of independent churches and various fringe sects."[68]

As the above description suggests, an important differentiation between great and little tradition churches regards their indigeneity and independence from foreign origins. To help analyze their indigenous character, Hedlund makes a distinction between "indigenous" and "indigenized" churches. He explains, "Indigenisation, contextualization and Indianization are expressions of the effort by a non-indigenous body (one of alien origin and pattern) to reincarnate itself in the local culture and idiom."[69] The prominent example of indigenization are the efforts of some of India's great tradition churches to change foreign worship patterns and structures into those that reflect Indian culture.

Hedlund applauds the efforts of great tradition churches to indigenize, but contrasts this with churches that are indigenous by origin and nature. He explains, "Indigenous Indian Christianity is found in the Little Tradition of the so-called fringe sections largely (not exclusively) of Pentecostal, Charismatic or Evangelical origin."[70]

One of the reasons that the indigenous little tradition churches have been under-valued is that the great tradition churches have labeled them as sects. To better conceptualize their role in Indian Christianity, Hedlund argues that little tradition churches should instead be understood as "revitalization movements" within the larger Christian movement.[71] Great tradition churches, Hedlund hopes, will recognize and embrace little tradition churches as important and new expressions of Christianity.[72]

---

68. Hedlund, "Present-day Independent Christian Movements," 51–52.

69. Ibid., 51.

70. Hedlund, *Quest for Identity*, 3.

71. Hedlund develops the concept of "revitalization movements" as originally developed by anthropologist Anthony F. C. Wallace. See Wallace, "Revitalization Movements." For further missiological examples and applications of the concept see Tippett, *Church Growth and The Word of God*; Tippett, *Introduction to Missiology*; Hiebert, Shaw and Tienou, *Understanding Folk Religion*.

72. Ibid., 18–19; Hedlund, "The Witness of New Christian Movements in India," 19.

Hedlund's focus on "New Christian Movements" is, I believe, a helpful contribution to this and other studies. In particular, his application of revitalization movements helps highlights that many new churches and movements are responses to tension and stagnation in existing churches. However, I contend that his application and categorization of the great/little traditions, and his distinction between indigenized and indigenous churches can inhibit the conceptualization of the process of identity formation.[73] As some of Hedlund's own examples seem to show, the origins of a church may say very little about its actual identity and character and how this has been shaped. Though the categorization of great/little traditions and indigenous/indigenized churches has helped Hedlund shine a spotlight on an under-researched segment of churches, it does not conceptually advance research regarding the processes through which various New Christian Movements are influenced and shaped.

The second of Hedlund's contributions that relates to this study are his critiques of the *Yeshu Bhaktas* in light of the IIICs. In earlier writings Hedlund cites work by Hoefer and acknowledges that "this category forms a significant component of South Indian religious life and represents one aspect of indigeneity of Christianity."[74] However, in more recent writings Hedlund questions "A widely-promoted but controversial 'churchless Christianity' project (that) attempts to circumvent the stumbling block of the church by plotting a new paradigm that does not take into account the ecclesial community."[75] Citing Hoefer and Richard, Hedlund summarizes that "Devotees of Christ are encouraged to retain their ethnic and caste community identity as practicing Yishu bhaktas without membership in a church."[76] Hedlund expresses reservations about such a "project" on several grounds. The core of his critique regards the importance of establishing gatherings known as "churches." He explains:

---

73. As anthropologist Steven Kaplan, in his introduction to *Indigenous Responses to Western Christianity*, summarizes, "The transformation of Christianity as a result of local initiatives has assumed diverse forms and has been guided by a variety of principles and motives. While blanket terms such as enculturation, adaptation, indigenization, and contextualization may be of some use in characterizing the general processes which occurred, when applied to specific cases they tend to obscure rather than clarify important distinctions." Kaplan, "Introduction," 4.

74. Hedlund, *Quest for Identity*, 70.

75. Hedlund, "Present-day Independent Christian Movements," 56.

76. Ibid.

> *Biblically*, the norm from Jesus onward has been the formation of communities of believers known as the "church." *Theological-ly*, the church is the worldwide community of those who confess Christ as Lord and strive to express the values of his Kingdom. *Historically*, the church as the gathered faith community has existed for two thousand years. *Missiologically*, formation of visible fellowships of believers has been the outcome of missionary witness worldwide . . . . *Strategically*, one must consider Hinduism's capacity to absorb—witness the demise of Buddhism in the land of its birth as well as the disappearance of early Christian communities beyond Kerala."[77]

Hedlund highlights a theological versus sociological view of church. In this regard, and as my discussion of Hoefer and Richard showed, both of the latter would probably affirm Hedlund's statements, including the importance of local gatherings and of the global and historic church. In addition, both would probably disagree with Hedlund's assessment that they "do not take into account the ecclesial community."

While Hoefer and Richard encourage *Yeshu Bhaktas* to remain outside of existing Indian churches in order to remain a part of their Hindu communities, they affirm the *Yeshu Bhaktas*' membership in the worldwide church and encourage the idea of some form of gathering for discipleship. But are such gatherings a "church" theologically? Would these be an expression of an IIIC? Hoefer and Richard are unclear on this point. Unfortunately, and similar to Tennent, Hedlund's critique becomes blurred over Richard and Hoefer's ambiguity regarding what is and is not a "church."[78] As such, Hedlund's critique again highlights the need for greater theological and sociological clarity regarding the ecclesial identity of New Religious Movements such as *Yeshu satsangs*.

In summary, Hedlund helpfully highlights the wide presence of IIICs as expressions of New Religious Movements in India, and I concur that these can be viewed as engaging a process of revitalization in relation to their socio-cultural context and the existing church in their area.

---

77. Ibid., 57. Italics original.

78. In email correspondence regarding the contents of this chapter H. L. Richard adds, "I have proposed affirming *ekklesia* of Yeshu groups while denying 'church.' Church simply has too many connotations that are problematic in both biblical (primary current meaning is a building) and current identity terms." Richard, Jun 20, 2011. He thus affirms gatherings that are theologically shaped as "church," but clarifies that the actual word "church" carries unhelpful sociological meaning. However, this "proposal" has not been outlined in any published documents.

However, though I find it helpful to highlight the distinctive characteristics and contributions of the IIICs, I contend that Hedlund's application of the categories of great and little traditions and the differentiation between indigenous and indigenized churches do not give adequate attention to the processes that, in actuality, blur these distinctions. In addition, Hedlund's particular critique of *Yeshu Bhaktas* further highlights the need for theological and sociological clarity when addressing the issue of ecclesial identity. In light of this, I suggest that a theory with attention to process, such as an Emergentist theory of identity formation, will add new theoretical dimensions and insight into discussions of ecclesial identity. Before turning to this, however, I will discuss the contributions of one additional scholar.

Jonas Adelin Jorgensen

In 2004, Jonas Jorgensen conducted an ethnographic study of a group of "Christ Bhaktas," or devotees of Christ, in Chennai. Coupled with a second study of Muslim "Jesus Imandars" in Bangladesh, Jorgensen interviewed twenty-three people who were a part of a mandali, or Christ Bhakta fellowship. Several of the bhaktas were also members of local "missionary churches," several attended services in local charismatic churches, and others participated exclusively in the mandali. Jorgensen analyzes the gatherings and narratives of these respondents to better understand their theology and practice, and the ways in which they engage in what he calls a "syncretistic process"[79] and the formation of "interreligious hermeneutics."[80]

Jorgensen's study traverses a wide range of theories and theoretical frameworks. Of particular importance to my study, however, are his foci on identity formation and ecclesiology. Regarding the former, Jorgensen gives attention not only to the identities of *Yeshu Bhaktas*, but also seeks to highlight the processes through which these identities were formed. In

79. In brief, Jorgensen contends that syncretism should be viewed as a process versus an outcome. He acknowledges that there is "some point" in viewing syncretism through the framework of "legitimate and illegitimate syntheses," but concludes that such a framework is simply a theological interpretation "of the outcomes and consequences of the process." Jorgensen, *Jesus Imandars and Christ Bhaktas*, 116.

80. The concept of "interreligious hermeneutics," according to Jorgensen, helps conceptualize "the theoretical understanding of religious communication across cultures and religions" (ibid., 25). Though he focuses on the specific examples of Jesus *Imandars* and Christ *Bhaktas*, his overall interest is to conceptualize how these relate to the wider, globalizing Church.

particular, Jorgensen discusses ways in which particular theologies and identities are the result of "syncretic" interactions with the ideologies and cultures of a context. It is important, he argues, to view this interaction as an ongoing process.[81] However, though the theoretical basis of his theory is quite developed, it seems to be less helpful to him in interpreting the empirical data of the *Yeshu Bhakta*s of his study. For example, in tracing some of the main factors of the bhaktas' testimonies, he finds and acknowledges that many, if not most, of the *bhaktas* "converted" from Hinduism, "became Christians" through Christian institutions such as schools and churches, and continue to be a part of some churches.[82] He also indicates that the various practices, concepts and terms that the *bhaktas* use sometimes combine Hindu and Christian meanings. However, he does not probe the process through which the *bhaktas*' practices and beliefs have been impacted by their interaction with Christian churches and teachings. Thus, whereas I concur with Jorgensen's overall interest in the process of identity formation, I suggest that other theoretical frameworks may be more helpful for analyzing ecclesial identities of *Yeshu Bhakta*s and *satsangs*.

A second contribution related to this study is Jorgensen's analysis and discussion of ecclesiology; or what he calls the *Yeshu Bhaktas*' "ecclesiological ideal." In this, Jorgensen's analysis of what exists is clearer and more helpful than his discussion regarding the process of its formation. Regarding their present ecclesiology, Jorgensen—and perhaps the *bhaktas* themselves—are most articulate about what they dislike in the existing churches. In their view the local, institutional churches are characterized by their western and foreign practices and emphasis on structures and clergy. In contrast the *mandali* fellowships of the *bhaktas* are more "Indian" and focus on "fellowship and relations in opposition to structure."[83] Relatedly, in observing their current *satsangs*, Jorgensen concludes that the *Yeshu Bhakta*s are using the "style" of Hindu *bhakti* but doing this within a "Christian theological universe" or Christian system of meaning.[84] This, he says, has important implications for the identities of the *Yeshu Bhakta*s and their fellowship. He says:

81. Ibid., 115.
82. Ibid., 333, 401–2.
83. Ibid., 383.
84. Ibid., 396–97.

> [The] manipulation of symbols and elements has clear theo-
> logical implications: the meaning of central Christian teachings
> gains new significance through refashioning of Hindu symbols.
> However, the refashioning of rites and symbols serves not only
> a theological but also a social purpose: it seems that indigenized
> rituals become tools in the release from and re-integration into
> Hindu society rather than into any Christian church. In this
> profound sense, the liminal *bhakti* groups facilitate a recovery
> not only of theological meaning but also of their Hindu social
> identity as truly and interiorly Indian.[85]

This analysis of "symbols" and practices reflects Jorgensen's symbolic anthropological framework, and seeks to account for the theological and social aspects of these practices. Jorgensen's framework, however
does not address questions regarding the interaction between this social
identity, the influence from Christian churches, and their relatively new
project of creating *Yeshu Bhakta* identities. Such information is important to understand the formation of ecclesial identities, but unfortunately
lies outside of Jorgensen's framework.

In summary, Jorgensen has provided an important and pioneering
study of a group of *Yeshu Bhakta* and helpfully considers their beliefs and
Hindu practices. He also gives attention to aspects of the current ecclesiology of this group of *Yeshu Bhakta*, which he formulates through symbolic anthropology and other theoretical frameworks. However, though
he proposes to look at the process through which the *bhaktas'* beliefs and
identities have been shaped, his framework and its application does not
fully develop crucial questions related to this, including how and why
their practices contribute to their ecclesial identity, and the influence that
interaction with local churches have on the continuing ecclesial identity
of the *satsang*. It is questions such as this that an Emergentist theory of
identity formation will help address.

Summary of Recent Scholarship

In summary, early Indian pioneers such as Upadhyay and Subba Rao
critiqued the church's lack of cultural engagement and tried to offer conceptual and practical alternatives. As well, recent scholars have developed
various sets of data regarding *Yeshu Bhaktas* and theories to interpret
this data. How does this contribute to and guide the current research

---

85. Ibid., 402.

of the *Yeshu satsangs* in northwest India? First, the work of early Indian pioneers show that questions regarding an authentic expression of Indian Christianity are not new. Similar to what the *Yeshu Bhakta* expressed in the studies of Hoefer, Jeyraj and Jorgensen, the early pioneers were not comfortable with the way some churches called them to separate and disassociate from their Hindu communities. In response, both the early pioneers and the contemporary *Yeshu Bhakta* sought to retain aspects of their Hindu culture and practices while changing the object of their devotion to Jesus.

Second, though some studies have discussed various practices, identities and theologies of *Yeshu Bhakta* and *satsangs*, this survey highlights the need for greater precision when talking about ecclesial identities. Hoefer's ecclesiology, Hedlund's critique of this, the Richard/Tennent debates, and Jeyaraj's discussions regarding "followers of Jesus outside of the church" have all, I contend, suffered in part from a lack of clarity regarding the theological and sociological definition of "church."

Third, there is a need for further theory and discussion regarding the processes through which groups such as the *Yeshu satsangs* form and shape their identities. How do *Yeshu satsang* leaders seek to shape their group's identities in relation to their culture? In what ways have their interactions with Christian and Hindu and Sikh contexts helped *Yeshu satsangs* emerge? Emergentist theory can help answer these questions and shed light on the ways in which the interaction of people with different structural and cultural properties lead to the emergence of new structures, culture and identities. In the next chapter, I will develop this theory and describe how it can help with understanding ecclesial identities.

CHAPTER 2

Social Theory Framework

An Emergentist Theory of Identity Formation

MY CENTRAL ARGUMENT THROUGHOUT this study is that an Emergentist social analysis and theological analysis of *Yeshu satsangs* will help clarify the ecclesial identities of *Yeshu satsangs*. Ecclesial identities, including those of the *Yeshu satsangs*, consist of shared practices formed over the course of time through interactions between members' contexts and their faith in Jesus. To analyze the social nature and formation of these identities I formulate what I am calling an Emergentist theory of identity formation, comprised of four theoretical components. The first, an Emergentist theory of agency, draws primarily on Pierre Bourdieu and the Critical Realist theory of Margaret Archer. The remaining three— Analytical Dualism, the morphogenetic process, and retroduction—are drawn from Archer and other theorists. I will describe each of these in turn.

AN EMERGENTIST THEORY OF AGENCY

How do people make decisions? Specifically, how do *Yeshu satsang* leaders decide about what practices to use in their *Yeshu satsangs* and what guides these decisions? These questions have been at the heart of recent debates in cultural sociology regarding the role of reflexive agency and unconscious influence on our actions and practices.[1] These debates often refer to two competing theories to account for peoples' actions.

1. For example, see Adams, "Hybridizing *Habitus* and Reflexivity"; Bottero, "Inter-subjectivity and Bourdieusian Approaches to 'Identity.'"

On the one side, some theorists assert that people are conscious of their decisions and exercise a high level of agency in implementing them. Margaret Archer, for example, in her extensive work on Critical Realism[2] is particularly concerned to show that "We are simultaneously free and constrained and we also have some awareness of it."[3] While, according to Archer, most theories conflate people's agential abilities into the social and cultural systems, Critical Realism contends that people have the ability to conceive of and execute various "projects" according to their own interests, and to reflexively deliberate about their own roles and identities in relation to others.[4]

On the other hand, some theorists contend that people often act unconsciously according to socially shaped habits. Pierre Bourdieu, for example, argues that most of what people do is not the product of reflective, conscious thought but rather formed by a largely unconscious *habitus*. Practices, according to Bourdieu, " . . . have as their principle not a set of conscious, constant rules, but practical schemes, opaque to their possessors, varying according to the logic of the situation . . . "[5] These "practical schemes" are formed in persons' early years as they respond to their contexts in ways they are told are appropriate. Eventually this becomes a *habitus*, an unconscious repertoire from which people draw to

---

2. Realist social theory has emerged in recent years as a response to postmodern, linguistic and deterministic theories. A core tenet is the defense that " . . . it is possible for human beings to have knowledge that is about the world as it is (and) that we are not caught in the 'prison house of language' to such an extent that we can know nothing about the world at all." Alcoff, "Who's Afraid of Identity Politics," 315–16. Among Realist social theorists there exists quite a fair level of diversity regarding specific approaches and emphases, but in general most affirm that objective truth exists and acknowledge that its apprehension is subjective. Hiebert, *Missiological Implications of Epistemological Shifts*, 69. Ontologically, therefore, realist theory asserts that there are objective systems that exist independent of, to differing degrees, human beings and that create emergent properties that we observe and experience. Epistemologically we do not have pure, unmediated access to this world. Rather, our knowledge is always locally and historically relative, though there are grounds for choosing between competing views. Beyond these basic tenets there exists diversity regarding specific epistemologies and methods. In this paper I utilize the approach of a particular school of Realist theory called Critical Realism. Even within this school lies diversity, and as such I am focusing upon the work of one of its main (British) proponents, Margaret Archer.

3. Archer, *Realist Social Theory*, 2.

4. Archer, *Structure, Agency, and the Internal Conversation*, 122.

5. Bourdieu, *The Logic of Practice*, 12.

respond to particular circumstances but which they rarely, if ever, reflect upon.[6]

Thus, Archer and Bourdieu at first glance account for peoples' actions in very different ways. However, as Matthew Adams has summarized, numerous scholars see potential for and are exploring ways in which reflexive and *habitus* theories such as these can be hybridized.[7] Drawing on the work of Elder-Vass in particular, I suggest that aspects of both perspectives can be helpfully combined through a Critical Realist ontology and what Elder-Vass calls an "Emergentist theory of action."[8] Elder-Vass contends that " . . . many and perhaps most of our actions are co-determined by both our *habitus* and our reflexive deliberations, and that despite the apparently conflicting implications of these two perspectives for our sense of our ability to choose our actions, they in fact represent two complementary moments of one and the same process."[9] Rather than being opposite explanations, reflexive deliberation and *habitus* actually represent complimentary parts of an overall process. People make decisions but also employ a host of unconscious actions and responses while implementing the decision. For example, a person may reflexively deliberate about whether or not to go to a location, and then utilize *habitus* responses when implementing the decision.

Building on Elder-Vass' theory, I suggest that it is helpful to conceive of agency as a continuum. On one end of the continuum are decisions that require little reflexive deliberation, such as those that are made quite regularly and for which we draw on responses from our *habitus*. On the other end are those decisions upon which we reflect carefully. In these we consider options in light of our concerns and what will help us realize

6. Bourdieu does allow for a certain level of reflexivity apart from the *habitus*. As he explains, "It is, of course, never ruled out that the responses of the *habitus* may be accompanied by a strategic calculation tending to perform in a conscious mode the operation that the *habitus* performs quite differently . . . " (ibid., 53). On the whole, however, Bourdieu believes that the influence of the *habitus* leaves " . . . a very variable margin for choice." Ibid., 50. As he says, " . . . How can one fail to see that decision, if decision there is, and the 'system of preferences' which underlies it, depend not only on all the previous choices of the decider but also on the conditions in which his 'choices' have been made, which include all the choices of those who have chosen for him, in his place, pre-judging his judgments and so shaping his judgments" (ibid., 49–50).

7. Adams, "Hybridizing *Habitus* and Reflexivity."

8. Elder-Vass, "Reconciling Archer and Bourdieu in an Emergentist Theory of Action."

9. Ibid., 335.

those concerns. In the middle of the continuum are decisions for which we mix reflection and *habitus*.

What is it about a decision that affects the mix of deliberation and *habitus* used to implement it? Bourdieu asserts that peoples' *habitus* are usually created within particular social "fields," such as social classes or vocations. As Williams summarizes, a field is a "structured system of social positions . . . which is both the product and producer of the specific *habitus* appropriate to it."[10] In fact, Bourdieu's theory of *habitus* is largely formed around the assumption that people stay within these fields, and he gives less attention to what happens when one crosses fields, or when fields change because of crises (as in changing or forming new religious communities). However, it can be argued that decisions that cause people to cross "fields" require more deliberate reflection, and we could expect to find more reflexive deliberation in times of transition or crisis. As people move through changes or crises, they will adapt old practices to a new context or adopt new practices. In such cases people will become highly conscious of their adapted or new practices, and remain so for a period of time. However, as people find their identity in the new situation, these adopted or new practices will again eventually form into a new *habitus*. Thus, *habitus* can be disrupted and new practices introduced through change or crisis. Over the course of time, the new practices and reflexive deliberations will then again form into new *habitus*.[11]

The concept of an agency continuum thus helps highlight the ways in which *habitus* and reflexive agency co-determine identity formation. In the case of ecclesial identity formation, I will consider how *Yeshu satsang* leaders make conscious choices regarding their practices and identity—particularly when facing crises or changing religious communities or "fields"—but also draw on many unconscious actions (*habitus*) when animating that identity. An Emergentist theory of identity formation, with its focus on reflexive deliberation and *habitus*, thus gives close attention to the "projects" of these leaders to create an ecclesial identity. Particularly because of the "fields" or systems they are often traversing between religious communities, these leaders are quite aware of this project and the decisions they are making. However, they also bring with

10. Williams, "Theorising class, health and lifestyles," 587. Italics in original.

11. O'Mahoney, in his study of cultures of ethics in businesses, contends that reflexive deliberation eventually weaves into, shapes, and becomes the fabric of the business' culture. O'Mahoney, "Constructing *Habitus*." In short, the reflexive deliberations of today become the *habitus* of tomorrow.

them certain *habitus* that impact the ways they frame their choices. It is helpful and important to first recognize that such a mix of dispositions exists, and to further understand that these impact the ecclesial identity that they are trying to shape.

ANALYTICAL DUALISM

The second theoretical component important to an Emergentist theory of identity formation is what Archer calls Analytical Dualism. I will describe this and also define the concepts of culture, structure, and agency.

Integral to Analytical Dualism is the tenet that agency and structure/culture can and should be analyzed separately so as to understand them and their interplay. Doing so links structure/culture with agency while avoiding the risk of sinking one in the other via conflation.[12] Through Analytical Dualism, cultures, structures, agents and their interplay are analyzed temporally, since the changes that take place in these systems emerge over time. Analytical Dualism, claims Archer, " . . . is a methodology based upon the historicity of emergence."[13]

On one side of Archer's dualism is that of people and their agency. Archer deals with this extensively, particularly in her later work. People, asserts Archer, are influenced but not determined by cultural and structural emergent properties (CEPs and SEPS). In addition, people have the potential of developing their own personal identity as they interact with those CEPs and SEPs, as well as with other individuals and groups.

On the other side of the dualism is culture and structure. Archer asserts that, though these often relate closely to each other, culture and structure each have their own systemic realities and a difference can and should therefore be maintained between them. Not only are culture and structure distinct, but each also has unique "emergent properties" that exert influence upon persons.

For Archer, structural systems (SS) mainly consist of and are defined as social institutions. Though helpful, I find that Archer's description of these structures can be helpfully supplemented by cultural sociologists such as Wendy Griswold and Cornell and Hartmann.[14] A social structure, according to Griswold, is a "network of relationships among

---

12. Archer, *Culture and Agency*, xiv.

13. Archer, *Realist Social Theory*, 66.

14. Cornell and Hartmann, *Ethnicity and Race*; Griswold, *Cultures and Societies in a Changing World*.

members, its institutions, and its economic and political life."[15] Similarly, according to Cornell and Harmann, such structures form various "sets of relationships" through which people can pursue various interests that "may include everything from extended families to credit associations to educational systems to political parties."[16] By extension, such institutions would also include religious groupings, such as various Hindu and Sikh sects. According to Archer, from such structures come "structural emergent properties" (SEPs) whose causal powers include things such as material distributions, roles, organizations, and institutional power.[17] For example, if a person is a part of and cares about a family, the family exerts causal powers on the person's decisions, perhaps through affirmation or social sanctions.

The task of defining culture has in general been more problematic for cultural sociologists than has that of structure. Because of this Archer spends considerable time and energy working out a theory of culture. In developing this, Archer first critiques the "myth of cultural integration."[18] This approach, held by many theorists, defines culture as "a community of shared meanings."[19] Archer argues that this definition harbors many difficulties, including an inability to clearly distinguish between and analyze culture apart from community. Instead, Archer asserts that the cultural system (CS) has an objective existence apart from the Socio-cultural Community or realm (or S-C). If cultural systems are analyzed separately from agents, then researchers can not only more clearly understand their separate properties and powers, but also analyze the various ways in which culture and agents interact.[20]

What, however, is a cultural system (CS)? According to Archer, "At any given time a cultural system is constituted by the corpus of existing intelligibilia—by all things capable of being grasped, deciphered, understood or known by someone."[21] From the CS come "cultural emergent properties" (CEPs), which are those aspects of the cultural system that people have engaged and which have thus begun to influence them. Ex-

15. Griswold, *Cultures and Societies in a Changing World*, 12.
16. Cornell and Hartmann, *Ethnicity and Race*, 86.
17. Archer, *Structure, Agency, and the Internal Conversation*, 5.
18. Archer, *Culture and Agency*, 2.
19. Ibid., 4.
20. Ibid., 21.
21. Ibid., 104.

amples of this would be propositions, theories or doctrines that a person or group create or study.[22]

I find that Archer's definition of culture can again be supplemented with concepts from Griswold. Culture, according to Griswold, consists of language, practices and symbols that guide peoples' "thinking, feeling, and behavior."[23] Each of these components of the cultural system exert causal powers that can influence people in particular ways. For example, in the study of ecclesial identities, theology and doctrines about God and his work can be analyzed as a religio-cultural system that, when engaged and activated, have emergent properties (CEPs) that impact peoples' socio-cultural system.

Before moving on from a discussion of Analytical Dualism, I find Swidler's metaphor of the "cultural toolkit" or "repertoire" a helpful supplement to Analytical Dualism for describing the relationship between culture, structure and people. Rejecting the idea that cultures are overarching systems that determine social structures, Swidler instead proposes that culture exists as a "toolkit" consisting of the "symbols, stories, rituals and worldviews, which people may use in varying configurations to solve different kinds of problems."[24] This toolkit contains a vast array of different "pieces" of culture from which people may draw as they construct "strategies of action."[25]

This is not to say that people always make choices based on rational deliberation. Indeed, drawing on Bourdieu, Swidler says that an equally helpful metaphor is the "repertoire" that has cultivated "skills and habits in its users so that one can be more or less good at the cultural repertoire one performs . . . "[26] As people move among various situations, they draw on pieces from their toolkit or repertoire that help to orient them and their actions.[27] Thus, similar to an Emergentist theory combining Archer and Bourdieu, Swidler asserts that people select and draw on elements of culture in skilled, conscious ways but also cultivate habits (*habitus*) that unconsciously draw from the same repertoire.

22. Archer, *Structure, Agency, and the Internal Conversation*, 5.

23. Griswold, *Cultures and Societies in a Changing World*, 12.

24. Swidler, "Culture in Action," 273; See also Swidler, *Talk of Love*.

25. Swidler, "Culture in Action," 273.

26. Swidler, *Talk of Love*, 24–25.

27. Swidler, "Culture in Action," 277.

In this study, Analytical Dualism, together with the concept of the cultural toolkit, will help me to analyze the nature and formation of ecclesial identities in two ways. First, separating culture, structure and people will allow me to analyze the multiple systems that *Yeshu satsang* leaders engage in their attempts to shape identities for their *satsangs*. Secondly, analyzing the practices and cultural objects that *Yeshu satsang* leaders draw from their cultural "toolkits" will help me consider the reasons they choose particular practices and objects and the properties and associations that those have for the leaders and *satsangis*.

MORPHOGENETIC PROCESS

As Analytical Dualism suggests, ecclesial identities consist of cultural and structural properties. Such identities do not instantly appear. Rather, they emerge over the course of time as people, cultures and structures interact. The third theoretical component, termed Morphogenetic Process by Archer, helps conceptualize the ways these components interact and transform each other over time.

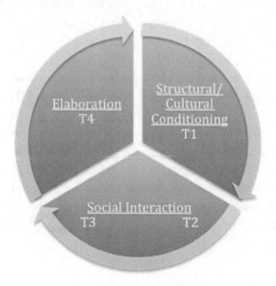

Figure 1: The Morphogenetic Process

As can be seen in Figure 1, there are three stages to the morphogenetic process. The first (T1) is "structural/cultural conditioning" and involves the structural and cultural properties that exist at the beginning of the process. In the second stage of social Interaction (T2), the structural/

cultural system exerts its influence upon people at the Socio-cultural (S-C) level through emergent properties. These properties shape peoples' situations " . . . such that they have the capacity to operate as constraints and enablements."[28] Concurrently, (T3) people and groups interact with systems and their constraints and enablements. The last stage (T4) is "structural/cultural elaboration." In this the interaction between people and systems creates elaborations in the structural/cultural realm, as well as new social roles and identities for people. This elaboration becomes the new context (or T1) that sets the stage for the next cycle.

The elaboration that occurs in systems and the S-C can take one of four general combinations, depending on T2, T3 and their interaction. I will describe two that are of particular importance for this study.

Constraining Contradictions

The first combination occurs if, in T2 there is a contradiction between two ideas in the cultural system (CS), but a fair amount of unity (constraint) at the S-C level (T3). If, by example, we imagine contradicting ideas A and B at the CS level, Archer explains that, in a Constraining Contradiction, " . . . invoking A also ineluctably evokes B and with it the logical contradiction between them . . . . ."[29] In this type of situation, neither A nor B can stand alone, even though B might, " . . . constitute the hostile environment in which A is embedded and from which it cannot be removed."[30]

However, because they contradict, cultural tension is created and the adherents of A and B have to respond to each other. Some people certainly have the option of opting out of their commitment to A or B altogether. However, if they remain committed to their ideology, the response is usually to try and correct and repair the contradiction.[31] Though certain amounts of correction are possible, this is not the norm. Rather, what most often results is some form of syncretism. The main strategy usually becomes "the sinking of differences" between A and B so

28. Archer, *Structure, Agency, and the Internal Conversation,*132.

29. Archer, *Culture and Agency,* 148.

30. Ibid., 148–49.

31. By way of example, Archer cites Durkheim's analysis of early Christianity and Classicism. Though the Church tried to stand apart from the contradictory aspects of Classicism, it was inherently immersed in the latter's ideologies and logics. The Church thus tried to correct the contradictions, often by utilizing Classic logic in theology. Ibid., 150–51, 157.

as to bring union between them.[32] This then requires the redefinition of one or both parts.

Competitive Contradictions

In some situations there exists a contradiction between idea A and idea B at the CS level and a division based on interests or resources at the S-C level. In these cases A and B represent not only clearly different ideologies, but also clearly distinct communities that are aligned with the ideologies. The logic of this situation forces everyone involved to make choices " . . . by accentuating differences, by insisting on their salience, by undermining indifference and by making the question of alignment inescapable."[33]

In addition to forcing choice, the Competitive Contradiction encourages one side to eliminate the other on the ideational (and sometimes literal) battlefield. People A challenge and confront people B, with the goal of having victory over the other. The unintended consequence of this, however, is usually "ideational pluralism" or sustained differentiation, such as between different religions, different civilizations, etc.[34]

As I have stated, ecclesial identities emerge over time as leaders and people are shaped by past and present experiences and form ideas and structures in light of those experiences. Because of this, the morphogenetic process provides a framework through which to analyze the interaction of cultures, structures, and people. In particular, and as will be seen in Chapter 9, the morphogenetic process, including constraining and competitive contradictions, helpfully analyzes and explains some of the ways in which the *Yeshu satsangs* are responding to the Indian Church.

RETRODUCTION

The final theoretical component of this study is retroduction, which Critical Realists suggest can be used to understand the morphogenetic process.[35] Retroduction is the process of looking back to see what processes have helped create the current situation, or elaboration. For this study I combine this with a focus on induction to create a two-part method. The first focuses on inductively generating a theory regarding the markers of

32. Archer, *Realist Social Theory*, 234.

33. Ibid., 240.

34. Archer, *Being Human*, 176.

35. Bhaskar, *The Possibility of Naturalism*; Blundel, "Critical Realism; Sayer, *Realism and Social Science*.

ecclesial identity.[36] In this, I first inductively analyze the existing situation, or elaboration, to understand the context, the practices and ecclesial identities of the *Yeshu satsangs* and what they understand themselves to be doing. I correspond this to stage four (T4) in Archer's morphogenetic process.

In the second step I retroductively seek to explain this theory by identifying the mechanisms and structures that produced them.[37] I link this to stages one and two (T1-T3) of Archer's process, seeking to understand how peoples' *habitus* and the interaction of different emergent properties created the current ecclesial identity.[38] This is done through archival work to understand some of the systems at work in a given context, and through the oral narratives of the people themselves. I will briefly discuss how each stage of the Morphogenetic process relates to the formation of ecclesial identities and how I will investigate these in this study. Referring to Figure 1, I will begin first with an analysis of the present elaboration (T4) of the *Yeshu satsangs'* ecclesial identity markers, and will then move to the previous stages of formation (T1-T3) to describe the ways in which these helped to form these markers.

Step One: Elaboration (T4)

In the Morphogenetic process, the current ecclesial identity of a *Yeshu satsang* is an elaboration (T4) stemming from previous interactions. In Chapters 5 through 8 I seek to answer the second and third research questions: How do *Yeshu satsang* leaders in northwest India use, modify and resist various practices to shape their ecclesial identities, and what are the ecclesial identity markers of six Hindu and Sikh *Yeshu satsangs* in northwest India? I do this by first inductively analyzing the structural and cultural emergent properties of the *Yeshu satsang* practices, and how the *Yeshu satsang* leaders and *satsangis* reflect on these. In Chapter 8 I then consider by way of coded analysis the themes, or markers, that these practices suggest, thus addressing my fourth research question: How did the *Yeshu satsang* leaders' Hindu and Sikh backgrounds and interaction

---

36. Gibbs, *Analyzing Qualitative Data*, 4–5.

37. Sayer, *Method in Social Science*, 107.

38. As Sayer explains, "We need to know not only what the main strategies were of actors, but what it was about the context which enabled them to be successful or otherwise . . . . Often the success or failure of agents' strategies may have little or nothing to do with their own reasons and intentions" Sayer, *Realism and Social Science*, 26.

with Christian churches help shape the ecclesial identity markers of their *Yeshu satsangs*?

Step Two: Structural/Cultural Conditioning (T1) and Interaction (T2 and T3)

After understanding some of the markers of their current ecclesial identities, in Chapter 9 I then retroductively investigate the ways in which the ecclesial identity markers were created. I consider the histories of the *Yeshu satsang* leaders and their stages of development, and particularly their interactions with various cultural and structural systems and the formation of particular *habitus*. I also analyze how this interaction led them to develop a *Yeshu satsang* and choose certain practices. Further analysis shows how this process, together with their *habitus*, shaped the particular markers of ecclesial identity. This gives insight into the processes that helped to shape the current ecclesial identity markers and addresses my fourth research question; How did the *Yeshu satsang* leaders' Hindu and Sikh backgrounds and interaction with Christian churches help shape the ecclesial identity markers of their *Yeshu satsangs*?

CHAPTER SUMMARY

Church, or eccesial communities, including those of the *Yeshu satsangs*, have social identities that are shaped by many factors. To help analyze and explain the formation of these identities we need a theory that considers how these emerge through the interactions of people and their context over the course of time. I contend that an Emergentist theory of identity formation as outlined in this chapter provides social theorists as well as missiologists the theoretical framework to describe and analyze the markers and formation of the ecclesial identities of groups such as the *Yeshu satsangs*.

CHAPTER 3

Ethnographic Methodology

HAVING DESCRIBED THE SOCIAL theory for this study, I will now discuss the specific research methodologies used to study and understand the *Yeshu satsangs* and how these relate to or complement my theoretical framework.

DATA COLLECTION

This study was preceded and prepared for by a pilot study of individual *Yeshu satsangis* (*Yeshu satsang* members) in New Delhi in 2007, and periodic visits with a primary *satsang* leader-consultant in the state of Punjab (northwest of New Delhi) from 2006–2009. The core data for this study, however, was collected during a six-month period in 2010 from leaders and members of six *Yeshu satsangs*. Four of the leaders and *Yeshu satsangs* are among majority Hindu communities and two sets of leaders with *Yeshu satsangs* are in Sikh villages. I interviewed fifty *satsangis*, most of whom were current members of one of the six *satsangs*. However, seven of the *satsangis* that I interviewed currently do not regularly attend a *Yeshu satsang* for various reasons, though have done so or are familiar with them. Three of these became helpful consultants[1] for understanding the context and issues of the *Yeshu satsangs*. For a full list of the leaders, see "Appendix B: Summary of *Yeshu satsangis* and Leaders."

To ensure that the data I collected for this study was reliable (consistent and trustworthy) I utilized three research methods. This also corresponded with a process that has been called Critical Realist Discourse

---

1. I follow the lead of some scholars who use the term "consultant" rather than "informant." See Bernard, *Social Research Methods*, 346.

Analysis,[2] and is particularly well-suited for eliciting information for Emergentist/Critical Realist analysis.

The first step[3] was a literature review researching extra-discursive factors of culture and structures that impact the lives and talk of *Yeshu satsangis*. I focused in particular on literature regarding the ways the Christian community has been historically shaped in northwest India, and on studies regarding the formation of caste and religious identities.

The second step involved ethnographic research (participant observation) of the *satsangs* and related meetings, including prayers, *kirtans* or *bhajans* (worship songs), sermons, announcements, material objects, participation, and physical set-up.[4] From these observations I identified the ways in which *satsang* leaders speak about, practice, and shape the ecclesial identities of the *satsang* community, indicating some of the cultural and structural systems that they are influenced by and to which they are responding.

The third step employed semi-structured ethnographic interviews with *satsang* leaders and members in Hindi or Punjabi as appropriate. The questionnaires, translated into English, can be seen in Appendix C and D. The sampling for *satsangi* interviews was determined through consultation with the *satsangi* leaders. Though the sampling and choices of interviewees often followed pragmatic issues, such as who was available and comfortable with interviews, I sought to obtain a number and sampling representative of a given *satsang*. I interviewed most *satsangis* once, and these interviews lasted anywhere from thirty minutes to two hours. Three people, whom I will describe below and who have led and participated in *Yeshu satsangs* proved to be particularly helpful and available consultants. *Yeshu satsang* leaders were interviewed multiple times. At least one interview normally followed most or all of the Leadership Questionnaires, with follow-up interviews then exploring questions regarding the leaders' *Yeshu satsang*, *satsangis*, practices, vision, and challenges.

As can be seen from the leader and *satsangi* questionnaires, the semi-structured interviews (Appendix C and D) began with the invitation for an open narrative regarding the persons' testimony of how they came to follow Jesus or, if only recently attending the *satsang*, how they

2. Riley, Sims-Schouten, and Willig, "Critical Realism in Discourse Analysis."

3. Though I present and followed these steps chronologically, they also functioned cyclically. Information from an interview, for example, would prompt new literature research, or would open-up new things to look for in participant observation.

4. Jorgensen, *Participant Observation*; Spradley, *Participant Observation*.

came to attend the *satsang*. This then led to "grand tour questions" and "experience questions" that probed the persons' specific experiences with their family's religious practices, how they began following Jesus, how family and friends reacted to this, and how the *satsang* leaders and members responded.[5] I then asked a series of descriptive questions that tested and explored particular domains, or themes of practices and teachings of the *satsang*.[6] The interview questions provided the data to answer my second, third and fourth research questions.

To further ensure that data was reliable, I utilized translators to help in the process of some interviews; a limitation that I will describe further below. I also recorded all interviews (with the participants' permission) and most *satsangs*. This allowed me and a team of transcribers that I trained to make and crosscheck transcriptions and translations for accuracy.

One threat to the reliability of my data that I had to address regarded the "deference effect," or the potential desire of some interviewees to answer questions in a way that would please me as a foreigner and guest to their village or town.[7] To address this, I introduced myself (and the *Yeshu satsang* leaders introduced me) in general terms, not discussing the exact focus of my study. I was thus there to study, or "write a book," about the way their *Yeshu satsang* worshipped and about their testimonies of following Jesus. I further formed my questionnaire in a way that began with general questions regarding their testimony and experiences, and later focused on more specific issues of Hindu and Sikh community identity. The interviewees were thus largely unaware of the specific types of answers and foci in which I was interested. Though these precautions partially obscured some of my specific interests, I recognize that my identity as a Christian and my questions focusing on following Jesus may have caused some respondents to answer questions in ways that would reflect favorably on Jesus and the *Yeshu satsangs*.[8]

---

5. Spradley, *The Ethnographic Interview*, 86–88.

6. Ibid., 88, 126.

7. Bernard, *Research Methods in Anthropology*, 241–42.

8. In light of this it is interesting that many respondents, as I will show, reflected favorably on Hindu/Sikh-oriented practices and communities, even while speaking positively about Jesus. Such responses would not always have been the natural deference and opinion given to a foreign Christian.

To ensure that findings were valid, I took steps to achieve face validity and content validity for each of my research methods.[9, 10] For face validity in the participant observation of *satsang* meetings, I tested the factors that I should look for with the *satsang* leaders. Content that was gleaned from these observations was then periodically brought back to the *satsang* leaders for discussion and to validate its interpretation.

For the face validity of semi-structured interviews, questions were initially developed through consultation with a primary *satsang* leader and then fine-tuned after pilot interviews with *satsangis* and through subsequent meetings and interaction with the leader and consultants. This process ensured that questions were asked that elicited the needed information with a minimal level of confusion. Where translators were used, I reviewed questions and question-asking techniques so that main questions were asked in consistent ways. The content validity of my findings was tested through regular discussions with *Yeshu satsang* leaders and others. In this the three consultants were particularly important, with whom I was able to discuss the content analysis of my findings and alternative interpretations.

DATA ANALYSIS

As indicated above, my interview questions primarily elicited oral narratives from my respondents. I thus analyzed these narratives using both "paradigmatic" and "narrative" analysis.[11] The former analyzes narratives and interview responses for themes and categories, and is sometimes called "content analysis."[12] Narrative analysis, by contrast, looks for the "holistic content" of the narrative, including the patterns, development, and reoccurrences of wider themes.[13] This was combined with Critical

9. Bernard, *Research Methods in Anthropology*, 56; Elliston, *Introduction to Missiological Research*.

10. Face validity answers the question "Does the instrument appear to measure what it claims to measure from a popular perspective?" To answer this, the researcher elicits the opinion of consultants and others who observe the method. Content validity answers the question, "Does the instrument indeed test or measure the issues about which conclusions will be drawn?" To answer this the researcher determines whether the method is testing the various meanings of the subject area. Elliston, *Introduction to Missiological Research*, 44.

11. Polkinghorne, "Narrative Configuration in Qualitative Analysis."

12. Gibbs, *Analyzing Qualitative Data*; Lieblich, Tuval-Machiach, and Zilber, *Narrative Research*.

13. Gibbs, *Analyzing Qualitative Data*; Lieblich, Tuval-Machiach, and Zilber,

Realist Discourse Analysis to consider how structural and cultural systems constrain and enable not only the content of their stories but also
the way they are sharing their stories with me, and what this suggests
about their identity formation process. In particular, I observed such
textual features through the questions: "Where do they start their story?"
"What narrative markers do they use to organize their stories?" and
"How do micro-narratives create, contrast or affirm themes?" To help
with the analysis process all transcripts were translated into English and
then analyzed through the NVivo software program.

LIMITATIONS AND MODIFICATIONS

Throughout the course of the study I encountered various limitations
that would potentially impact the reliability of my data, and made corresponding modifications. The first limitation regarded language. Though
I am able to speak the Hindi language to a certain degree, I do not know
Punjabi and some Hindi dialects. To address this limitation I utilized
the help of translators, particularly when in areas with other languages
(Punjab) and dialects (parts of Himachal Pradesh). These translators
also often helped as consultants with whom I regularly discussed and
tested observations and concepts. In addition, I developed a small group
of transcribers who helped me with transcribing and translating transcripts, and who crosschecked my manuscript and each other's to ensure
accuracy.

A second limitation regarded the ways in *Yeshu satsangis* and local
non-*satsangis* might respond to my presence as a white foreigner. As I
came to find out, people in the villages and towns sometimes suspect
that the *Yeshu satsangs* are associated with Christianity, and thus sometimes associate any white person connected to it as a type of missionary
and financial sponsor. This can further fuel rumors and accusations that
churches, *satsangs* included, use money to coerce and "convert" people.
Satsang leaders and members were sometimes highly sensitive to this
discourse in their communities. To overcome this limitation and ensure
reliable data regarding *Yeshu satsangs*, the leaders and I first decided on
particular *satsangs* that would be helpful to my study but whose communities were less sensitive to the presence of a white foreigner.[14] In addition,

---

Narrative Research: Reading, Analysis, and Interpretation; Riessman, *Narrative Analysis*.

14. In one case a *satsang* leader and I decided against research with a particular
Yeshu satsang because of negative experiences they had in recent years due to the

we considered and agreed on the ways in which they or I would introduce myself to the *Yeshu satsangs* and the best locations for interviews so as to minimize misunderstandings based on my presence.

A final limitation I encountered pertained to the types of questions that I could ask. I had intended to ask questions regarding the marginalized in and around the *satsang*—which would invariably reference caste distinctions—and the role of leadership styles in shaping the *satsangs*. These issues, however, proved very sensitive for direct questions, and threatened the reliability of my initial interview design. I was able to overcome the limitation of caste questions to a degree by adjusting the design of questions and looking for indirect references to these issues during the course of conversations and attendance at *satsangs*. The issue of leadership style proved too sensitive to overcome, and I thus decided to adjust my research design and not include this as part of my query.[15]

WRITING CONVENTIONS OF THIS STUDY

As per the agreement that I made with respondents, I have changed all names and have been careful to obscure specific geographic markers so as to keep identities and locations confidential. Though not all respondents were concerned with confidentiality, some were, and it was easiest to adopt the same standard for all participants and *satsangs* involved. In addition, respondents spoke Hindi, Punjabi or English, and sometimes a mixture of these. Because of this, when quoting a respondent I place an [H] (for Hindi), a [P] (for Punjabi), or an [E] (for English) at the end of the quote to specify the original language of the quotation.

Analyzing the practices and factors that shape ecclesial identities in general, and those of the *Yeshu satsangs* in particular, requires careful ethnographic research that corresponds theoretically with the social theory guiding the study. The research methodology I have described in this chapter was designed to generate data that helps to illuminate the identities that emerge from the *satsangs'* practices and socio-religious contexts. It is now time to give a brief introduction to the location, leaders and characteristics of the *Yeshu satsangs* themselves.

---

presence of a foreigner.

15. Some leaders were sensitive to what could seem like foreign scrutiny of their leadership of *Yeshu satsangs*. In particular, one of the leaders central to my research and through whom I networked with other *Yeshu satsang* leaders had recently experienced a bad conflict with and criticism from a foreign missionary, and was thus very sensitive to any questions regarding his leadership.

CHAPTER 4

An Introduction to *Yeshu Satsangs* and Their Context

IN THIS CHAPTER I give an overview of the region in which the *Yeshu satsangs* are located, the main characteristics of the *Yeshu satsangs* themselves, and the characteristics of the Christian church in that area. In the chapters that follow I will then analyze the practices and histories of the *Yeshu satsangs* and their leaders through an Emergentist theory of identity formation to better understand the ways in which the leaders are attempting to use practices to shape their *satsangs'* ecclesial identities, and how they themselves have been shaped and impacted by cultural and structural systems.

REGIONAL AND RELIGIOUS LANDSCAPE OF NORTHWEST INDIA

Northwest India is comprised of the five states of Punjab, Rajasthan, Haryana, Himachal Pradesh, Jammu-Kashmir, the National Capitol Territory of Delhi, and the Union Territory of Chandigarh. Though *satsangs* are located in various places, I focus on *satsangs* located in Punjab, eastern Himachal Pradesh, northern Haryana, and Chandigarh (see Map 1).

Map 1: Regional Locale of the Six *Yeshu Satsangs*

The religious demographics of these states, according to the most recent 2001 census data, shows that Sikhs form a majority of the population in the state of Punjab, and Hindus make up the majority in Haryana, Chandigarh, and Himachal Pradesh (see Table 1). Christianity is a minority in all areas, though there are certain districts in Punjab where the population is slightly larger.

Table 1
2001 Census Data: Religious Community Populations by State[1]

	Chandigarh	Haryana	Himachal Pradesh	Punjab
Hindu	78.61%	88.23%	95.43%	36.94%
Muslim	3.95%	5.78%	1.97%	1.57%

1. Census Commissioner of India, "Census of India."

Christian	0.85%	0.13%	0.13%	1.20%
Sikh	16.12%	5.54%	1.19%	59.91%
Buddhist/Jain/Other	0.46%	0.31%	1.28%	0.37%
Total	100%	100%	100%	100%

OVERVIEW OF THE YESHU SATSANG LEADERS AND PRACTICES

The present study focuses on eight leaders representing six *Yeshu satsangs*, as well as the data from interviews with fifty *satsangis*. Each of the six *Yeshu satsangs* that I studied uniquely reflect the religious communities in which they are located and the preferences of the leaders and *satsangis*. These *Yeshu satsangs* can be grouped into three general categories, corresponding to the different communities in which they are set (see Appendix E: Summary of *Yeshu satsang* Leaders by Community). I will in this section introduce the different *Yeshu satsang* leaders and give an overview of the distinct characteristics of the *satsangs* in each category, taking note of both the similarities and respective differences between leaders.

Yeshu bhakti Satsangs

Three of the leaders that I studied—Gaurav, Dinesh and Ravi—conduct *Yeshu satsangs* in Hindu, or predominately Hindu communities, along eastern Punjab, West Himachal Pradesh and West Haryana respectively. All three are from Hindu families, became followers of Jesus[2] as adults, and originally led Christian churches. Of the three, Gaurav has been leading a *Yeshu satsang* the longest, having made a switch to this style approximately ten years ago when he moved to his present location. Dinesh led a house church for four years but, after meeting Gaurav and receiving training, changed to a *Yeshu satsang*. Ravi began leading a *Yeshu satsang* around five or six years ago after joining staff with a large international mission organization and receiving teaching in contextualization.

A common Hindu tradition that all three leaders embrace is the Hindu *bhakti* tradition. The Hinduism of many in the northwest,

---

2. The *Yeshu satsang* leaders, and the *satsangis*, never used the word "convert" or any Hindi or Punjabi equivalents. Instead they often expressed their move towards faith in Jesus as "coming to this line."

according to these leaders, contrasts with that of South India or from orthodox pilgrimage sites such as Varanasi.[3] Hindus in such regions tend to emphasize elaborate temple-based rituals and symbols, and the *Yeshu satsangs* of the same regions consequently utilize and adapt some of the elaborate symbols and rituals associated with these traditions. In contrast, many Hindus in the northwest are influenced by the *bhakti* traditions. These tend to de-emphasize temple rituals in favor of devotion to and following the teachings of a guru.[4] Ravi describes the contrast:

> Varanasi is a main place for many Hindus. And it is the place of religious pilgrimages, and so the whole of Hindu influence starts from [there]. And Haryana is Hindi . . . and Hindus are there but mostly it has been influenced by Punjab. That is, most of the influence of the [Sikh] gurus have come here, and now because of the gurus we have to bring a little Punjabi style and Hindi style (in our *satsangs*) and we have to mix both." [H][5, 6]

Relatedly, the *Yeshu bhakti satsang* leaders argue that *satsangs* with simpler rituals are more appropriate for their context, since the Hindus of the area are, as another *satsang* leader says, "not very ritualized."[7]

Another reason that these *satsang* leaders appeal to and draw on the *bhakti* tradition is that all three, and particularly Gaurav's urban *Yeshu satsangs*, tend to attract people from diverse religious and caste communities, including Hindu, Sikh, Christian, and tribal. Whereas highly ritualized Hindu *satsangs* do not easily accommodate such diversity, these leaders find that the *bhakti* tradition advocates and creates a less-ritualized, socio-religiously inclusive community that is still a part of the Hindu framework.[8]

---

3. The Yeshu bhakti *satsang* leaders sometimes used Varanasi as a point of comparison and contrast. This because Varanasi, along with its many temples and ceremonies, represents one of the most sacred pilgrimage sites for Hindus and Brahminical Hindus in India. In addition, Varanasi is also the center of an influential network of *Yeshu satsangs* that have patterned themselves according to some of the orthodox Hindu rituals of the region.

4. The most prevalent expression of this is Sikhism, which began as a *bhakti* sect.

5. Interview with Ravi, Jun 24, 2010.

6. For this and all other interview quotes refer to Appendix B for the list of leaders and *satsang* members.

7. Though they opt for less use of symbols, these *satsang* leaders do utilize symbols in particular instances.

8. This again is also reflected in the *bhakti* origins of Sikhism, which has traditionally opposed caste divisions and advocated equality among people from diverse

Gaurav's *Yeshu satsang* is the largest, and is actually comprised of four *satsangs* that meet throughout the city with a total of eighty to one hundred *satsangis*. Periodically Gaurav hosts a "special *satsang*" which regularly draws 200 or more people who are at the fringe of the *satsang* in relationship or spiritual understanding. Of all the *Yeshu bhakti satsangs*, Gaurav's *satsang* is the most diverse in its membership, consisting of people from Hindu, Sikh, Christian, and tribal communities, as well as a variety of castes and socio-economic levels.

Dinesh's *Yeshu satsang* meets in his home and consists of approximately twenty to thirty people. Having only recently begun to change his approach, Dinesh's *satsang* displays a hybrid of Christian and Hindu influences, as will be described below. The people that attend the *satsang* are largely from Dalit and OBC castes[9], though at least one *satsangi* from a high-caste Hindu family regularly attends.

Ravi's *Yeshu bhakti satsang* also meets in his home with thirty to forty people on average. Though Ravi is more intentional and experienced at designing *Yeshu bhakti satsang* worship settings, he admits that his *satsang* also displays a mix of Hindu and Christian influences, the latter coming from the worship style promoted in his mission organization. Nonetheless, as will be discussed below, Ravi has taken clear steps to shape the worship and teaching of the *satsang* in a way reflecting his and his community's Hindu culture and structure.

Arya Samaj Yeshu satsang

The second type of *Yeshu satsang* is one led by a lawyer named Padman. Every weekend Padman and his family travel from their home in a city to his parent's home in a small village to conduct a *satsang* for parents, brothers, and their families. Currently, approximately five to ten members of Padman's family attend the *satsang*. In addition Padman sometimes hosts *satsangs* with other families in the village, and also has trained two other leaders in nearby towns to lead *satsangs*.

Padman's high-caste family comes from a particular Hindu sect called the Arya Samaj.[10] Ten years ago while working at a mission

backgrounds.

9. OBC stands for "Other Backward Caste," a government classification that includes castes such as Sudras who are "above" the Dalits but not as "high" as Brahmins, Rajputs, and other such historically privileged castes.

10. The Arya Samaj began in the nineteenth century as a Hindu reform movement and gained a strong following in northwest India. The founder, Swami Dayananda

hospital[11] Padman came into contact with some short-term western missionaries and, through a course of events, began to follow Jesus and attend a church. Because of his baptism and "western" style of worship and discipleship, Padman's family threw him and his family out of the family house. However, three years ago Padman's antagonistic elder brother died, making Padman the eldest son and giving him opportunity to renew relationship with the family and assume a role of leadership. At the same time he attended a training seminar hosted by Ravi's mission organization on "contextualization" and received some advice from one of its leaders. As a result, two years ago he began an Arya Samaji-style *Yeshu satsang*.

The distinctive identity, teachings, and rituals of the Arya Samaj sect have led Padman to incorporate a set of symbols and practices quite distinct from the Hindu *Yeshu bhakti satsangs*. In particular, and as will be discussed further below, Padman has translated and regularly recites portions of the Gospels in Sanskrit, and he utilizes a number of objects and practices that are important aspects of a distinctly Arya Samaji *satsang*.

Padman still retains associations with churches and meets and networks with various pastors in his area. He feels, however, that such churches do not relate well to his Arya Samaji people. He thus readily embraces his Arya Samaj, Hindu identity, calls himself a Hindu *Yeshu Bhakta*, and hopes that his family will also in time become drawn to Jesus through his example and *satsang*.

Sikh Yeshu satsangs

The third category type of *Yeshu satsang* is represented by two sets of leaders who conduct *satsangs* in their Sikh communities. The first set of leaders is a married couple, Jagdeep and Manpreet, who live in a town in eastern Punjab. Jagdeep works as an engineer in a local thermal power plant and Manpreet is the principal of a nearby school. Both are from Majhabi (Dalit or low-caste) Sikh[12] families. Twenty-five years ago

---

among other things condemned idol worship and emphasized the importance of monotheism.

11. Padman originally trained and worked as a medical doctor and, three years ago, received training in law and now works in the region's high court.

12. The main Dalit caste of the northwest is officially and traditionally called the Chuhras. While the name is used in history books and official documents, no one, particularly from within the community uses the name, which in its spoken form has derogatory connotations. The term *Majhabi*, which literally means "one who observes

Manpreet and Jagdeep became followers of Jesus and began attending a pentecostal church[13] in their area. Six years ago they started a church in their own home and, approximately three years ago met Pastor Sandeep Singh, a pastor from Singapore from a Jatt Sikh background.[14] After hearing Pastor Sandeep's vision to start Sikh *Yeshu satsangs*, and receiving some teaching from him, Jagdeep and Manpreet changed their gathering to be more like a Sikh-style *satsang* so that they would be more effective in relating to and evangelizing Jatt Sikh people. However, the gatherings continue to display a hybrid mix of Christian and Sikh worship styles and vocabulary, and to attract people from a variety of castes. Ten to twenty people regularly attend the *satsang*. Most are from Majhabi Sikh families but at least one from a Hindu family regularly comes as well.

---

religious practices," has in recent decades become the more common alternative term.

13. There is no consensus on how to classify non-mainline churches in the northwest. However many of those that scholars and leaders have referred to, and virtually all that I have visited over the past several years, have practices that show pentecostal influence, such as raising hands, exuberant worship, and an emphasis on miracles and spiritual power. Many of these church leaders also exhibit a highly charismatic style of preaching and stage presence. In this study, when referring to such churches and practices I have adopted the nomenclature of what James K. A. Smith and other pentecostal scholars call "small-*p*" Pentecostalism. Jacobsen, *Thinking in the Spirit*, 8–12; Smith, *Thinking in Tongues*, xvii. For Smith "'pentecostal' is meant to be a gathering term, indicating a shared set of practices and theological intuitions that are shared by pentecostals, charismatics, and 'third wavers.'" Ibid, xvii. Though James and others use this primarily to describe the different groups as they have emerged in the West, this can be used to aptly describe the shared sets of practices and "theological intuitions" of groups in northwest India. Jacobsen adopts this terminology to describe the historic plurality of pentecostalisms and says, "In a general sense, being pentecostal means that one is committed to a Spirit-centered, miracle-affirming, praise-oriented version of Christian faith, but as soon as one begins to ask more specific questions . . . pentecostal opinion begins to diverge, sometimes in rather marked ways." Jacobsen, *Thinking in the Spirit,* 12. In a similar way Webster notes that the pentecostal churches in the northwest tend not to emphasize ecstatic speech as much as "divine healing in response to fervent prayer." Webster, *A Social History of Christianity*, 298. Churches that in the West generally do not embrace pentecostal practices, such as the Baptists, sometimes do so in northwest India. While not all newer and growing churches in the northwest are pentecostal in style and influence, there is much evidence to show that many, if not most, are.

14. Jatt Sikhs are the main landowners, religious and political leaders in Punjab. They are known as a proud people who uphold Sikh beliefs and strongly resist conversion to other faiths. Though he grew up in Singapore, Pastor Sandeep still considers himself a Jatt and has developed a mission vision to start *Yeshu satsangs* in the Punjab, particularly among Jatt Sikh families. As part of this vision he regularly visits and conducts seminars sharing this vision.

The second set of leaders, Navdeep and Naveen, together lead two *Yeshu satsangs* in different villages. Navdeep and Naveen each live in separate towns and travel to the villages together at least once each week to conduct the *satsangs* and to visit families. Navdeep is the main leader and Naveen is the songwriter and leader, having composed numerous Sikh-style *kirtans*. Navdeep and Naveen are supervised and financially supported by Pastor Sandeep. Though Pastor Sandeep has a high level of influence on the *satsangs* and their practices, Navdeep and Naveen embrace and add to this in particular ways.

Both Navdeep and Naveen are from Majhabi Sikh families and started following Jesus through the influence of pentecostal-style pastors. Both spent several years working for various Indian mission organizations before meeting Pastor Sandeep six years ago. Pastor Sandeep's *satsangs* initially had a typical pentecostal style, including loud singing, shouting "hallelujah," and exuberant preaching. However, approximately five years ago Pastor Sandeep went to a Christian conference on contextualization, made changes in the two village *satsangs*, and started teaching seminars on contextual *satsang* ministry.[15] Navdeep and Naveen embraced these changes and began making changes in their own styles and lifestyles.

Yeshu satsang Consultants

In addition to the *Yeshu satsang* leaders described above, three people became invaluable consultants. Two of these were from Sikh families, and one from a Christian/Hindu family. Because of their distance from *satsangs*, among other reasons, the consultants do not regularly attend *satsangs* at present. However, each have previously led or attended them, are sympathetic to them, and reflect deeply on many of the issues that motivate the formation of *Yeshu satsangs*. I will introduce each briefly in turn.

Jasbir is from a Jatt Sikh family and became a follower of Jesus around ten years ago. Shortly after this he was forced to leave his family

---

15. Pastor Sandeep shares that early in his ministry among Punjabis in Singapore a turning point came when he realized that the prevailing mode of evangelism was, as he says, "totally 'foreign' to my people." Because of this he developed a desire to "see my people worshipping Jesus in a fully indigenous church and contextualized way." However, in his outreach work, including that to the Punjab, he was constrained by and ultimately adopted the (pentecostal) norm of ministry of those areas. The second and more immediate turning point came five years ago when the conference on contextualization "confirmed that what I had in my heart was of God."

home and began living with pentecostal pastors and doing church ministry. Jasbir soon began to lead his own groups and churches and, approximately five years ago, was asked by Pastor Sandeep to lead his *Yeshu satsangs*. Jasbir adopted this approach but soon after had leadership conflicts with pastor Sandeep and left his ministry. Since then Jasbir has been involved in Christian pastoral ministry and training in his region, but has also remained sympathetic to a *satsang* approach. Jasbir occasionally leads *Yeshu satsangs* and has plans to begin them in his region.

Nandita is also from a Jatt Sikh family. Five years ago, through a series of miraculous events, she and her parents became followers of Jesus and eventually joined a pentecostal church in their area. Nandita gained experience in church ministry, attended a regional Bible college, and began a small house church in her area. Though her church closely resembles the pentecostal-style churches that she has attended thus far, she has also come into contact with Jasbir and pastor Sandeep, and learned about Sikh *Yeshu satsangs*. In October 2009 she and her parents invited Jasbir to help organize and lead a *Yeshu satsang* as a memorial service for an uncle who had just died. The experience was positive for her family, and also received a good response from their Sikh community. Since then she has reflected more on the merits of a Sikh *Yeshu satsang* approach, and particularly the dynamics of this for the Sikh community.[16]

My third consultant, Ruth, is originally from a nominal Christian family. Ruth's family, however, did not regularly attend churches, nor does she remember hearing or learning much about Christian faith and beliefs growing up. When she was seventeen, she and a Hindu boyfriend decided to get married, and she subsequently learned much about Hinduism and its practices which she appreciated; particularly the *satsangs*, *pujas*, and associated music and symbols. Though she did not worship a specific god in their home, her daughters and son grew up under the influence of her husband's extended family and considered themselves Hindu; and Ruth accepted and affirmed this. When her husband left her to follow a Hindu guru, however, she entered a period of crisis and, through a series of events, attended a pentecostal church with her daughter. They

16. A particularly important issue, which will be addressed below, is Nandita's desire to get married. She and her parents are very interested in finding a follower of Christ from a Jatt Sikh background, which is quite rare. Her extended Sikh family watches, and sometimes taunts her about whether she will have to marry someone from outside their community, such as a Dalit Christian. The community issues surrounding this highlight important dynamics regarding ecclesial identities.

became followers of Jesus but eventually left the church over conflict and joined Gaurav's *Yeshu satsang*, where they attended for nearly ten years. Recently Ruth and her family left Gaurav's *satsang* because of a dispute with Gaurav. Though the break was painful for both Ruth and Gaurav, Ruth continues to appreciate the *Yeshu satsang* style and the ecclesial identity that Gaurav is establishing, and particularly for how it fit her Hindu-oriented family.[17]

HISTORIC CONTOURS OF THE CHRISTIAN CHURCH IN NORTHWEST INDIA

One of the characteristics that the *Yeshu satsang* leaders all share is that all came to faith in Jesus through and were discipled in churches, Christian ministries, or both. Because of this, most of their *Yeshu satsangs* were originally Christian house-churches before transitioning to a *Yeshu satsang* style. As I indicated above, this transition is quite recent for most of the leaders. Thus, though the leaders are all from Hindu and Sikh communities, all have been influenced by and are responding to the identity and practices of the Christian churches in their region. Because of this I will briefly consider some of the general characteristics of the Christian community in northwest India and how this developed. In addition I will give attention to what Archer calls the "situational logics" that emerged from the morphogenetic interaction between missionaries, Indian people, and cultural/structural systems.

Foreign Legacy

The history of Christianity in the northwest is closely tied to the legacy of the mission efforts that began in the area in 1818[18] and that expanded throughout the nineteenth century.[19] Though the results of missionary's work during the first half of the nineteenth century were modest,[20] at least

17. The conflict between Ruth and Gaurav was still very fresh, emotional, and related to another couple that Ruth had befriended and with whom Gaurav had had previous conflict. I delimited my study to focus on practices of religious identity and, because of this, did not deal directly with the issues surrounding this conflict.

18. Prior to this the Jesuits had a brief "Mughal mission" and two Roman Catholic churches had been built in Delhi. These, however, did not last long and had been abandoned by 1818.

19. Webster, *A Social History of Christianity*, 40–48.

20. For the first forty to fifty years, missionaries engaged the people of the northwest largely from within select urban centers, with the occasional venture into the

in terms of the number of conversions, this began to change in the latter half of the century due to two developments. The first was an increase in the number of missionaries to the area after a major uprising in 1857, and the related increase in evangelical and evangelistic engagement with Hindus, Sikhs and Muslims.[21] The second development was the rise of the so-called "mass movements" which, as I will describe below, resulted in tens of thousands of converts over the course of three to four decades.

The rise of the Christian missionary presence, the increase of their evangelistic efforts, and the dramatic rise of converts not only increased the overall number of Christian converts and churches in the region, but also fueled the concurrent development of a series of religious reform movements throughout India, and particularly in the northwest.[22, 23] The various Hindu, Sikh and Muslim reform groups that emerged during this time each had a unique history and origin, but all shared a common cause of defending and strengthening their religious community over-and-against perceived threats, including that of the Christian missionaries and church.[24]

---

rural countryside. Missionaries were thus in various ways disconnected from the majority of Indian communities, and the overall size of the church community did not grow to a large degree during this time, never exceeding 200 people. Ibid., 73.

21. The 1857 "great uprising" was a series of mutinies initiated by disillusioned Indian soldiers in British-led infantries throughout north and northwest India. After the British regained control, there was a marked difference in the exercise of political power, but also a substantial shift in the way missionaries approached their task. Politically, the British firmly cemented their hold of empire and assumed direct rule (rather than through the East India Company). At the same time a new wave of missionaries arrived from Britain and elsewhere, bringing with them a new fervor for evangelism, fueled by the rise of Evangelicalism and new confidence in how to spread it.

22. Webster, *A Social History of Christianity*, 135.

23. Five of these coalesced into associations and helped set the stage for further organizations. These included the Brahmo Samaj (1863), the Anjuman-i-Punjab (1865), the Anjuman-i-Islamia (1869), the Amritsar Singh Sabha (1873), and the Arya Samaj (1877).

24. Interestingly, many of the leaders of these movements were themselves educated in Christian mission schools and used the forms of Christian dissemination and argumentation to later resist aspects of Christianity. As they went on to strengthen and re-articulate aspects of their Hindu, Sikh and Muslim traditions for modern India they imitated the Christian mission and created organizations "to articulate, redefine, defend, inculcate, and spread their respective faiths through preaching, the dissemination of religious literature, and the creation of schools." Webster, *A Social History of Christianity*, 135.

An analysis of this aspect of the Christian church's history and interaction reveals that one of the unexpected results of the missionary's actions was what Archer calls a "constraining contradiction"[25] within the religious context of northwest India. As described in Chapter 2, a constraining contradiction occurs when the engagement and promotion of one idea invokes another, contradictory idea. In this case, the post-1857 missionaries brought a high level of assertiveness and confidence regarding the supremacy of Christianity and its importance for the Indian context.[26] This message, however, combined with the growing assertiveness of the British Raj, provoked a reaction among some Hindus, Sikhs and Muslims. This was particularly so among those who were gaining British and western educations. The unintended result of this combination of messages was the belief that Christianity was a threat to Indian religious traditions and structures and thus needed to be resisted.[27]

In a constraining contradiction, according to Archer, the contradiction is "constrained" due to a relatively stable social context.[28] In this situation one of the normal outcomes is either: 1) for the advocates of each to attempt to correct the other; or 2) to "sink the differences" through some form of syncretism.[29] Examples for both of these outcomes can be found in the decades at the end of the nineteenth and beginning of the twentieth centuries. Webster notes examples of both in the case of the Arya Samaj, which proved a particularly aggressive interlocutor for the Christian missionaries. On the one hand missionaries such as the Rev. T. Williams in Rewari attacked and attempted to "correct" the Arya Samaj teachings and writings, seeking to expose the Vedas as foundations made

---

25. Archer, *Culture and Agency,* 148.

26. Webster quotes Robert Clark, a missionary who, in 1878, asserted, "Mohammedan and Hindu objections to Christianity have been fully answered; and Christianity (instead of Mohammedanism) now stands forward in the eyes of many learned, earnest, thoughtful Natives as being unassailable" Clark as quoted in Webster, *A Social History of Christianity,* 129.

27. Whereas previous modes of resistance to British colonialism and Christian teaching sought to overturn British structures, particularly in the 1857 uprising, the resistance two decades later instead began to use the very structures of education and modes of thought that missionaries had used to promote Christianity. Though Hindus, Sikhs and Muslims had resisted Christianity on ideological levels throughout the previous decades, the resistance was now articulated more clearly using some of Christianity's structural and cultural systems.

28. Archer, *Culture and Agency,* 148–49.

29. Archer, *Realist Social Theory,* 234.

of "sand." On the other hand, Dr. H.D. Griswold, who was trained in the "new theological liberalism" of the West, upheld a high view of Christ while also appreciating the moral and spiritual vision of the Arya Samaj and their vision to create a new India.[30] Griswold and other missionaries like him thus changed their stance and apologetic towards Hinduism. As Webster summarizes, "Instead of juxtaposing Christianity as true and Hindu religion as false, they offered a much more positive assessment of Hinduism's moral and spiritual power . . . ."[31] Though they upheld some distinctive qualities about Christ, they sought to "sink" other differences that the contradiction had highlighted.

In addition to the two outcomes suggested by Archer, the developments within the religious landscape of northwest India suggest an additional outcome. This played upon the fact that the Indian social context was not homogenous and stable, and was prone, like any society, to form groupings based on cultural and structural interests. Though, as argued above, the definitions of religious groups were not always strong or firm, people resolved the tension of the constraining contradiction by strengthening the identities of discrete religious groups. These types of groups, which Archer calls "corporate agents," form around a collective project and seek for means and roles to accomplish their objectives within the wider social context.[32] As the corporate agents involved in the northwest religious milieu mobilized their constituencies and strengthened their cultural and structural bases, the tension morphed to what Archer calls a "competitive contradiction." In this, contradictory ideas become adopted by groups that are divided by various socio-cultural factors.[33] The contradictory ideas—Christianity as superior to Indian religious communities and Christianity as a threat to Indian religious communities—helped to mobilize and define groups who competed with each other and Christianity for adherents. Thus the threat that Christianity represented to the religious cultures and structures of northwest India resulted in religious leaders further bifurcating the socio-religious landscape along already-existing but latent lines of religious tradition, education, and caste affiliation.[34] The goal of such interaction is usually some form of victory

30. Webster, *A Social History of Christianity*, 141–43.

31. Ibid., 143.

32. Archer, *Being Human*, 265.

33. Archer, *Realist Social Theory*, 240.

34. Webster notes that the division of groups along religious lines became particularly strong in the northwest in the early twentieth century, such that the British

and the elimination of the Other or its power. However, as Archer points out, the unintended consequence is usually "ideational pluralism" or sustained differentiation.[35] In the case of the emergence of northwest Indian religious identities, the sustained differentiation became expressed through increased structural and cultural boundaries between religious groups, including between Christian and other groups.[36]

Just as the properties of religious interaction contributed to the emergence of religious reform movements, so the reform movements provided properties towards the emergence of yet another development with which missionaries soon had to engage. In this, the combination of renewed articulations of Indian religious thought, the effective propagation of this through organizations and institutions, and the added assertiveness of Indians in political leadership contributed to the emergence of Indian nationalism, particularly at the tail end of the nineteenth century.[37] As a result, Christianity, as a religious Other, began to be framed more and more as a foreign religion that was "unIndian,"[38]

Christian missionaries, particularly in urban areas, began to search for ways to respond to this new cultural ideology. Non-Christian religions were not, as they had hoped, acknowledging the "superiority" of Christianity, but were rather finding new vitality through reform movements. Because of this the missionaries began to reshape their apologetics in two ways. The first was to hope for and envision, together with the Indians, a "new India," but argue that Jesus Christ provided the best foundation upon which to build this vision. A second approach critiqued the "foreign" approaches to church and evangelism and sought for ways of presenting Christ in authentically Indian styles.[39] A promi-

---

government had to alter its policy of not regarding the religion of those it hired in favor of a policy that sought to "balance the competing claims made on behalf of the Hindu, Sikh, and Muslim communities" (Webster, *A Social History of Christianity*, 138).

35. Archer, *Being Human*, 176.

36. It should be noted, however, Sikh, Hindu, and Muslim reforming corporate agents did not, on the whole, succeed in articulating ideologies and forming structures that embraced everyone in their religious spheres. This was particularly true of Hindu and Muslim reform movements, but less true of the Ludhiana/Amritsar Singh Sabhas, who succeeded in winning a large majority of Sikh power structures to their vision of Sikhism as a distinct religion. Even with this, though, alternative structures and visions persisted and continue to persist.

37. Hardgrave and Kochanek, *India*, 39.

38. Webster, *A Social History of Christianity*, 146.

39. Ibid., 147.

nent figure and spokesperson to arise in the midst of this critique was Sadhu Sundar Singh,[40] who wrote about and practiced a Christian faith that was essentially evangelical but expressed through Indian thought-forms. Unfortunately, despite his popularity in some circles, he did not develop a movement or group, nor is there evidence that his example vastly changed the competitive contradiction that had come to dominate the religious landscape.[41]

Thus, as missionaries became more confident of and assertive in their task, their efforts combined with the emergent properties of other concurrent developments to create a constraining contradiction. In this, the insistence that Christianity was superior to Indian religious traditions elicited the interpretation that Christianity was a threat to Indian cultures and structures. One result of this ferment was the formation of various Hindu, Sikh and Muslim reform movements, which sought to strengthen the ideological foundations of their communities and mobilize those within them. The constraining contradiction quickly gave rise to a competitive contradiction, as groups divided themselves on social and ideological lines. Seminal literature and the testimonies of various *Yeshu satsangis* and Indian Christians show that the competitive contradiction that arose one hundred years ago and more continues to have significant power in the ongoing engagement between religious communities.[42] Even though the Church has emerged and shaped itself as a

40. Shortly after his conversion to Christ through a vision, Singh became baptized in 1905 and took the vows to become a sadhu. As Webster notes, though there had been other Christian sadhus before him, Sundar Singh had a much wider appeal, and was the first to appeal to educated urban people. Ibid., 147. Many Christians in India and abroad, and several missionaries embraced Singh's vision for expressing Christianity in a way congruent with Indian religious traditions. As Singh is alleged to have expressed it, "We are offering Christianity in a Western cup and India rejects it. But when we offer the water of life in an Eastern bowl, then our people will recognize it and take it gladly." Davey, *The Story of Sadhu Sundar Singh*, 66.

41. This is in contrast to Kathettu who asserts that "Sadhu Sundar Singh was the pioneer of the indigenous Christian movement among the Sikhs in Punjab." Kathettu, *The Sikh Community and the Gospel*, 85–86. Whereas I concur with Kathettu that Singh was "an excellent example of indigenization in the Indian context," there is no evidence that his work has led to a "movement" among Sikhs or Hindus.

42. These days this contradiction is often bolstered by the suggestion that Christians offer (foreign-based) money and other incentives to lure converts, a belief that is common also in other parts of India. Although it has not been studied carefully, several other factors may reinforce the perception of Christianity as a foreign-based religion, including the regular presence of foreign speakers and evangelists, and cable television channels such as the "God channel" that feature North American speakers.

member among various Indian religious structures and is led by Indians, and despite its arguments regarding its approximate 2000-year history in India, Christianity's foreign reputation and the competitive contradiction that this represents continues to persist.[43]

Diverse but Largely Dalit

Another factor impacting the character of the Christian church in northwest India was the rise of Dalit converts and the new situational logic this helped to create. Though conversions in this region between 1818 and 1873 were minimal and from a range of castes, between 1873 and 1900 over 100,000 people from the rural Chuhra Dalit community converted to Christianity.[44, 45]

The influx of Chuhras into Christian institutions, and the establishment of churches within and for this community dramatically impacted the identity of the Christian church in northwest India and eventually created a different type of competitive contradiction from the one described above. One side of the equation affirmed that Christianity responds to and addresses the needs of the Dalits. While many religious and caste communities in India suffered from injustice and discrimination, no community experienced this more so than the Dalits. As missionaries began to nurture the growing numbers of converts and organize churches, they began to orient their teaching and efforts towards the unique needs of that community. As a result, Christianity in these areas became socio-culturally tied to the Dalit communities and their needs. Non-Dalit Hindus came to embrace the other side of the contradiction, believing that Christianity's adaptation and response to the needs of the Dalits, and

---

43. Kathettu, in his assessment of the outreach ministries of churches in the Punjabi city of Pathankot concludes, "though churches and mission organizations are indigenous in origin, traces of foreign influence are very visible to the common person" Kathettu, *The Sikh Community and the Gospel*, 92. Aside from the choice of language, he unfortunately does not identify what characteristics are "indigenous" or "foreign."

44. Webster, *A Social History of Christianity*, 168.

45. These movements occurred primarily within the Chuhra community, and were initially begun by itinerant lay-Christians who worked independently of any mission oversight and whose "informal agency" mobilized many along family networks. Pickett, *Christian Mass Movements in India*, 44–45; Harding, *Religious Transformation in South Asia*, 248. Missionaries at first responded cautiously, giving teaching and baptism to enquirers who came to them. Within ten years, however, it became apparent that a large movement was underway, and more missionaries began to move from urban centers into the rural districts to further encourage it.

the latter's widespread embrace of Christianity, meant that Christianity is the religion of the Dalits, and no other. Thus, for missionaries to follow the idea that God was saving the Dalits, and to create churches and efforts that supported it, meant invoking a contradictory message in society.

It is important to note here that a constraining or competitive contradiction is not the same as a genuine "logical contradiction." Rather, it is a mechanism that is triggered when people pursue certain objectives in a certain way. When encountering the contradiction, missionaries and Indian believers would logically refute the idea that Christianity was a threat to Indian society or that it was only for the Dalits. In response they also sought to, in some ways, address the "foreignness" of their evangelism and to reach out to and integrate higher-caste people. None of this, however, could significantly alter the morphogenesis that was occurring and the resulting elaboration and perceptions of the emerging Christian community. The legacy of the mass movements can still be seen in the Christian demographics of Punjab districts (see Table 2).

Table 2
Census Data: Punjab Religious Community Population By District[46]

District	Sikhs	Hindus	Christians	Muslims
Gurdaspur	55%	37%	7%	
Amritsar	78%	21%	1%	
Kapurthala	62%	38%		
Jalandhar	40%	59%	1%	
Hoshiarpur	40%	59%		1%
Nawanshahar	40%	60%		
Ludhiana	49%	48%	3%	
Moga	91%	9%		
Bathinda	78%	21%		1%
Faridkot	78%	22%		
Firozpur	51%	47%	1%	
Mansa	85%	14%		1%
Sangrur	70%	22%		8%
Muktsar	80%	20%		
Fatehgarh Sahib	75%	23%		1%

46. Census Commissioner of India, "Census of India."

Patiala	68%	32%		
Chandigarh	16%	79%	1%	4%
Rupnagar	61%	39%		

Of particular significance in this table is the higher number of Christians in Gurdaspur and Ludhiana districts, which were central locations for the mass movements. In addition, the city of Ludhiana has a sizeable Christian district formed in part around Christian Medical College.[47]

Another legacy of the mass movements that is still visible is the competitive contradiction that emerged from it. In his assessment of the social status of northwest Christians, Webster notes that Christians "are perceived and often perceive themselves as a caste; almost all are Dalits and carry a Dalit image."[48] Though there have been changes in socio-economic status, and though many rural Christian Dalits have moved to urban areas, the Dalit caste image of Christians has in many ways grown stronger. Of those people who convert to Christianity or join the newer churches, most come primarily from Dalit communities, as well as from mainline churches.[49] The strengthened Dalit identity of the church thus further enhances the competitive contradiction that it unwittingly participates in.

Pentecostal

Up to the 1960s and 1970s most churches were affiliated with Roman Catholic or historic Protestant groups.[50] However, since the 1960s a new,

47. Also of interest in this table is the low percentage of Muslims. Prior to 1947 most districts had a significant, if not majority population of Muslims. Missionaries often communicated in a mix of Punjabi and Urdu, as did the more educated Indians. Sadhu Sundar Singh, for example, wrote his devotionals in Urdu. Webster, *A Social History of Christianity*, 215. The residuals of this can be seen particularly in the hymns and liturgy of mainline churches. More widely, vestiges of this history can be seen in the Muslim "pirs" or graves that dot the northwest landscape and to which Hindus and Sikhs continue to visit and attribute spiritual power. However, with the 1947 partition and subsequent migration, the Muslim population shrunk drastically, as did its linguistic and cultural influence. By contrast, and as discussed above, Sikhism rose in power and influence, particularly following the creation of the smaller state of Punjab 1966. It is now Sikhism, rather than Islam, that is more strongly influential.

48. Ibid., 323, 31, 32.

49. Kathettu, *The Sikh Community and the Gospel*, 86–90; Webster, *A Social History of Christianity*, 357.

50. After national independence in 1947 many of the historic, mainline churches

rapidly growing movement of pentecostal-style churches has proliferated through the efforts of missionaries from south India as well as leaders from the northwest itself.[51]

The nature and characteristics of this new wave of evangelical and pentecostal churches has yet to be thoroughly assessed. Webster, after a brief study of various churches and locations, concludes that most of these churches emphasize healing and exuberant worship, and are typically led by pastors with high levels of "evangelistic zeal, initiative, skill, charisma, and entrepreneurship."[52] Katthethu also notes how the worship style of these churches is often distinct from other historic churches, and can include loud, simultaneous praying, the singing of short, lively choruses, standing, raising hands, and shouting words such as "hallelujah."[53] In addition, Webster assesses that these churches are "winning by far the most converts from outside the Christian community and are thus giving to Christianity whatever sense of movement it still has in the region."[54]

From archival resources such as Webster and Kattethu, as well as the testimonies of the *Yeshu satsangis* and leaders, I suggest that another constraining contradiction is being formed through the pentecostal practices of these churches. In his assessment of ministry in the Punjab, Katthethu notes that many pentecostal churches have active healing and prayer ministries. He does not critique this, and instead states in his conclusion that, among other things, churches need to present Jesus Christ as the one who "has the power to cure diseases, raise the dead and also chase evil spirits away forever." If they do this "It will be a breakthrough for the Sikh people who believe in attacks of evil spirits . . . ."[55] However, at the same time he laments that, "the church has not yet been able to adequately incarnate itself to the Punjabi context or to communicate fluently in the Sikh language . . . Instead somewhere in its zeal the church

---

focused on consolidating their communities and maintaining their organizations.

51. Though the main growth of these types of churches came in the 1960s and 1970s, pentecostal groups such as the Assemblies of God and Indian pentecostal Church had been establishing churches as early as the 1930s. These churches had enjoyed modest growth, particularly from among Dalit Hindus and Sikhs, and mainline Christians Kathettu, *The Sikh Community and the Gospel*, 84.

52. Webster, *A Social History of Christianity*, 357.

53. Kathettu, *The Sikh Community and the Gospel*.

54. Webster, *A Social History of Christianity*, 357.

55. Kathettu, *The Sikh Community and the Gospel*, 110.

communicated more of western culture as Christianity and thus won for itself the label of being a western religion."[56]

The ideology represented by these two points—that Jesus Christ can heal and deliver people from demons, and that Christianity is experienced as a foreign religion—do not in and of themselves contradict each other. The healing power of God does not logically mean that Christianity will be seen as an Other. In fact, as Kattethu and Webster note, some non-Christians come to the churches out of a desire to be healed. Nonetheless, the pentecostal practices, as learned and replicated by the leaders of these churches, start a mechanism that leads to the second. In the case of many pentecostal churches in the northwest, the learned practices of eliciting God's power, such as using words like "hallelujah" and shouting "praise Jesus!" (in English) perpetuates the perception that Christianity is "western" or Other.

I will return to this theme in Chapter 9, but here suggest that pentecostal churches in the northwest have, through some of their practices, created a type of constraining contradiction within the church community. Because expressions of God's power have been important for the growth and vitality of these churches, the practices are retained and any internal tension is resolved through educating or socializing the people into the practices of the church.[57] However, these practices also at the same time add to the competitive contradiction, referred to above, that portrays Jesus and his followers as members of a different, foreign, or Other community.[58] As churches in India have found, this contradiction

56. Ibid., 120.

57. Katthethu narrates a humorous story that illustrates the point in another way. While at a "seekers meeting" in one location, he says, "We invited a pastor from Punjab. The meeting went on well. After the meeting in the first day someone came to me and said *bhaiya* (older brother), preaching is good but one thing I did not understand why is the preacher asking us always to shout *allukuya* in between. Alookuya is *subji* (a vegetable dish) which is made from *aloo*, potato and *kuya*, a kind of tuber. I was literally shocked hearing this. With a smile I clarified, that it is not *alookuya* but it is hallelujah and also I shared the meaning of hallelujah" (ibid., xxv). Of particular interest to me is Kattethu's conclusion. "We fail," he says, "to teach them the meaning of certain biblical terms" (ibid.). Similar to many pentecostal churches, Kathettu does not question the role that the practice had in generating confusion, but sought to diminish the tension by explaining the practice. Even if it creates confusion, a practice is kept because it is "biblical" and (for pentecostals) an avenue for accessing God's power.

58. In speaking about the morphogenesis of social structures such as the Christian church I find helpful the concept of the excluded "Other" in discourse, such as developed by Stephen Riggins. Riggins, "The Rhetoric of Othering," 3. I would disagree with

is not so easily alleviated, particularly as they elicit practices and mechanisms that support this perceived contradiction.

In sum, Hindus and Sikhs who perceive or learn of the church's foreign legacy, Dalit character, and pentecostal style regard the church as what social scientists refer to as an Other, or as something radically different from themselves. In an Emergentist framework, this corresponds with the establishment of a separate social structure and culture. Christians of course dispute these assessments, and particularly any accusations that the Christian church is somehow non-Indian and foreign. Unfortunately, however, the church is caught in a dilemma where the worship of Jesus and the proclamation of the Gospel (as they practice it) invoke contradictory messages in the minds of the Hindu and Sikh hearers. That is, though churches do not say that Christianity is foreign, Dalit or Other, their identity and practices nonetheless communicate this to Hindus and Sikhs, albeit unintentionally. It is against this backdrop, and the contradiction that many of the Christian churches of the northwest embody and perpetuate, that we can best understand the actions of the *Yeshu satsang* leaders.

CHAPTER SUMMARY

In this chapter I have provided an introduction to the demographics of northwest India and to the *Yeshu satsang* leaders themselves. In addition, because each of the *Yeshu satsang* leaders has been influenced by and interacted with Christian churches in the area, I have also described some of the historic background and characteristics of the Christian church. Of these, I have highlighted three characteristics and related situational logics that have shaped the Christian church. The first characteristic and situational logic, stemming from the original missionary origins of the Christian church, asserts that the Christian church promotes a foreign religion and is in some way structurally and culturally non-Indian. The second situational logic contends that the Christian church and its religion belongs to the Dalit community. Indian Christians and *Yeshu satsangis* continue to hear and face this logic and reputation from among Hindus and Sikhs. The sense that the Christian church is somehow the religion of an Other, whether foreign or Dalit, is finally affirmed through

Riggins, however, that the creation of the Other is something that only happens in the realm of discourse. Rather, I would contend that discourse is one factor that people use, in the course of structural and cultural interactions, to help shape structural and cultural Others.

some of the practices promoted by the growing pentecostal churches of the area. As I will discuss more below, the power that comes through pentecostal practices is highly popular among Hindus and Sikhs, but the latter sometimes view the practices themselves as relating to a community different from their own, thus perpetuating the situational logic that the Christian church is Other.

I will more fully describe the ways in which the *Yeshu satsang* leaders have interacted with these characteristics in the following chapters, particularly Chapter 9. First, however, I will describe and inductively analyze the particular practices that the leaders are using to shape these new *Yeshu satsangs* and consider the ecclesial identities that these are forming.

PART II

The Formation and Markers of Ecclesial Identities of *Yeshu Satsangs*

CHAPTER 5

Structural Emergent Properties Of Hindu/Sikh Practices

As DESCRIBED IN CHAPTER 2, an Emergentist theory of identity formation can identify the themes and processes of identity formation. In particular, social researchers can analyze peoples' practices and experiences in terms of the morphogenetic process and Analytical Dualism. Such an analysis will help identify the cultural and structural emergent properties (CEPs and SEPs) of these practices and the ways in which these have enabled and constrained the peoples' interests and desired identities.

In terms of a *Yeshu satsang*, the practices play an important role in the emerging ecclesial identities and markers of the *satsangs*. Through a variety of practices such as religious music, sermon, prayers, the use of material objects and setting, and social interaction, the *Yeshu satsang* leaders attempt to shape new ecclesial communities with identities that will relate to the wider Hindu, Sikh and Christian communities. In addition, these practices embody the ways the *satsangis* and leaders perceive or desire God to be at work within the *Yeshu satsang* community. In the next two chapters I will analyze the practices of the *Yeshu satsangs* and address my second research question: How do *Yeshu satsang* leaders in northwest India use, modify and resist various practices to shape their ecclesial identities?

The practices that leaders use in the *Yeshu satsangs* can be grouped into two basic categories. One set of practices are those that emerged from within and are strongly connected to Christian social structures, and whose meanings are so important to the leaders that they retain the practices and take steps to minimize the structural associations and SEPs. I will discuss these practices more in Chapter 7.[1]

The other set of practices that the *Yeshu satsang* leaders use consists of those that are Hindu or Sikh in origin, and that are viewed as "Hindu/ Sikh" by the leaders and *satsangis*. These practices have Hindu or Sikh CEPs and SEPs and are particularly important to *Yeshu satsang* leaders in their attempt to make the *Yeshu satsangs* look and feel similar to a Hindu or Sikh *satsang*. Leaders choose these practices based on their religio-structural association with the Hindu/Sikh communities, but also because they are practices whose meanings can be changed over time by associating them with Christ and biblical meaning. In the following chapter I will analyze the ways the *Yeshu satsang* leaders seek to change the meanings of these practices according to Christian properties. Presently, I will discuss the ways in which the leaders use and reflect on the Hindu/Sikh religio-structural properties of these practices, first focusing on worship and speech practices.

WORSHIP PRACTICES

Yeshu satsang leaders use a variety of worship practices and objects. Of high importance to these leaders are the areas of music and the use of worship objects.

Yeshu satsang Music: Bhajans and Kirtans

The *Yeshu satsangs* typically use a form of worship music called a *bhajan* or *kirtan*.[2] The *bhajan* genre has a long history that is intimately tied to the Hindu and Sikh *bhakti* traditions. Because of this the use of *bhajans* can invoke for *satsangis* some of the associated emergent properties of these traditions. For further discussion on the use of *bhajans* in *Yeshu satsangs*, see Appendix F.

---

1. A sub-set of these are various pentecostal practices that were learned in prior churches and that continue to be used, though as unconscious or near-unconscious *habitus*. I will discuss these in Chapter 9 in relation to the leaders' backgrounds in various churches.

2. In the *Yeshu satsangs* of the northwest the Hindu *Yeshu satsangs* tend to use the word "*bhajan*" and the Sikh *Yeshu satsangs* use "*kirtan*." In other parts of northern India, however, they are sometimes used interchangeably, and "*kirtan*" sometimes refers to a type of *bhajan* that features call-and-response lyrical patterns. Because *Yeshu satsangs* did not use these terms in a uniform way, in this section I will use "*bhajan*" to refer to both.

The *Yeshu satsang* leaders, and some *satsangis* themselves are highly aware of the Hindu and Sikh properties of the *bhajans* they use and compose. There are two in particular that they identify as holding particular importance: (1) the sense of continuity and connection with their Hindu or Sikh community structure; and (2) the feeling of reverent devotion to God. Though both properties are important to leaders, it is the *bhajans'* association with the Hindu or Sikh social structures that is most important to leaders at this stage in their ecclesial development.

For example, when deciding which types of songs and which songbook to use for his *satsang*, Ravi decided against the songs commonly used by others in his organization. Though he himself has learned and sung these, he decided against them because they reflect "a Western style of worship"[3] Instead he chose a book of *bhajans* compiled by some *Yeshu satsangs* in Varanasi. These, he says, sound more like the Bollywood *bhakti bhajans* that the Hindu people in his area like. Such an association is important for Ravi, since he is conscious that his Hindu neighbors hear the music that his *Yeshu satsang* sings. Though some know his gathering is focused on *Yeshu*, and is thus possibly related in some way to the Christian church, he tries to foster a close connection to the Hindu community. The use of *bhajans* is one way he does this.[4] Thus, for Ravi, the Hindu SEP that people associate with the *bhajans* helps foster a religio-structural connection between the *Yeshu satsang* and Hindu communities.

Though this is of high importance to leaders, they and *satsangis* also value the devotional connection to God that *bhajans* help them to foster. Interviews with the leaders and *satsangis* show that *bhajans* convey a certain affect, a feel that evokes a sense and atmosphere of devotion.[5] Emotions, as Archer argues, are "commentaries upon our concerns."[6] When experienced in a social environment, such as a *satsang*, such emotions "tell us how we are doing in pursuing (our concerns) in the social

3. Interview with Ravi, Apr 11, 2010.

4. Ravi proudly talks about when, during a time of sectarian tension, police were investigating various Sikh and Christian sects. When they came to his neighborhood because of reports that a group met at his house his Hindu neighbors told the police that Ravi simply conducts *satsangs*, which satisfied the police and caused them to move on. Interview with Ravi, Apr 11, 2010.

5. For example, one *satsangi* comments, "Yes, *bhajans* is something that you can concentrate more on the Lord with your eyes closed. You're singing, you FEEL closer to God [says this dreamily, with a smile]. It's a different thing. I love it. I just love it" [E] Interview with Ruth, May 10, 2010.

6. Archer, *Being Human*, 195.

environment of which they are part."[7] Archer focuses on how agents experience and negotiate emotions in various circumstances, but in doing so only partially explains the importance of affect.

Another important dynamic regards the unconscious role of emotions and the past that they reflect, or how they express *habitus*.[8] In this the good or enjoyable feelings created by singing *bhajans* are, as described by some *satsangis*, closely tied to past experiences of worship. For them *bhajans* create a sense of peace and the right atmosphere through which to approach and relate to the divine. For example, one of Gaurav's *satsangis*, who always enjoyed *bhajans*, reflects on those that she now sings in the *Yeshu satsang* saying, "When we sing *bhajans*, when we pray with the *bhajans*, then I feel very good at that time. Because we feel that we are not on the earth. It seems that we are flying in the heaven. I like this part very much" [H].[9]

Ruth, one of my consultants, also expressed her enjoyment of the *Yeshu satsang bhajans* because they remind her of the *bhajans* she began to learn soon after marrying her Hindu husband and participating in some of the Hindu family rituals. She says, "Though in my childhood I never worshiped, like throw flowers, or burning incense, or doing things, still I enjoyed it. I enjoyed it. Because in my in-laws house I had seen all these things and somehow it attracted me" [E].[10] In this the *bhajans* reminded her of a time in her life when her new marriage was particularly new and exciting. Thus *bhajans*, for Ruth and others like her, evoke memories of a positive family experience as well as a structure in which devotion to God can be properly expressed.

Many Sikh *Yeshu satsangis* also have much previous experience worshipping with *kirtans* in the peaceful setting of a *gurdwara* (Sikh temple). Such settings and experiences emphasize a reverence for God, and Sikh *Yeshu satsang* leaders invoke this same feeling of reverence by using *kirtans*. As Navdeep shares in one of his sermons, "When we go to the *gurdwara* and they recite the *kirtan*, there is much silence. Have

---

7. Ibid., 220.

8. Curiously, though Bourdieu refers to emotions and feeling as an expression of class, he does not extensively pursue the connection between emotions and *habitus*. Very recent studies are beginning to explore the possibilities of this connection. See Flach, Margulies, and Söffner, eds., *Habitus in Habitat I*.

9. Interview with G-1, Mar 6, 2010.

10. Interview with Ruth, May 10, 2010.

you heard it? When we listen also to cassettes and listen to these kinds of *kirtans* we feel good" [P].[11]

Navdeep and the *satsangis* go on to talk about the peaceful qualities of Naveen's *kirtans*, which many Christian "preachers" do not understand, and in fact oppose because of the association with the Sikh community. Navdeep and Naveen persist, however, because as Navdeep says, "God wants to change people so that they may come to Christ. That's why Paul says, 'For the Jews I became a Jew. For the Greeks I became Greek'" [P].[12] The *kirtans* help these leaders and their *satsangis* to become Sikh culturally by stimulating feelings of reverence and peace that are associated with *gurdwaras* and are important to feeling a part of the Sikh community structure.

As another example, Jasbir, who is interested in Sikh-style *Yeshu satsangs* but currently leads a Christian pentecostal church, reflects on this feeling of reverence as conveyed through Sikh styles of prayer and worship,

> Jasbir (J): Our, uh, Sikh style, I like their way of praying. We [Christian church] are too loud and uh, they [Sikhs] are very, they are well-behaved people in their *satsangs*. Christians are not. I think if we will bring that level of spirituality, which they profess, they have, in *gurdwaras* to the churches, the churches can be transformed.
>
> Darren: Huh! Really?
>
> J: Yeah. That's a very radical statement, but that's what I feel. The level, their level of worship. How they, how they revere, how they have reverence towards God. I do believe that we have a personal relationship with God, but that doesn't mean that we [always have a] buddy-buddy kind of relationship . . . taking God very casually. [E][13]

For Jasbir, the peaceful and reverent manner of worshiping, including *bhajan* singing, exhibits and invokes a *habitus*-like quality, a preconscious logic established by prior experiences about the proper way of approaching God. In particular, *bhajans* invoke for *satsangis* a particular type of order, approach, and devotion. When memories of such practices elicit good feelings they are, as Archer says, reflecting the affirmation that

11. From Navdeep *satsang*, May 1, 2010.

12. Ibid.

13. Interview with Jasbir, May 20, 2010.

people received from a certain "normative order." of society.[14] In these cases, the feelings of "rightness" evoked when certain *bhajans* are played in part reflect a sense that a positive social structure has been replicated.

However, it is also the case that some *bhajans* are closely associated not only with prior Hindu or Sikh social structures, but also with prior Hindu or Sikh cultural systems. Such associations are most strong for *bhajans* that were composed for a Hindu community, such as movie *bhajans* and popular puja *bhajans*. In such cases there is disagreement among *Yeshu satsang* leaders about the degree to which the lyrics, and even the melody of the *bhajans* is helpful for the *Yeshu satsang*. In Emergentist theory terms, these leaders debate about if and how certain CEPs of these *bhajans* can be redefined and the object of devotion redirected. For example, *Yeshu satsang* leaders disagree on whether or not they can include in their *Yeshu satsangs* a version of the popular *bhajan* known as the *aarti bhajan*. This *bhajan*, often sung in temples, Bollywood movies, and elsewhere, begins with the line *"Om jay jagadishi harai"* (Victory to the Lord/sound/word, Lord of the Universe). The beginning syllable *Om* is generally understood by Hindus to be the "sound" or word associated with the creation of the universe. Because of this some church leaders contend that using *Om* to invoke religio-structural properties will invariably, and harmfully, invoke and remind *satsangis* of unbiblical religio-cultural properties as well. Padman, however, sings the *bhajan*, believing that this ideology can be helpfully reinterpreted to refer to the *Logos*, or "Word" which the Bible equates with Jesus. In this he argues that both the *Logos* and *Om* refer to the power through which everything was created and through which everything is sustained. Though there are many dissimilarities as well, Padman believes that *Om Jai Jagadishi's* association with the social structures of the Hindu community and the possibility of reinterpreting it to align with the Christian beliefs of its cultural system makes the *bhajan* valuable.

Gaurav tends to be in between the two poles of this debate. Though he sometimes uses *Om Jai Jagadishi* and appreciates its Hindu associations, he also says that they are "a bit careful when we use it because some Sikhs do not like it" [E].[15] This because it reminds them of the Hindu community, but also because of the associations it has with idol worship. Gaurav thus recognizes that some practices contain strong SEPs and

---

14. Archer, *Being Human: The Problem of Agency*: 215.
15. Email correspondence with Gaurav, Dec 30, 2010.

CEPs that some in his *satsang* may not like or appreciate because of the associations that those practices have for the Sikh (or Christian) communities from which some *satsangis* come.

Bhajans, movie *bhajans* and others like *Om Jai jagadishi* thus have SEPs whose associations with the Hindu social structure are appealing to some *Yeshu satsang* leaders. However, as in the case of the latter, these also have potentially negative impacts among some *satsangis*. To try and mitigate these negative impacts, Gaurav and the other leaders sometimes limit their use, and also try to re-interpret them via new CEPs of Christian beliefs. I will, in a later section, discuss the ways in which the *Yeshu satsang* leaders seek to shape these practices with CEPs so as to help shape the current religious structures and cultures of their *satsangs* and their ecclesial identities.

Worship Objects

Similar to *bhajans*, some worship objects are meaningful to *satsangis* because of their religio-structural associations. When preparing for communion, Gaurav sometimes uses the *diya* (oil lamp), incense, and coconut. These objects, and the coconut in particular, are important signs for some Hindus. He says, "We are taking (the coconut) into Hindu communities . . . because they are having, they relate to the coconut a lot. We all Indians do in some way relate to the coconut" [E].[16] However, he also explains that the socio-structural associations are not always positive, particularly for non-Hindus. "Practically," he says for example, "taking a coconut into a, uh, Sikh culture is foolishness" [E].[17]

The SEPs are nonetheless positive when used in the right way and among the right people. One of Gaurav's assistants argues for the occasional use of these objects, saying, "This is our Indian culture. That's why we are using this. (We) want to give the message to others (Hindus) that we can serve the Lord in an Indian style" [H].[18] In this instance, Gaurav's assistant champions the use of these objects as a response to an implied accusation—that followers of Jesus are not "Indian" and have departed from their Indian heritage. Using the associated SEPs of such practices

16. Interview with Gaurav, Mar 10, 2010.

17. Ibid.

18. Interview with G-13, Feb 17, 2010.

in these instances is one way of demonstrating their association with the Indian (Hindu) social structure.[19]

Another of Gaurav's *satsangis*, who was converted from Hinduism and discipled in another church before coming to Gaurav's *satsang*, shared about the first time she saw the use of the coconut. She explains, "When a big *satsang* was organized they decorated flowers like this and, in the midst of them, put a coconut like this in a *kalash* (small pot). They were doing this, and it shocked me!" [H].[20] She had not, up to that point, seen these objects used in the context of worshipping Jesus. However, after listening to some teaching on this she now says, "I think that this is right. It is not necessary to change your external appearance. We need to change our heart" [H].[21] As will be seen further, the change of the external versus change of the heart is a reoccurring theme among many *satsangis* who value the worship objects in part because they give a sense of continuity with the Indian, or Hindu, community structure.

At the beginning of his *Yeshu satsangs*, Dinesh blows a *shankh*, a large seashell that creates a sound like a trumpet.[22] The *shankh*, he explains, is something Hindus are familiar with, and which they use to start their *satsangs* and *pujas* (worship).[23] For Dinesh and his *satsangis*, the use

---

19. When people talk about "Indian" culture they most often imply "Hindu" or related socio-religious cultures, such as Sikhs or Jains. Never, for example, did I encounter anyone discussing Indian culture using examples from Muslim practices or architecture. Also, *satsangis* often use the term "culture" in various ways and to refer to different things, but quite commonly use it to refer to practices that are associated with a particular social structure.

20. Interview with G-3, Feb 17, 2010.

21. Ibid.

22. The *shankh* is a common symbol in Hindu worship, and in Hindu epics. In the Mahabharata, for example, Krishna blows a powerful *shankh* to declare war.

23. Dinesh debated this point with a Christian friend:

> Friend (F): What is the importance of the *shankh*?
>
> Dinesh (D): Here they blow the *shankh* in the temples.
>
> F: They blow it everywhere. But you . . . ?
>
> D: We (blow it) for starting, I mean, to start (the *satsang*), just as the battle in the (Hindu epic) Mahabharata started with the *shankh*.
>
> F: But in the Christian context, how can we blow the *shankh*?
>
> D: Just as the worship starts we blow the *shankh* three times, then after that a song begins. We start the song and blow the *shankh* three times in order that the people, I mean, we do it to show to the (Hindu) people. Brother, we are also in your line. We also believe as you, but we have this

and sound of this invokes particular SEPs related to the Hindu community and temple. Dinesh blows the *shankh* three times at the beginning of the *Yeshu satsang*, because "here they blow the *shankh* three times in the temples" [H].[24] Gaurav also uses the *shankh* in some of his *Yeshu satsangs*. One of Gaurav's *satsangis* reflects on this saying:

> Whenever we take our relatives or somebody else with us (to the *Yeshu satsang*) they should feel that, no, this is not a separate religion. Because we are told that we have become Muslims, that we became something. This is how people speak. Then (after coming to the *satsang*) they say, "No, they do nothing there." It seems whenever my relatives went there then they say, "No, they do like Hindus, because they also have the *shankh* with them. They also lights *diyas*." So I like this, uh, when somebody comes with me. My faith is in the Lord only . . . But those who come with us they feel that, no, these people are also doing like us. So I like to take them also with me. [H][25]

The SEPs of these practices, in this case, helped to counter the perception of the *satsang* as an Other, including Muslim. In addition, such practices open opportunities for relationship. Dinesh discussed this in light of his father's opinion of his *satsang*. Previously his father told him, "You have not done the right thing" by following Jesus and worshipping in his previous style. However, Dinesh says, "Now that we have started doing these things (*shankh, bhajans*), we have started playing (Indian) instruments, he says, 'Now you have come into the right way'" [H].[26] His father subsequently stopped opposing Dinesh and his *satsang*. Also, Dinesh has had further opportunity to share about Jesus with his father, has seen "a lot of difference in his life."[27]

One of the desired effects of using Hindu or Sikh SEPs, as the above illustrations show, are the opportunities that *satsangis* hope to have to share their faith with others without the barrier of invoking a religio-structural Otherness. However, and similar to the *bhajans*, such objects and practices also help create a certain feeling or affect for some *satsangis*.

---

style. All believe in Shiva *bhagwan* (Shiva god), but we believe only in Yeshu *bhagwan* (Jesus god)" [H]. Interview with Dinesh, Mar 20, 2010.

24. Interview with Dinesh, Mar 20, 2010.

25. Interview with G-1, Mar 6, 2010.

26. Interview with Dinesh, Mar 20, 2010.

27. Ibid.

Ravi explains why, in his *Yeshu satsang*, he has started using the coconut, banana and milk instead of juice and bread for communion. He says:

> Sometimes we break coconut . . . and sometimes we try to use banana and curd or milk and banana. Because it has a very sacred place in Hinduism . . . So most of the people use it as a *prasad* (offering). Hindu people use banana and milk. In temples breaking coconut is considered holy. If there is an inauguration of a shop, and if they have purchased a new thing, car or house, then also they break a coconut. So the coconut is considered holy. We use it and we use banana and milk also. [H][28]

For Ravi, the sense of sacredness and holiness that Hindus feel concerning the coconut, banana and milk is the same "feel" that he wants to invoke when taking communion. This, he says, helps convey the sense of communion being the *Mahaprasaad* (great offering) that "we will do with God one day" (referring to Matt. 26:29).[29]

Though the Sikh *Yeshu satsangs* use fewer objects in accordance with the Sikh tradition, those that are used can also convey a sense of affect. Manpreet likes to use a *rehal* (wooden stand) to hold her Bible during her *Yeshu satsang*. At one point she comments on this and on a *satsangi* who kept her Bible in a plastic bag and placed in on the floor during the *satsang*:

> Manpreet (M): Look, I mean, we place the Bible in the midst of us. I have purchased a wooden stand and put a cloth on it, wrapped the Bible. This is our respect for the Bible. But some [people] put the Bible this way and that way [carelessly]. Like we put it into a plastic bag, like that sister, and she left the Bible there on the ground. You were walking along, and your foot might have touched the Bible. This is why, I mean, we need to give honor to God. This is a good thing.
>
> Friend: Yes. Many people stumble because of this thing, that we have put the Bible on the ground.
>
> M: They stumble. Yes. Those who are non-Christians, they say this, I mean, "They are not respecting their sacred book. They are moving around, taking this in their armpit." Meaning, many pastors do this when they go somewhere . . . [But] that is God's

---

28. Interview with Ravi, Jun 24, 2010
29. Ibid.

holy word. This is written by God's spirit. So we must give honor, to this [Bible]. [P][30]

Of interest on this point is that, though Manpreet herself was discipled for many years in Christian churches and has retained some Christian practices in her *Yeshu satsang*, she and her husband nonetheless display certain sensitivities common among Sikhs. In this case, the use of the *rehal* connects with the sense of how "God's word" should be reverently treated.[31] Whereas some Christians treat the Bible in ways that Sikhs would deem disrespectful, Manpreet has adopted a practice that reflects past experience in the Sikh community structure, as well as certain Sikh cultural concepts regarding the reverence and honor that should be given to scripture.

DRESS

The use of dress, and discussion over proper dress, is a theme that several leaders and *satsangis* discuss. For Dinesh, taking off shoes in the *satsang* space and wearing appropriate clothes have clear religio-structural emergent properties. Like the other *Yeshu satsangs*, Dinesh has his *satsangis* practice taking off shoes before entering the *satsang* room. Though this is a standard practice in many rural churches in other parts of northwest India, the Hindus in Dinesh's town have observed Christian gatherings and rallies that do not practice this. Dinesh explains:

> What happens in churches is, what happens in big, big rallies are that we sit there with our shoes. But what happens in our place [house] when we go to *satsang* we remove our shoes outside. But it does not happen among Christians. That is why [Hindu] people say, "Christian people sit with their shoes in the meetings!" . . . That is why we have to keep a watch on these things. [H][32]

30. Interview with Manpreet, Apr 4, 2010

31. In Sikh *gurdwaras* respect for the Sikh scriptures, the *Guru Granth Sahib*, is expressed in a number of ways, including giving it its own "bedroom" with a bed and linens. The book is placed in this place every night by the *granthi* (priest), and retrieved every morning. When reading from the *Guru Granth Sahib*, an attendant regularly waves a brush made of long horse-hair over the scripture, a practice originally and allegedly done for royalty and people of importance to keep insects off of them.

32. Interview with Dinesh Mar 22, 2010.

In a similar way, Dinesh is conscious of the impact that clothing makes regarding religio-structural association. It is common, for example, among Christian youth in churches in his town and elsewhere to wear casual clothes to the church service. Whereas this may reflect the globalized youth culture of the area, for Dinesh it also invokes unhelpful SEPs associated with the foreign Christian church. In contrast, girls should come to the *Yeshu satsang* with their head covered, as is common among Hindus. As Dinesh explains:

> Like the clothes they [girls] wear to go [to church]. Girls just wear a kind of [inappropriate] clothes and go there. We have seen these things. If girls come they should come with their head covered, so that we can stay safe in our culture. So that the people would not feel that Jesus Christ is a foreigner. Then it will not be seen as a foreign religion. [H][33]

Among the Sikh *Yeshu satsangs* a common issue regards cutting hair and wearing a turban.[34] Though many Sikh youth are cutting their hair because of modern styles and international influences, many in the Sikh community still value and keep this tradition. Traditionally, in some Christian churches cutting one's hair and no longer wearing a turban was a sign of conversion. Though this is no longer a universal practice among churches, the *Yeshu satsangs* have made a special point of retaining the turban.[35] Both Navdeep and Naveen have re-adopted the practice, having previously cut their hair and leaving their turban, while ministering in Christian churches. Naveen describes the reaction he received from Christians, and his rationale for again wearing a turban:

> For some time, people used to ask me questions . . . saying, "We have seen so many pastors keeping themselves clean shaven. Then who told you to wear this [turban]? Why do you do this?" So I have to tell them in a very systematic way. Slowly, slowly I

33. Ibid.

34. The last of the Sikh Gurus, Guru Gobind Singh, instituted the *khalsa* (brotherhood), the members of which vow to wear five things, including the *kesh*, or uncut hair worn under a turban.

35. According to Navdeep, Pastor Sandeep from Singapore once expressed this, saying "If we don't wear a turban it is okay. But neither is there any harm in wearing a turban. But if somebody listens to us (talk about) Christ because of wearing that turban, is that a difficult task?" Interview with Navdeep, May 2, 2010. Thus, though they do not require people to retain a turban, it is strongly encouraged for the sake of being able to communicate the gospel effectively.

tell them this is only for Jatt Sikhs, because this is the culture of Punjab . . . First they look at your beard, and after that [we can talk] about God. This beard is the main thing, a mark for them. Because of this thing we get a bridge. We start sitting in the midst of them . . . Otherwise, is it easy to put a turban weighing a kilo on your head? [Laughs]. It makes me sweat! [Laughs]. [P][36]

Naveen's comments have two implications regarding the structural properties of the turban. First, and as I will discuss further below, Naveen shows that wearing the turban is a practice that facilitates social interactions beyond the *Yeshu satsang*, and particularly among the Jatt Sikh caste community. Second, and for our purposes in this section, the turban holds a strong religio-structural property, particularly for Jatt Sikhs. In this the turban helps Naveen and Navdeep to relate to the Jatt Sikh social structure.

SPEECH PRACTICES

Just as *Yeshu satsang* leaders desire to invoke structural emergent properties (SEPs) through Hindu and Sikh worship and dress practices, they try to do something similar in their preaching and speech practices. When discussing discourse or speech events, it is important to consider the variety of ways in which speech is used. Dell Hymes has developed a typology of the various components of the speech event. Of particular importance and relevance to the *Yeshu satsang* setting are what Hymes calls the speech content or topic, the speech setting, and the speech form or instrumentality.[37]

In their preaching or discourse style, all leaders have adopted the standard Hindu and Sikh speech setting and form of sitting on a special mat on the floor or a platform, sometimes placing the scriptures in front of them on a small wooden *rehal*. Generally the leaders stay in this position for most, if not all of the *satsang*. This is particularly important in the Sikh context since, according to Naveen, this approach adds to the peaceful setting that Sikhs are accustomed to. Contrasting the way in which they used to preach and approach Sikhs, Naveen says that now, "We teach them with a proper manner, with peace, with ease, so that they may understand" [P].[38] However, while retaining the SEPs of the practice

36. Interview with Naveen, May 2, 2010.

37. Hymes, "Models of the Interaction of Language and Social Life," 53–71; Hymes, *Foundations in Sociolinguistics*, 55–57.

38. Interview with Naveen, May 3, 2010.

the leaders change the propositional CEPs, or content of the discourse, which is usually taken directly from the Bible and often reflects doctrine learned from, or shared with, Christian churches or institutions. They thus seek to retain the Hindu and Sikh structural practices of preaching and invoke properties that shape and characterize Hindu and Sikh religious structures, but interpose Christian cultural properties.

Some speech practices of self-ascription also have SEPs that are connected to the Hindu and Sikh communities of origin, as many of the *Yeshu satsang* leaders and *satsangis* are aware. Some of the *satsangis* in Dinesh's *satsang*, for example, come from outlying villages where there are no churches or Christians. For the Hindus of these communities the main contrasting community, or religious Other, is Islam. When the friends and family members of new *satsangis* learn that the person is attending a *satsang* or receiving prayer from a person they are not familiar with, they sometimes accuse the *satsang*i of becoming a Muslim.[39] One *satsang*i, who started attending the *Yeshu satsang* two months prior to our initial meeting said, "They [extended family] say that I go to a Muslim (place). But I answered them, 'Who said that he is Muslim? He is *Yeshu Bhagwan* (Jesus-god). I go to Jesus'" [H].[40] When I asked further about how she calls herself she explained, "We are Hindus. We are not Muslims [laughs] . . . Now we are Hindus only, Hindus only. We are not Muslims. This is *Yeshu Bhagwan* [Jesus God]. It is Jesus . . . No, we believe in Jesus and we will follow *Yeshu Dharma* [Jesus path/religion]" [H].[41]

This *satsang*i's speech in this and other parts of her testimony show how the *satsang* is allowing her to retain an association to her Hindu community via her self-ascription while she also begins to build an understanding of her new faith. First, in the face of accusations of following and becoming a Muslim, she affirms that she remains a Hindu. In this instance, the main way she defines this is simply in opposition to the Other of the Muslim community. Second, she affirms but also qualifies the nature of her association through two distinctly Hindu terms: *bhagwan* and *dharma*. The former commonly refers to the plural nature of

---

39. This accusation, which is faced by other *Yeshu satsangis* in other areas, also stems in part from what Jasbir calls the "old church language" of the Christians. Colonial-era missions and churches used many Urdu words to relate to Muslims, since this was the majority religious community in the region pre-partition. See Krishan, "Demography of the Punjab (1849–1947)."

40. Interview with D-2, Mar 21, 2010

41. Ibid.

Hindu gods and goddesses, and is often rejected by Christians because of the possibility of Jesus simply being identified simply as one choice of deity among many. Though her use of this with "Jesus" could be a pluralistic association, it is also a highly unusual one for a Hindu to affirm, particularly in the midst of criticism. The use of *dharma*, though often used by Christians, Hindus and others to refer to "religion," also can refer to a person's duty or path that, when followed, leads to righteousness. It is of significance that here she couples it not with the phrase of a community (such as Christian or *Masihi*) but with the object of her devotion, Jesus.

Thus this *satsangi's* use of vocabulary illustrates that she is orienting herself towards Jesus. When her family accuses her of associating with a structural Other (wrongly ascribed as Muslim) she claims her structural connections with her Hindu family community by affirming that she is Hindu. She also begins to integrate her understanding of Jesus into her ideology and express it in distinctly Hindu language.

To help their *satsangis* create distinctions between the SEPs and CEPs of self-ascriptions, and to affirm Hindu/Sikh religio-structural associations, *Yeshu satsang* leaders have introduced various terms that often use "Hindu" and "Sikh." In their *Yeshu satsangs*, Gaurav, Dinesh, Ravi and Padman have introduced the phrase *Yeshu Bhakta*. This phrase draws on the association with the Hindu *bhakti* tradition, emphasizing devotion to God or a guru, while specifying Jesus as the focused object of devotion. Such a phrase invokes SEPs in an attempt to create links with a particular part of the Hindu social structure while also re-framing the CEPs in relation to Jesus.

One woman, who had started coming to Dinesh's *Yeshu satsang* only one month prior to my initial visit, has adopted this self-ascription. She explains her own use of this term, saying, "We are generally Hindus, *Yeshu Bhaktas* . . . The Christians and other castes are also made by humans. But God is one. And now in the circumstances we live in, I mean, it is hard to change our religion. But nobody can stop us from believing in God, since God is one" [H].[42] Of interest in this explanation is how the *satsangi* associates herself with the Hindu community and specifies that the Christian community is a caste that, like others, was made by humans. For her, in this context, "changing religion" relates to changing a human-made community. Her *satsang*, however, has created a space where she can remain Hindu while being devoted to God through Jesus.

42. Interview with D-7, Mar 21, 2010.

For some *satsangiṣ* the *Yeshu Bhakta* self-ascription is closely connected to and helps to describe the *satsang* community in light of the other worship practices of the *Yeshu satsangs*. Another of Dinesh's *satsangis* explained to my interpreter/research assistant and me:

> Satsangi (S): I am called a *Yeshu Bhakta* . . .
>
> Interpreter (I): Is there a reason for this?
>
> S: There is only one reason for this. When we came here we have seen that here, as with Hindus, there are rituals. In the same way the *diya* is lit here, they blow the *shankh*, and they keep flowers, etc. They do it here in the same way as they do it in the temples . . .
>
> I: So that is why you call yourself a *Yeshu Bhakta*?
>
> S: Yes, because that is according to Hindu ritual. [H][43]

These *satsangis* have learned the self-ascription of *Yeshu Bhakta* from Dinesh, and have generally followed his example in using it. However, though Dinesh calls himself *Yeshu Bhakta*, he also nuances it in ways that shows some ambiguity in his relationship to the Hindu community. This is because, as will be discussed further below, Dinesh's family has been closely tied to the Ravidas community, which was established in part as a movement resisting high-caste power and hegemony.[44] Dinesh has developed this further by studying and joining other organizations that were inspired by B. R. Ambedkar and other Dalit movements of recent decades.

A general characteristic of many of these movements, beginning with Ambedkar himself, has been the equation of "Hindu" with the upper-caste Brahminical Hindu community that has oppressed the lower caste groups for centuries.[45] When speaking about this Dinesh often as-

43. Interview with D-5, Mar 22, 2010.

44. Guru Ravidas was a fifteenth century *bhakti* saint from a Dalit caste. In the northwest the Ravidasi sect has grown among Dalit castes. The Ravidasis are related to Hindus and Sikhs in beliefs and practices, but particularly embrace a Dalit identity.

45. This politicization and the Dalit resistance of this term has been championed by Kancha Ilaiah, among others. Ilaiah, *Why I am Not a Hindu*. Ilaiah and many others from low-caste/Dalit backgrounds contend that high-caste Hindus unjustly categorize all non-Christian, non-Muslim, and non-Buddhist Dalits as "Hindu" in the hopes of further strengthening the Hindu communal block against other groups. In reality, however, most low-caste/Dalit persons do not experience or understand their religion as "Hindu" in terms of its Brahminical traditions and philosophy. Rather, such people

serts that he is actually not in favor of any religion, including Hinduism, and thus does not consider himself a Hindu per se. However, he readily admits that his birth registration, like that of his children, still says "Hindu," and he values the close ties that he has with the Hindu leaders of his area and how they counsel him to stay away from "the Christians." Similarly, he at times refers to the Hindu community as "my people," particularly when contrasting himself with the Christian community.

As these examples suggest, Dinesh is making a distinction between Hindu SEPs, though he is not consistent about the exact distinction. On the one hand he resists the "Hindu" self-ascription and critiques the higher-caste Hindu power and hegemony that this implies. On the other hand, when discoursing about "Christians," Dinesh stresses his association with Hindus. Though he sometimes stops short of saying that he is a Hindu, he readily associates himself with the wider *bhakti* tradition that shares many practices with Hindus but that have often critiqued high-caste hegemony. In these cases he is more interested to align himself with the general Hindu community of his area (which include higher-caste) and to disassociate himself from the Christian community and certain Christian self-ascriptions. The exception to this latter point is Dinesh's use of the self-ascription "*Masihi*," which has clear Christian connotations but which he tries to define in particular ways.

Gaurav also tries to nuance his identification with the Hindu community through various speech practices. As seen above, Gaurav's *Yeshu satsang* has a diverse group of people coming from various religious backgrounds and castes. Because of this, and while he is comfortable to call himself a Hindu *Yeshu Bhakta*, he recognizes that the self-ascription "Hindu" is difficult for some in his *satsang*. He explains:

> I can call myself a Hindu *Yeshu Bhakta*. [But if] someone comes from a Christian background I don't want to force him. I just tell him, "You don't have to be a Christian, just a *Yeshu Bhakta*." . . . [Some] don't like the word [Hindu]. A Dalit comes to our *satsang*, [name]. I'm not forcing [him] to call him, call himself HINDU *Yeshu Bhakta*, because he doesn't LIKE Hindu guys. So I tell him, just call himself *Yeshu Bhakta*. We're in the *bhakti*

---

understand their beliefs in terms of the (primarily local) deities that they worship. This redefinition of Hinduism attempts to separate the more populous Dalit/OBC community from the higher castes and thus minimize the power that the high-caste has traditionally exerted over the others.

movement, or *Yeshu satsang* movement. So [there is a] range of scope within our *satsang*. [E].[46]

Similar to Dinesh, Gaurav is sensitive to the connotations that the self-ascription "Hindu" hold for some in the Dalit community. Because of this, and because he values a multi-caste and multi-religious community, Gaurav tries to be selective of the Hindu SEPs that he invokes. Though he still uses some Hindu worship practices to foster a connection with the wider Hindu structure, and will call himself "Hindu," he more commonly draws on the more general concept of *bhakti*. As mentioned above, many Dalits have historically started and participated in *bhakti* movements and, even though these have often focused on Hindu deities, they have not been associated with the higher-caste "Hindu" power structures. The SEPs of the *bhakti* self-ascription thus invoke a structure that, in Gaurav's experience, appeals to people from various castes and communities.

Relatedly, another term that Gaurav sometimes introduces is the more general term of "Indian." It is and has been important, and popular, to speak of the Christian church as "Indian" or becoming "Indian" or "Indianized." This word uses a national category in place of a religious or caste category, and is very popular among Indian churches. Gaurav explains his own understanding:

> It has to be, you know, done [according to] Indian context, Indian culture, Indian language usage, Indian practices. When you say "Indian," then . . . many other cultures and practices are there. We can all accommodate all of them within the *satsang*. And so everybody feels, "We are a part of *bhakti*. Jesus loves us. *Yeshu* is compassionate, loving, and accepts me in his, you know, group or *satsang*." [E][47]

Thus, for Gaurav and Dinesh, the concept of "Indian" and "*bhakti*" invokes SEPs that transcend the Hindu community, as it is sometimes more narrowly defined, particularly as understood by Dalits and OBCs.

Padman and Ravi are more favorable to the Hindu associations and SEPs of the "Hindu" self-ascription, but, similar to Dinesh and Gaurav, also make distinctions between those and its CEPs. Ravi states:

> I always say it like this, uh, "I am not a Christian, I am Hindu *Yeshu Bhakta*." Then I am ready for their questions, like, "You believe in Jesus, then how are you a Hindu?" Then I said, "On

46. Interview with Gaurav, Mar 6, 2010.

47. Ibid.

my (birth) form and my father's it is written 'Hindu.' And I live in Hindustan (India) and I speak Hindi. That is why I am a Hindu. And also Hindu is not a religion, it's a community." And then I say to them, "If you go to a *pir*, to a Muslim *pir*"—many Hindus go to Muslim *pirs* in Haryana and in Punjab and also in UP. They go everyday—"do you bow down, do you offer *prasad* . . . ? After doing all of this, have you become a Muslim?" They said, "No." "And then I follow the teachings of the Lord Jesus. So how have I become a Christian?" [H][48]

Ravi's use of the Hindu *Yeshu Bhakta* self-ascription is a conscious attempt to remain associated with the Hindu community. In explaining his choice of words to his hypothetical interlocutor, Ravi extends the logic of a similar distinction made by many Hindus themselves. In a practice common particularly in the northwest, many Hindus (and Sikhs) go to the graves of Muslim *pirs* (saints) and pray to the spirit of that saint for various blessings. However, showing devotion to the spirit or god associated with a socio-structural Other does not necessarily identify the person with that socio-structural group. In the same way, Ravi retains his socio-structural relationship with the Hindu community through the SEP of "Hindu *Yeshu Bhakta*" while also creating space within that structure for an alternative devotion, or CEP, directed to Jesus.

The Sikh *Yeshu satsang* leaders and consultants also use self-ascriptions with SEPs that relate to the Sikh social structure. However—and similar to Dinesh—the Sikh *Yeshu satsang* leaders and consultants tend to nuance this depending on their caste background. Jasbir and Nandita, for example, are Jatt Sikhs—a higher-caste and wealthy community among Sikhs in the Punjab, and the group that has been traditionally most resistant to becoming followers of Jesus. Both Jasbir and Nandita readily use and accept the self-ascription "Sikh," and only qualify it by specifying that they are "followers of Jesus." Nandita, for example, recently attended a Christian conference in Singapore and, when showing her invitation letter to the airport immigration official, was met with a confused look. The airport official asked Nandita if she was aware that the letter regarded a Christian conference. When Nandita affirmed this, the official responded, "But you, your name is Sikh!" Nandita stated that she is indeed a Sikh, but a follower of Jesus. When, on one occasion, I asked her what it meant for her to be Sikh, she responded that one of the literal meanings of "Sikh" is "learner." She went on to explain:

48. Interview with Ravi, Jun 24, 2010.

> I am still Sikh. Yeah. That's why I told so many people . . . Uh,
> people said that, "You are now, uh, Christian." And, uh, we told
> them, "We don't have any change in our clothes, in our, like that.
> So we change only our heart. We change only our life. So how
> you can say that we are now *Isai*,[49] we are now Christian? We are
> still Sikh. We are learning." [E][50]

Recently the contrast in self-ascriptions has become more pro-
nounced for Nandita as she and her family search for a suitable young
man for her to marry. Her and her family's preference is to find someone
who is a Jatt Sikh follower of Jesus. However, the number of young men
who are both Jatt Sikhs and followers of Jesus are few. Because of this they
face much pressure from their extended family to prioritize the Jatt Sikh
identity and forego the requirement that he should be a follower of Jesus.

On the other side, Nandita and her family face pressure from the
pentecostal church they presently attend, and whose pastor is a Dalit
Christian, to prioritize the follower of Jesus and be open to someone
from a lower *Majhabi* caste. Though they were initially open to this,[51]
Nandita eventually shifted her opinion and began to strengthen her resolve to find someone from a Jatt Sikh family. This was important, she
indicated, so that her extended family would accept the alliance, and
also because it would show her family that God could provide someone
who fit both criteria. Her pastor, however, has become angry regarding
this re-emphasis of the Jatt Sikh identity, and has begun to teach against

---

49. "*Isai*" is an Urdu word that has also long been associated with the Christian
community. Churches with liturgies and heritages dating back to the missionary
involvement of the late nineteenth and early twentieth centuries sometimes include
Urdu religious words. This reflects the high population of Urdu-speaking Muslims
that resided in northwest India prior to partition.

50. Interview with Nandita, Jan 29, 2010.

51. When we first met, Nandita sometimes spoke passionately about the need for
inter-caste marriages, a strong teaching from her pastor. At one point she and her
mother shared:

> Mother (M): (Our relatives) are saying, 'Where you will marry your chil-
> dren? You will marry with the *Majhabi* people. Why you are talking to
> those people?' (laughs).
>
> Nandita: My uncle also said to my aunt (who is a follower of Jesus) . . . ,
> "Where will we marry our children? Only *Majhabi* people accept Jesus."
> My aunt said, "We will do it in their community."
>
> M: Don't they also have souls? [P]. Interview with Nandita mother, Jan
> 29, 2010.

caste associations.[52] The discourses that this conflict generates shows the value that Nandita and her family place on Sikh structural associations, including their attempt to embrace the (Jatt) Sikh self-ascription while also honoring their belief in Jesus.

In a similar way Jasbir also distances himself from the SEPs of various Christian self-ascriptions, even though he is clearly involved in the Christian community as a pastor.[53] Initially, in the years following his decision to follow Christ, he distanced himself from the Sikh community. However, in recent years he has again started thinking of himself as a "Sikh." Part of this change stems from his association with Pastor Sandeep and others who are conducting Sikh *Yeshu satsangs*. In addition to this, however, and similar to Nandita, another reason for this change is in part due to a life event that moves Jasbir back towards a Sikh identity. Whereas for Nandita the life event is marriage, for Jasbir the event is the growth of his young children who, similar to and because of him, are growing up estranged from his Jatt Sikh family and disconnected from this religio-structural heritage. Reflecting on his children causes him to reflect on the value of his Sikh social structure, as well as aspects of its culture, and to embrace some of the SEPs of Sikh self-ascription.[54] Thus,

---

52. In particular, the pastor began to preach that Jesus taught against believers putting names like "Jatt Hindu" or "Jatt Sikh" on identifying documents. Nandita disagrees with him, saying that she does not think this was Jesus' teaching. She continues by saying that the pastor only has Christian family and friends and so cannot understand her situation. He preaches against Sikh practices like taking *prasad* and going to the *gurdwara*, but he does not have Sikh family members. For her and her family, to not take *prasad* when it is offered would create a "wall" between them and their family and they would no longer be able to share about Jesus. Interview with Nandita, Jun 1, 2010.

53. We discussed this when talking about the time when he became a follower of Jesus:

> Darren (D): How did you think of it at that time? Were you thinking of it as follower of Jesus, or Christian, or do you remember what was in your mind at that moment?
>
> Jasbir (J): I think more like a follower of Jesus. Never, this Christian word never appeared.
>
> D: Mmm hmm. Or *Masihi* or anything like that?
>
> J: No. No *Masihi*!
>
> D: Or *Isiai*?
>
> J: No. Never. Never really became uh, acquainted with these words, *Masihi*, Christian. Even today I don't call myself a Christian. I call myself a follower of Jesus. Interview with Jasbir, May 20, 2010.

54. Jasbir reflects on this in one of our conversations, saying, "I still struggle

for Nandita and Jasbir there is some interest in retaining the Sikh self-ascription, particularly as they face life events in which the Sikh social structure is traditionally very important. They are consequently becoming more attentive to some of the SEPs of these self-ascriptions.

The other Sikh *Yeshu satsang* leaders (Navdeep, Naveen, Jagdeep and Manpreet) also use self-ascription in order to connect with the Sikh social structure, but in so doing also nuance and sustain a more ambivalent relationship to the Sikh community than do Nandita and Jasbir. This difference in self-ascription parallels a difference of caste affiliation. Whereas Jasbir and Nandita are higher-caste Jatt Sikh, the other four leaders are *Majhabi* (low-caste) Sikhs. The Sikh self-ascription is important, says Navdeep, for the ability to stay connected with the Sikh community. However, as I will discuss below, Navdeep prefers to qualify this with the word "*Masihi.*" When I asked him how he prefers to think and call himself he replied, "Uh, for this now we have to add (or join) two-three words (laughs). Uh, I would like to call myself *Masihi* Sikh."[55]

For Jagdeep the Sikh self-ascription has two purposes. On the one hand it corresponds with caste reservations, an issue common among the Dalit community. When first applying for his government job, Jagdeep was offered his position as part of a quota of jobs given to Scheduled Castes, which includes low-caste Sikhs. As per the definition of a Scheduled Caste, however, if a person such as Jagdeep were to become and declare himself a Christian, the government would no longer consider him a member of a Scheduled caste and would most likely remove him from his position. Because of this Jagdeep maintains his Sikh self-ascription to, in part, maintain job security.

In addition to this, however, the Sikh self-ascription is also important to Jagdeep and Manpreet because it is part of the new *satsang* style and strategy that they have adopted to be able to more effectively communicate the gospel to Jatt Sikhs. In one conversation, a friend asks Manpreet why they felt the need to adopt this pattern of *satsang*. In her

---

though, sometimes, between uh, my identity. Sometimes I DO wonder that uh, am I a Sikh follower of Jesus or am I Christian? What would my kids be? . . . I don't want my kids to become like uh, some of the fellows I met in [a local city]. And uh, they had, their forefathers were Sikhs or Hindus and now they are Christians and they are TOTALLY in Christian, Christiandom. So do I want to see or do I want my kids to have more uh, attachment with their culture, more attachment with their families?" [E]. Interview with Jasbir, May 20, 2010.

55. Interview with Navdeep, May 2, 2010.

reply Manpreet reflects on the Sikh self-ascription and how it relates to other speech practices. She says:

> Because the biggest thing is that my husband likes this. Also, I mean, he wants it to be like this. Because . . . he is Sikh. This thing is still in his mind, I mean, the influence of coming from the Sikh community. And see, in the culture where we are living . . . Paul said when you go to the Greeks speak like the Greeks, and if you go to the Hebrews then be like the Hebrews. Then why can't we become like those for the Lord where we live? [P][56]

Self-ascriptions are one important aspect of speech practice that SEPs *Yeshu satsang* leaders seek to invoke. In addition, however, leaders have adopted a range of religious words that create associations with Hindu and Sikh religious structures. Several of these words offer what the leaders view as alternatives to Christian words for "God," "baptism," "amen," "hallelujah," and others. The structural importance of these words is most clearly seen in discourses where leaders reflect on and contrast their *satsangs* with Christian church structures.

For example, while talking about becoming "Greek to the Greeks," Manpreet goes on to reflect on the structural implications of certain speech practices for *satsangs*:

> When we bring someone into the *satsang*, I mean, if we start saying "hallelujah, hallelujah" more, then the other [Sikh] people feel awkward. They will feel that they are leaving something . . . We also need to see Sikh people in heaven . . . [But] if they don't understand our language they don't come to us. Then how can we take them towards Jesus? How can we make them to walk on His path? They are all from Sikh families. [P][57, 58]

While *Yeshu satsang* leaders sometimes discuss how Christian language such as "hallelujah" can cause people to feel that they are participating in something "foreign" or Other, Manpreet affirms this in another way. Such speech practices, she says, not only invoke the SEPs of

56. Interview with Manpreet, Apr 4, 2010.

57. Ibid.

58. In a similar way Naveen reflects on previous "Christian" ways of preaching and worshipping in their churches. He explained, "We used to tell them, 'Repent and take baptism' and also about 'Hallelujah.' And we used to say 'amen.' And they became happy for some time. They also used to get saved. But when they went outside and said our language, 'Hallelujah, Amen,' [others said], 'They make Muslims.' Some say, 'They make foreigners'" Interview with Naveen, May 3, 2010.

the Christian community, but can make Sikhs "feel that they are leaving something" of their own. In other words, Manpreet is sensitive to how speech practices may make someone feel that they are leaving their own community.

Other *satsangis* also reflected on the SEPs of speech practices through contrast. One of my informants, Ruth, reflects on speech practices in light of her interactions with Christians. She states:

> We use "*Satguru*" for Jesus. This is a Sikh word. [Christian] people have objections to this, saying, "This is a Sikh word, their religion's word" . . . I have seen so many Christians get offended by the greeting "*namaste*." This is a Hindu greeting. But they prefer "*jai masih ki*." Or older people prefer "*salaam*." But if you asked them the meaning of this and other such Christian words, they won't know. [E][59]

This *satsangi's* experience suggests that religious speech practices have strong SEP associations with particular religious structures that, in many cases, eclipse the meanings of those words in importance.[60]

Navdeep and Naveen regularly have to address and try to correct the Christian speech practices of their *satsangis*; particularly the practices of greeting. In the northwest, as elsewhere in India, peoples' form of greeting often identifies the community from which a person comes.[61] Because of this, Christians are often taught to say "*Jai Masih ki*" as a distinct form of greeting.[62]

---

59. Interview with Ruth, May 10, 2010.

60. I related to Ruth the argument of a Christian friend of mine who says that followers of Christ should use "amen" rather than the *Yeshu satsang's* Hindu-oriented "*tatasthu*." "Amen" was more appropriate than "*tatasthu*," he said, since the former is used in the Bible. Ruth responded that in her experience such arguments rarely regard the meaning of the word and instead are really about how the word makes them feel. Similar to what some said regarding *bhajans*, speech practices convey an affect that is related to the person's experience and connection to a social structure.

61. One Sikh website explains this, saying, "In Punjabi the greeting one uses is tied directly to the religion of the one being greeted. The proper greetings for Hindus is '*Namaste*' and for Muslims it's '*Assalam-o-Alaikum*.' If one does not know the religion of the person they are greeting, it is suggested that the neutral greetings "Hello" or "Hi" (both being emulated from English) be used." "Sat Sri Akal."

62. Manpreet shares an experience regarding the practice of greeting. She says, "When we first came to the Lord we felt very odd saying '*Jai Masih ki*' (Praise the Lord). And other members in the family started to object saying, 'What have they become now? They became Christian now, right?' I had to face these things."

In contrast, many of the *Yeshu satsangs* have encouraged their *satsangis* to retain and use the greetings of their socio-religious communities. These, however, are not always used consistently; often because people have been introduced to the Christian greeting through other pastors and churches. When I noted that some in their *Yeshu satsang* greeted me with the Christian greeting *"Jai Masih di,"*[63] Naveen explained that in the first two or three years of the *satsang*, people were taught to say this. As well, people get confused when they go to other churches and the pastors tell them to say *"Jai Masih di"* while the *Yeshu satsang* leaders counsel to say *"Sat Sri Akal."* From the *Yeshu satsang* leaders' perspective, the traditional Christian teachings on different speech practices are unhelpful and can cause a confusion of identity.[64]

THE CONSTRAINTS AND ENABLEMENTS OF PREVIOUS STRUCTURAL EMERGENT PROPERTIES

When viewed through the Morphogenetic process, the perceived associations of worship, dress and speech practices to Hindu and Sikh structures bring certain constraints and enablements to the *satsang*. As Archer has discussed, whereas the cultural and structural contexts do not determine the choices and elaborations of people, they nevertheless constrain and enable those choices.

I have already discussed some of the enablements that leaders have encountered as they have engaged the SEPs of various Hindu and Sikh practices. These have included structural associations with the Hindu and Sikh communities as well as a particular devotion towards God based on prior affect.

In addition, however, the SEPs of these practices also bring particular constraints.[65] Some of the constraints identified by leaders are positive.

63. The use of the word *"di"* in Punjabi is the same as *"ki"* in Hindi.

64. Naveen explains through the use of a parable. He says, "For example there was a bird, and that bird died. She gave eggs in her nest. And after that another kind of bird came there in that nest. And when the chicks came out from those eggs, those chicks were originally from the first birth that died. Then another bird started teaching them her language like *"ghugu ku."* And those chicks were doing *"chir chir chri."* They also learned a little bit of *"ghugu ku."* Then the chicks of the bird became *"chir ghug."* Now they were neither the first, original bird nor the other kind of bird" [P]. Interview with Naveen, May 2, 2010.

65. This is where Swidler's cultural "toolkit" falters, as Eiko Ikegami has shown, by not addressing fully the impact that cultural and structural systems have on those wielding the "tools." Ikegami, "A Sociological Theory of Publics."

, In particular, practices with strong Hindu or Sikh SEPs, when practiced consistently, constrain the elaboration of ecclesial identity towards one viewed as more Hindu/Sikh in structure and association. For example, *bhajans* (and particularly Sikh *kirtans*) frame worship in a more reverent and reserved style, which then makes inappropriate more boisterous expressions of worship, such as pentecostal-style clapping and shouting.

One *satsangi* attending Navdeep and Naveen's *satsang* identifies this constraint and reflects upon it with a mix of appreciation and frustration. On the one hand, he appreciates and agrees with some speech practices. He says, "I am glad with one thing: that (the *satsang*) says, "*Dhan Satguru Yeshu*" and "*satbachan*." I am happy because of this, because it is our Punjabi culture and (people) like this thing [P].[66]

On the other hand, having recently gone to some pentecostal churches and experienced the excitement and miracles of those, he now feels constrained by the Sikh *kirtan* style that Navdeep and Naveen encourage in the *Yeshu satsang*. In particular, he believes that this style should not, but easily can, replace an emphasis on God's power. He says:

> But what happens, I mean, more people do not get saved just by saying "*Satbachan*" or "*Dhan Satguru Yeshu*." And less people do not get saved by saying "hallelujah." Because it is written in the Word of God, "Whatever work you want to do, you pray to me." And I pray to God to save people and plead in front of him, sitting at home. Whenever I get a chance, immediately I pray to God. [P][67]

When I probed further about his experiences with churches that practice saying "hallelujah," clapping hands, and having exuberant worship, he explained that these pastors preach against the Sikh style of worship:

> When [we] used to worship there, the Holy Spirit truly used to come down there. Truly it was felt . . . But when we, uh, I mean, worship here by folding our hands, we don't feel [the Holy Spirit]. But that was the thing we had been told [at the church], "Satan has bound your hands." So we have to glorify our God by opening our hands [by raising and clapping]. But our hands have been bound again [in this *satsang*] [laughs]. [P][68]

66. Interview with N-5, May 20, 2010.

67. Ibid.

68. Ibid.

One implication of this discourse, which I will discuss in Chapter 7, is the leader's and *satsangis'* desire for expressions of God's power, which many have been seen more through the use of pentecostal practices. Another implication, however, is that the structural properties of the *Yeshu satsang* style constrained other forms and styles of church worship; some of which are valued by current *satsangis*.

Most *Yeshu satsang* leaders, as we have seen, embrace the enablements and are aware of and comfortable with the constraints of these practices. However, some are more ambivalent of certain properties and their constraints, particularly when the leaders feel constrained towards high-caste and power identifications with which they are not comfortable. For example, Manpreet in her *Yeshu satsang* integrates Christian practices, particularly Christian *geets* (songs) with Sikh practices. This hybrid style reflects to a certain degree her discomfort with aspects of the Sikh structure. Whereas she and Jagdeep want to identify with the Sikh community for the purposes of evangelism, they nonetheless display ambivalence, and even resistance, towards the power that the Sikh structure has wielded in their experience.[69] Such ambivalence seems to parallel and reflect the reticence to yield to the constraints and SEPs of a consistent set of Sikh practices.

Relatedly, another constraint that some leaders resist is the restrictions of caste and religious structures. Some practices, such as using a coconut during communion or using the self-ascription "Hindu *Yeshu Bhakta*" are favorable to Hindus, and particularly high-caste Hindus. Used consistently, however, these practices would constrain the elaboration and identity of the *satsang* towards these groups while excluding others, such as Dalits or Sikhs. Gaurav, as I have shown, has responded to this constraint by using the practices periodically and mixing them with other practices acceptable to a broader category of *bhakti* sect.

---

69. Manpreet at various times in her discourses reflects on negative experiences with Sikh leaders, *gurdwaras*, and their power. She explains, for example, how she became disillusioned with the Sikh religion even before becoming a follower of Christ. She says, "I was very much devoted to the Sikh religion. I used to go to the [*Baba Budda Sahib*] *gurdwara* with naked feet to serve there . . . And when nothing happened . . . [I went and] after getting down from the bus, I used to stand with my back to the face of the *gurdwara*. I used to yell at people saying 'I served so many years here with my whole heart and I have not received anything from here . . . '" [P]. Interview with Manpreet, Apr 4, 2010.

CHAPTER SUMMARY

In summary, leaders and *satsangis* are aware of the Hindu/Sikh structural emergent properties (SEPs) that are evoked by particular worship, dress and speech practices, and the ways in which these can enable desirable associations with the Hindi and Sikh communities. They are also aware of certain constraints that these SEPs may create, some of which are again partly positive. In addition, the *Yeshu satsang* leaders often draw on these practices in an effort to contrast the foreign or Other identity of the Christian church. The *Yeshu satsang* leaders are thus choosing practices that provide their *satsangs* with a high level of shared identity with the Hindu and Sikh structures.

What, however, are the practices and emphases that *Yeshu satsangs* rely on to form the unique contours of their ecclesial communities? How do leaders address the prior meanings that people attach to Hindu or Sikh practices such that the *satsangs* retain a distinct identity and focus on Christ? The next two chapters will address two overall strategies that *Yeshu satsang* leaders use in this regard.

CHAPTER 6

Inscribing New Cultural Emergent Properties on Hindu and Sikh Practices

IN THE ABOVE DISCUSSION I have highlighted the ways in which *Yeshu satsangis* and leaders use some Hindu and Sikh practices to alter the identities of their *Yeshu satsangs*, particularly in response to accusations that they are structurally Other to their Hindu and Sikh communities. This process, I suggest, is a key component for the creation of new ecclesial identities and holds keys to the themes important for these identities. Such identities relate to what Archer calls peoples' "projects," or enterprises through which people express what they care about most.[1] One of a peoples' goals for such projects is to create a *modus vivendi*, or a way of living in the midst of competing interests. In particular, a *modus vivendi* is " . . . a set of practices which, in combination, both respects that which is ineluctable but also privileges that which matters most to the person concerned."[2]

For the *Yeshu satsang* leaders, part of the process of creating a *modus vivendi* is to engage practices whose prior structural properties and associations positively relate to their intended identity. In addition, however, *Yeshu satsang* leaders have new cultural emergent properties (CEPs), or beliefs in Christ, that contrast some of those common in their Hindu or Sikh communities. Thus, as leaders incorporate practices with desirable SEPs, they also have to counter certain CEPs and infuse new ones into these practices, thus reinterpreting them in light of Christian beliefs.

1. Archer, *Structure, Agency, and the Internal Conversation*: 133.
2. Ibid., 149.

By linking their new Christian meanings and concerns to the object or practice, the *Yeshu satsang* leaders thus seek to shape a Christ-oriented ecclesial identity that also relates to the Hindu/Sikh social structures.

In this section I will discuss the ways in which the leaders are attributing new meanings to their Hindu and Sikh worship and speech practices. These new meanings are drawn from Christian teaching, scripture or churches, and function as cultural emergent properties (CEPs). Thus, though these leaders in various ways are trying to distance themselves from the structures of the Christian churches of northwest India, they have been influenced by and are seeking to align themselves with the Bible and with aspects of what they see as "correct" aspects of Christian theology. Before proceeding, it is important to discuss one common way that Christians interpret Hindu and Sikh practices.

PRACTICES, CULTURAL EMERGENT PROPERTIES, AND DEMONIC POWER

In general, Christians often object to Hindu and Sikh practices because of the traditions and meanings ascribed to those practices by Hindus and Sikhs. Indian Christians, for example, may reject the use of a coconut in worship because it is often used to worship Hindu gods and carries particular related meanings. However, it is not only the ideologies, such as the worship of Hindu gods, which make Christians uncomfortable with these practices; rather, a prominent teaching among churches regards the demonic nature of the Sikh or Hindu religions, and the demonic influence that their practices may have on the practitioners.[3] Because of this, some Christians can and do object to the use of Sikh and Hindu practices in *Yeshu satsangs* on the basis that they contain and promote evil power. The *Yeshu satsang* leaders encounter this perception and try to clearly distinguish their practices from the powers of Satan in various ways.

First, though they clearly believe in the power of Satan and regularly talk about this, they do not agree that Hindu and Sikh practices and scriptures are in themselves demonic. Navdeep discusses this by contrasting the view of Sikh practices that he first learned from Christian

3. As an example, Ruth describes how she once went to the house of a Christian friend. Close to the house was a Hindu temple that periodically and loudly broadcasted prayers and mantras. Ruth's friend was very upset at this, closing her ears and calling them "satanic prayers." "Do you know what they are saying?" Ruth asked. "Oh," the friend said, "I know that these are Satanic prayers." Ruth comments that she is sad about the many Christians who respond like this. Interview with Ruth, May 10, 2010.

pastors. He recalls their general teaching, saying, "They said . . . whatever Sikhs are doing they are doing, I mean, they are doing for Satan. And even it was said that if you bow down, or you take *prasad* . . . then still we will go to hell" [P].[4]

However, after learning about a *Yeshu satsang* approach through Pastor Sandeep, Navdeep began to change his views and allow for the possibility that Sikh practices and scripture were not inherently evil and could contain "some truth." At the same time he had a change in his "nature," and felt compelled to share more about God's love for people, than about His judgment. Whereas he before would often preach harshly against Sikh beliefs and practices, labeling them as "Satanic," he now prefers to share God's love and good news. Navdeep thus rejects the sense that Sikh practices, in and of themselves, contain evil properties that will affect people.

Padman, with his Arya Samaji *Yeshu satsang* also resists the idea that his people and family follow and worship Satan. Noting how some pastors label Hindu *satsangs*, including his own *Yeshu satsang*, as the "Devil's workshop" he comments, "So, if somebody will say to my father that you are worshipping a devil, so what will be the reaction?" [E][5] In contrast, Padman draws from Acts 17 and frames his Arya Samaji community as worshippers of "the unknown God."

One teaching that Padman and the Sikh *Yeshu satsang* leaders are able to take advantage of is the Arya Samaji and Sikh teaching against idol worship. Because both communities have historically preached against worshipping idols, these leaders are able to draw on this aspect of their beliefs.[6] In contrast, the Hindu *Yeshu satsangs*, in using practices that in their original contexts are more clearly connected to idol worship, cannot appeal to anti-idol teachings, as can the other groups. As a result, the Hindu *Yeshu satsang* leaders all feel the need to clearly teach against idol worship. However, and in contrast to other churches in their area, none say that Hindus worship Satan, or state that idol worship is the same

4. Interview with Navdeep, May 2, 2010.

5. Interview with Padman, Apr 19, 2010.

6. Though the Sikhs do not believe in "idol worship," some Christian pastors teach that bowing down to the *Guru Granth Sahib* is the same as bowing down to an "idol." There are differences among the Sikh *Yeshu satsang* leaders on this issue. Navdeep does not advocate bowing down to the *Guru Granth Sahib*, but stops short of calling it an idol. Jasbir, on the other hand, strongly believes that the *Guru Granth Sahib* is an idol, and bowing before it is the same as idol worship.

as the worship of demons. Though they believe in the power of Satan, and often pray against its manifestation in peoples' lives, they are reticent to publicly attribute it to Hindu social structures.

Another step that some leaders take, including Navdeep and Naveen, is to counter any Satanic power, or perceptions of Satanic power in the *Yeshu satsang* through prayer and teaching. Prayers along these lines often echo one made by Navdeep at the beginning of one *Yeshu satsang*. He prayed:

> Help us in this *satsang*, and we believe that no Satanic power will be at work here, and we bind it in the name of Jesus. Please give us power to speak and ear to listen to your *bani* [Word]. I want to thank you that you heard our *ardas* [prayer], and we ask this in the name of *Satguru Yeshu, satbachan* [amen]. *Dhan Satguru Yeshu* [Group: *Dhan Satguru Yeshu*]. [P][7]

It is important to note how, in this prayer, Navdeep juxtaposes a number of Sikh speech practices—*bani* (word), *ardas* (prayer), *Satguru Yeshu* (true-guru Jesus), *Dhan Satguru Yeshu* (praise Jesus)—and uses them within the context of opposing the presence of Satan's power. Thus, instead of distancing themselves from these practices and any possible association or property of Satanic power, they instead use the practices in the midst of prayer to mitigate any power or perceptions of evil power within the *satsang*.

The *Yeshu satsang* leaders also try to give consistent teaching in order to help counter any confusion *satsangis* may have on these issues. In one *Yeshu satsang* Navdeep preaches on the nature of Satanic power. Drawing from Jesus' teaching in Mark 16:18 he says:

> The word of God says that those who have bad things in their hearts, bad things will come out. Those who have good things in their hearts, good things will come out . . . Because in this world two powers are working, one is God and one is Satan. Satan wants to control the people . . . (But Jesus) said, "If you have faith, put your hand on the people they will be healed. If you eat poison you will not get sick. And you have authority over the demons. So go into this world and preach the good news." [P][8]

He continues by reading and talking about the story of Philip and Simon the sorcerer in Acts 8. To explain the story Navdeep uses the word

---

7. From Navdeep *satsang*, May 3, 2010.

8. Ibid.

"*jadugar*" to describe Simon, the same word used to describe shamans in Punjabi villages. Just as "in their (Simon's) village there was witchcraft and Satanic power," so also "today in every (Punjabi) village there is witchcraft" and the *jadugars* say, "If you give money to me I will do something and your relatives will be destroyed!" Navdeep thus does equate Satanic power with an existing structure in the Punjab society. However, instead of attributing Satanic power to Sikh structures and practices, he focuses on the *jadugars*. Though many Sikhs go to *jadugars* for healing and curses, Sikh scriptures and orthodox leaders teach against them and their practices. Navdeep thus attributes Satanic power to the *jadugars* who, as practitioners of magic on the fringe of the Sikh social structure, are not equated with Sikh structures per se.

In a similar way, many *Yeshu satsang* leaders talk about the demonic identity and power of *pirs*, or the spirits of Muslim saints, to which many Hindus and Sikhs pray. Because these spirits are "Muslim" and outside of the Hindu and Sikh structures, leaders can attribute to them Satanic power without implicating the Hindu and Sikh structures.

Yeshu satsang leaders and *satsangis* are sensitive to demonic power and speak about its manifestations and God's ability to overcome it. However, whereas Christian leaders in general respond to this by restricting use of certain Hindu/Sikh worship practices, the *Yeshu satsang* leaders seek to retain the practice (along with its structural properties) and minimize association with any demonic power by instead invoking the power of God through Jesus. In addition, they often attribute demonic power to spirits and shamans at the fringe of the religious community.

Such distinctions communicate important theological implications for the ways in which God is at work in and through structures and culture. Many Christian leaders regard Hindu/Sikh religious structures and cultures as inherently evil and formulate ecclesial identities that strongly counter these systems. However, the *Yeshu satsangs* are challenging this view of structures and culture, and particularly the ecclesial responses and identities that this has formed in their context. Aspects of this approach will be seen again below in reference to practices that extend beyond the *Yeshu satsang*.

WORSHIP PRACTICES: BHAJANS AND WORSHIP OBJECTS

As the *Yeshu satsang* leaders use various practices in their *satsangs*, they reinterpret them in various ways according to Christian propositional

CEPs. I will look at examples of this in the practices of *bhajans* and worship objects.

One crucial issue regards how to treat the propositional CEPs of various Hindu or Sikh practices, such as those of *bhajans*, that, in their original form and context, refer to Hindu deities or Sikh gurus. In these cases leaders in general give new meaning to these *bhajans* by changing lyrics to reflect CEPs, such as singing about their devotion to Jesus (expressed *as Satguru Yeshu*) instead of a Hindu deity. Gaurav and his *satsangis*, for example, have at times adapted and used popular *bhajans* from Hindi films. These and other popular *bhajans* often use generic words such as *Prabhu* (Lord) that, in the context of a Hindu *satsang*, could refer to any number of deities. However, when the *Yeshu satsang* leaders use these *bhajans* in their *satsangs*, they clarify through prayers and instruction that *Prabhu* refers to God or Jesus.

The *Yeshu satsang* leaders also inscribe new CEPs onto the religio-cultural objects that they utilize in the *Yeshu satsangs*. For example, Dinesh describes the way he talks about the *diya* (lamp) in his *satsang*. As background to this, he explains the general way he views Hindu CEPs, such as those coming through Hindu scriptures. He explains, "First of all . . . I make them understand that, you see, it [truth] is in our scripture, it is in the Vedas. The Gita is teaching us this, but there is another truth apart from this, and we have to find that" [H][9] To do so, Dinesh says, we need to turn to the Bible, "which is the conclusion of all" [H].[10] Thus Hindu beliefs, such as those found in Hindu scriptures, have some truths but require the truths of the Bible, and particularly the revelation of Jesus, to be complete.[11]

---

9. Interview with Dinesh, Mar 22, 2010.

10. Ibid.

11. The *Yeshu satsang* leaders at various times expressed convictions similar to this, stating that Hindu/Sikh scriptures and beliefs could contain some truth, but that Jesus and the Bible contained the ultimate and most important truth. Though the *Yeshu satsang* leaders never explicitly discussed their "theology" of other religions, some of their ideas parallel the early twentieth century "fulfillment theology" of J. N. Farquhar, and it was apparent that they had heard or had begun formulating their own teaching along these lines. A full discussion of fulfillment theology is beyond the scope of this paper, but the classic expression of this is Farquhar's *The Crown of Hinduism*, in which Farquhar states, "Christ provides the fulfillment of each of the highest aspirations and aims of Hinduism . . . In him is focused every ray of light that shines in Hinduism. He is the Crown of the faith of India" Farquhar, *The Crown of Hinduism*, 457–58; See also Boyd, *An Introduction to Indian Christian Theology*, 89–90.

Dinesh then uses this same methodology in his use and explanation of various worship objects. In addition to their structural associations, he acknowledges some of their cultural associations and engages those that can then be redefined or "completed," through Christian teachings. In discussing the *diya*, for example, he begins with the Hindu understanding and value of the practice and then reinterprets it via Biblical passages. He explains:

> We [Hindus] worship fire. We lit the fire. We lit the *diya*. We lit the fire, and then [believe that] the fire is pure. And the Bible says when God appeared to Moses, he appeared through fire. Moses was not allowed, could not see [God directly]. [God said], "If you see me you will become blind." Because he is a very holy God. Moses was given the vision of God through fire. We can make anything dirty. We can make water dirty, we can make everything dirty. But we cannot make fire dirty. God is holy like a fire. He is a light. And after that we see that Jesus Christ said the same thing, "I am the light of world." And he, when we see in the life of Paul, when Jesus appeared to Paul and when Paul saw him, he became blind. [H][12]

Hindus, as Dinesh interprets it, worship the *diya*'s fire as a revelation of God's purity. The Bible, however, clarifies and completes this understanding, showing the fire to be a representation of God's holiness, demonstrated finally in Jesus as the "light of the world."[13] Thus Dinesh incorporates CEPs regarding the nature of God and Jesus and incorporates these into his use of the *diya* to supplement and "complete" some of the CEPs that may relate to Hindu religious culture.

The Sikh *Yeshu satsangs*, though including fewer symbols and objects of worship, nonetheless sometimes use the *kadah* or *halwa prasad* (sweet offering) at the end of the *Yeshu satsang*. This practice is common in Sikh *gurdwaras* and involves distributing a sweet food to those that have attended the *satsang* as a way of distributing the blessing of God. Navdeep, in their *Yeshu satsang*, acknowledges the general Sikh understanding of the *prasad*. One reason Sikhs practice the *prasad*, he says,

---

12. Interview with Dinesh, Mar 22, 2010.

13. At a later point he explains in a similar way, saying, "We light the *diya* because in temples they have a light burning. That is why we tell them (*satsangis*) that this is also the temple of Lord Jesus Christ. He has said that this is his house of prayer and this light (illustrates that) God is holier than fire" [H]. Interview with Dinesh, Mar 22, 2010.

is simply for the refreshment and enjoyment it brings. However, it has another reason. He explains: " . . . those who are listening, they know that there is a special blessing on whatever is kept in the presence of God, whatever that thing is" [P].[14]

Similar to Dinesh's use of the *diya*, Navdeep acknowledges and embraces a general Sikh understanding regarding the *prasad*. In the *Yeshu satsang*, however, he also clarifies and supplements this with a Christian understanding, giving to it Christian CEPs. At the end of one *satsang* a family brought the *halwa prasad* forward and Navdeep asked a *satsang*i to pray over it. The *satsang*i prayed: "Lord I want to thank you for this *prasad* and fulfill the needs of those who made it. Heavenly father bless this *prasad*. When people eat, bless them and may they remain in you and every disease go in the name of Jesus. I ask this in the name of *Satguru Yeshu, satbachan* (amen)" [P].[15] Thus, while acknowledging and validating that the practice has some general CEPs that are truthful and valuable (God blesses the *prasad* kept in his presence) the invocation in this prayer of Satguru Yeshu over the *prasad* clearly seeks to build on and focus this general ideology towards Jesus.

SPEECH PRACTICES

The speech practices of the *Yeshu satsang* leaders include the use of various words that are familiar to Sikhs and Hindus. As the *Yeshu satsang* leaders use these to create religio-structural connections with those communities, they simultaneously integrate new CEPs regarding the ways in which these refer to Christian identity, doctrine and concepts regarding God.

One category of speech practices, explored in Chapter 5, constitutes the self-ascriptions of the leaders and *satsangis*. Some leaders, particularly those from higher-caste families, use "Hindu" and "Sikh" to describe themselves. In doing so, however, they also inscribe meanings that more closely align with their new faith commitment to Jesus. For example, Nandita calls herself "Sikh" and embraces the literal meaning of "learner" or "disciple." She qualifies this, however, with "follower of Jesus" or other descriptions that specifies Jesus as the one from whom she learns and the one whom she follows.

---

14. Interview with Navdeep, May 2, 2010.

15. From Navdeep *satsang*, May 2, 2010.

In a similar way, Ravi, Padman and Gaurav all embrace the self-ascription "Hindu" because of its religio-structural properties, and qualify it with "*Yeshu Bhakta*" to clarify the focus of their devotion. As a prior example from Ravi shows, this follows a logic that many Hindus understand—the object of their devotion and prayer does not necessarily determine the religious community to which one belongs.

Another category of speech practice is greetings. As discussed above, the greeting one uses—whether "*jai masih ki*" for Christians, "*namaste*" for Hindus or "*sat sri akal*" for Sikhs—has strong structural properties that link people to the respective socio-religious community. Though these also have cultural properties, these are often not the main association that people consciously consider. Correspondingly, *Yeshu satsang* leaders often reflect more on the structural merits for adopting this practice. However, some leaders also justify the use of Hindu or Sikh greetings by reinterpreting them via Christian CEPs. Manpreet, for example, reflects on objections she received from Christians when she and her *Yeshu satsang* began to use "*sat sri akal*." She says:

> But it is written in [the Bible] that *Sat Sri Akal* means "serving God." But some Christian people started saying, "Look, now they have started saying *Sat Sri Akal*. They are on the other side." I used to ask them, "Have you ever read the Bible? Because it is written in the Bible that *Sat Sri Akal* means "serving God." Right? Truly the one who is the ancient and beyond time is God. He is older than anyone else. We serve him. [P][16]

Manpreet here refers to 1 Thessalonians 1:9 which says, "for they themselves report what kind of reception you gave us. They tell how you turned to God from idols to serve the living and true God." Not all Punjabi versions of the Bible translate "the living and true God" as "*sat sri akal*," and neither are all Punjabi Christians aware of this translation. However, Manpreet uses this connection to give a Christian CEP to the practice, equating the God of the Bible as the one who is *sat* (truth), *sri* (honored) and *akal* (eternal).

Relatedly, another category of speech practice regards the ways in which people refer to God. Hindi-speaking Christians commonly use the word "*Parmeshwar*," which *Yeshu satsangs* sometimes also use. However, because of its Urdu origin, many people associate it with the Muslim, as well as the Christian communities. In light of this the leaders

---

16. Interview with Manpreet, Apr 4, 2010.

have re-introduced other words whose structural properties link them to the Sikh and Hindu communities. However, some Hindu and Sikh terms also carry CEPs regarding the nature of God, and some *satsangis* are thus reticent to use them. Nandita, for example, feels that the Sikh word for God, *Waheguru*, should not be used "because the Sikhs will say, 'We have a direct connection with *Waheguru* already, so why do we need yours?'" [E][17] Nandita is thus concerned over the ideological and identity confusion that could result when Sikhs hear "Waheguru" and concludes that, since it is the same God, there is no need for them to change their practices or allegiance.

Most other Sikh *Yeshu satsang* leaders, however, contend that *Waheguru*, as well as the related title *Akal Purkh* can reflect Christian truths, or CEPs, of God and his character. In order to inscribe new properties, the leaders seek to explain the terms in relation to Jesus. For example, in one conversation with a non-believing Sikh, Jasbir argues that two things have not changed about himself: he is still a Jatt Sikh and he worships *Waheguru*. What has changed, however, is that he has been forgiven and purified through Jesus. He explains:

> Let me tell you one thing, I do not call myself as a "Christian" [E] . . . I am Jatt. It's a very simple thing . . . But the heart of one Jatt has changed. The heart has become good . . . Earlier to whom was I bowing? . . . In front of *Waheguru* . . . Even today I call him *Waheguru*. Even today I call him *Akal Purkh* . . . And *Satguru Yeshu* has cleansed me of my sins so that I can embrace God . . . . But today if a person comes to know Jesus from Jatts, he is still the same even today. Whatever *jaati* he comes from he is still the same. [P][18]

In this, Jasbir's discussion about *Waheguru* is sandwiched in the midst of a discourse regarding social structures. In particular, he argues that his community identity has remained constant in spite of his faith in Jesus. To substantiate this to his Jatt Sikh friend, he argues that he was and still is bowing down to *Waheguru*. However, he explains that Jesus has helped him truly embrace God by cleansing him from sin. Jasbir thus uses *Waheguru* to harness its structural properties, while beginning to inform it with Christian CEPs so as to clarify the new meaning that he desires to convey through it.

17. Interview with Nandita, Jun 1, 2010.
18. Discussion between Jasbir and friend 2, May 20, 2010.

Another word used by the *Yeshu satsangs* is that of *Satguru* (true/ultimate-guru). This word is usually reserved for gurus who have been enlightened and can show the way towards divine power. There is disagreement, however, among sects that use the word regarding the uniqueness of a *Satguru*. Some may view the *Satguru* whom they serve as one among many of the various *satgurus* who have come throughout history. Others, such as branches of the Radha Soami, view their Satguru as unique and unsurpassed.[19] In most cases, though, *Satgurus* are understood as the givers of revelation and power, and through whom the path to *moksha* (salvation) can be attained.

The *Yeshu satsang* leaders readily embrace the revelatory aspect of the *Satguru*. In reflecting on his use of "*Satguru Yeshu*," Ravi says, "We use the word '*Satguru Yeshu*' because '*Satguru*' means 'true guru.' And *satya* means 'truth' and Jesus said, 'I am the truth, way and life' . . . We reflect on this and tell people that He is *Satguru*" [H].[20] At other times, the leaders juxtapose *Satguru* with God or *Waheguru*. When discussing this point Naveen says:

> Now we will say to the Sikhs, "The one who is *Satguru*, *Waheguru*, right? He is a very merciful God. He does not take money. Whatever sickness we have, the evil spirits that do not leave our houses, all those things go out. And he is the only God who made heaven, who made earth and made everything. That *Satguru* Yeshu is who, I mean, is written in the word." [P][21]

In most cases the *Yeshu satsang* leaders inscribe new CEPs to the term *Satguru* through their teaching and prayers. Typical of Navdeep's prayers in this regard is one with which he began a *Yeshu satsang*, where he prayed, "We thank *Satguru Yeshu*. We will close our eyes. We want to thank him for his blessing. Because of him we are together here and he protected us. We want to that thank you, *Satguru Yeshu*. You also forgive our sins. You love us. We want to thank you for your grace" [P].[22]

A final example of some of the ways in which *Yeshu satsang* leaders seek to inscribe Christian CEPs onto Sikh and Hindu speech practices regards the use of the word "*Om*." As described in Chapter 5, this word has strong connections to the Hindu community, and can convey particular

---

19. Juergensmeyer, *Radhasoami Reality*, 10.
20. Interview with Ravi, Jun 24, 2010.
21. Interview with Naveen, May 3, 2010.
22. From Navdeep *satsang*, May 3, 2010.

philosophical ideas regarding God. Ravi reflects on this, saying, "We have no objections to the terminology. According to my thinking the word '*Om*' is a symbol that Hindus use, but it is not for any [specific] god. '*Om*' has three hundred different meanings that are made" [H].[23] Because of this, he argues, he and his *satsang* can use it as well and inscribe their own meaning.

Padman, who uses *Om* regularly in his *Yeshu satsang*, describes his understanding of the term in a small pamphlet through which he teaches some young men whom he is training to be *Yeshu satsang* leaders. In this he explains:

> Hindu scriptures are pointing toward OM, but [the meaning of] OM remained buried under the heap of misinterpretation due to ignorance and lack of information. Before OM came to this world, God was revengeful and use to kill and punish using his power. But when Jesus-OM descended as human, through his life and teaching he revealed the nature of God . . . Maharishi Dayanand Ji [Apostle John] presented OM/Muktinath Ji as the mind of God in a person come to earth, and as the one person who possesses reality instead of shadows and able to lead men out of the shadows into the real world for which the entire construction of the Hindu world is crying. The omniscience of Eshu Ji/Taranaishwar Ji/Om [Jesus Christ] is well understood by Hindus if presented in its culture, thoughts and language. [E][24]

In summary, the *Yeshu satsang* leaders are aware that the worship and speech practices whose structural properties they appreciate have also contributed to various Hindu/Sikh cultural systems through CEPs. When the leaders use these practices, they are aware that people will associate them with the religious social structures with which they are familiar, but could also associate them with other understandings of God. In an attempt to create a *modus vivendi* that alleviates this tension, *Yeshu satsang* leaders seek to attribute Christian CEPs to these practices through explanation and by juxtaposing them with other Christian CEPs in the midst of prayer and teaching. In doing so, the leaders seek to shape ecclesial identities that ideologically aligned with Christian teachings from the Bible, but that are structurally associated to varying degrees to the Sikh and Hindu communities in their areas.

23. Interview with Ravi, Jun 24, 2010.

24. Email correspondence from Padman, Dec 19, 2010.

THE CONSTRAINTS AND ENABLEMENTS OF CHRISTIAN CULTURAL EMERGENT PROPERTIES

As *Yeshu satsang* leaders engage the Christian cultural systems and draw on Christian teachings, it is again important to recognize that emergent properties of these teachings bring certain constraints and enablements to the elaboration of their project or identity. This is to say that the leaders' cultural and structural contexts both limit and facilitate the "projects" whose *modus vivendi* expresses "that which matters most" to them.[25] How do the incorporation of Christian teachings, and the re-interpretation of Hindu and Sikh practices in light of these teachings, constrain and enable a "project" of a new ecclesial identity?

One constraint that these teachings bring is one welcomed and embraced by the *satsang* leaders themselves. The Christian teachings that the leaders draw on constrain the devotion and loyalty of *satsangis* to a Christian revelation of God through Jesus and the Bible. In this they specifically emphasize the centrality of Jesus and the need to stop idol worship and pray only to Jesus. Though they give new *satsangis* time to develop this exclusive devotion in their personal lives, *satsang* teachings clearly emphasize the centrality and importance of Jesus. Dinesh describes his approach in this manner:

> [W]e make the people clearly understand why we are totally against idol worshiping. I do not say this, but in my *satsang* when they get mature I tell them clearly that if you want to come to me for prayers then you have to trust only in God who is the creator of the world. Jesus is his son through whom God hears our prayers. And the Holy Spirit is there and working among us. [H][26, 27]

In this, the *Yeshu satsang* leaders embrace and allow themselves to be constrained by the same Christian teaching, or CEPs, as that of most other Christian churches and leaders in their contexts. The *Yeshu satsang* leaders' teaching on idol worship and the exclusivity of Jesus would thus in itself be very similar to the teaching of other Christian leaders. Where

25. Archer, *Structure, Agency, and the Internal Conversation*, 149.

26. Interview with Dinesh, Mar 22, 2010.

27. Gaurav and Ravi also maintain a similar stance. When among Hindus, Gaurav tries to counter some of the harsh-sounding ways that Christians denounce idols by using the analogy of the growth of children who need toys that they can touch and play with. Similarly, when people are spiritually "small" they may need idols that they can see and touch. But they should move beyond them towards faith in God through Jesus.

the *satsang* leaders differ, however, is that they challenge the extended restraints that Christian leaders have applied, particularly over the practices that have traditionally been associated with idol worship, such as the use of the coconut, *diyas*, and others. The *Yeshu satsang* leaders disagree with the Christian teaching that a restriction against idol worship must also include a restriction against the practices that are sometimes associated with idol worship. Rather, as the forgoing section has shown, the *Yeshu satsang* leaders argue that the religio-structural associations, or SEPs, of these practices can be separated from their religio-cultural associations, or CEPs, and that the latter can be critiqued and redefined according to Christian doctrine. The *Yeshu satsang* leaders thus embrace constraints that they feel are more in line with the original intent of the Bible.

In addition, the *Yeshu satsang* leaders generally allow *satsangis* more time to make changes in their practices. Padman, for example, feels that churches too quickly seek to constrain Hindus and their practices when they become followers of Jesus. Though he agrees that their practices should eventually change and, in essence, be constrained or redirected by a biblical understanding, he argues that Christian leaders should be more patient and allow changes to come more slowly.[28]

Though the *Yeshu satsang* leaders welcome the constraint of exclusive devotion to Jesus and do not advocate idol worship, this also brings constraint to the social interaction of *satsangis* with the Hindu and Sikh communities. Jasbir is very aware of the tension, for example, that is involved if he or other *satsangis* attend a village *gurdwara*. In a large *gurdwara*, such as the Golden Temple in Amritsar, people can enter and not bow before the *Guru Granth Sahib*, due to the large number of people. However, in a smaller village *gurdwara*, such an omission of practice would be noticed and highly scrutinized. I will return to the discussion of public practices below, but here emphasize that some of the CEPs

28. Padman shares about Hindu practices such as *prasad*:

> Padman (P): These (high-caste) people are really, they need, they need care. They need help. They need someone that can tell them who God is. If they are doing it [*prasad*] and, if we have to uh, associate with them, so . . . what they are doing let them do. Don't put don'ts and do's in the very beginning. So, okay, it may take some time. It is not overnight work . . . And after some time hopefully, definitely! It is a must! They will change. It is going to happen!
>
> Darren: What is the change? Meaning, that they will . . .
>
> P: Change, meaning, that they, that they will know the real God. [E] Interview with Padman, Apr 19, 2010.

embraced by the *Yeshu satsang* also constrain their religio-structural associations.

Devotion to Jesus not only restricts the types of religious practices that some *satsangis* are able to participate in, but it can also constrain other aspects of *satsangis'* relationships with their communities. Padman, for example, identifies the constraint that arises with the public use of "*Yeshu.*" Whereas some *Yeshu satsang* leaders identify this and try to alleviate some tension by using the title *Satguru Yeshu*, Padman points out that sometimes just the mention of "*Yeshu*" can be "offensive" because of its association with the social structures of Christianity. Because of this, he recommends sometimes using the name "*mukteshwar*" (Lord that gives salvation).[29] Doing so allows him to more carefully introduce and describe the qualities and person of Jesus.[30]

Relatedly, another constraint of Christian CEPs is the emphasis on the Bible. This is again a constraint welcomed by the *satsangis*, and in this they would again be very similar to many of the Christian churches and leaders in their areas. However, just as the *Yeshu satsang* leaders critique the Christian interpretation of what would be restrained or restricted by devotion to Jesus, so they also critique the interpretation of how an emphasis on the Bible restrains the perspective of other scriptures. As an example of this, Navdeep experienced a transformation in his perspective on Sikh scriptures. Following his conversion, Navdeep was discipled by pentecostal pastors who strongly denounced Sikh beliefs and scriptures as demonic and as unable to convey any truths. However, after meeting

29. As an example, he shares a story about how he was befriending a high-caste Hindu politician (Member of the Legislative Assembly, or MLA). While doing so an Indian missionary whom he knows also met the MLA and, in the course of conversation, told him that Padman is a baptized Christian who follows Jesus. This, according to Padman, "totally destroyed the relationship" he had been building. Still, Padman went to the MLA's home and explained that he is a Hindu that worships *Muktenath*, or *Mukteshwar*. The MLA said, "Oh, okay." Padman prayed for him, and the MLA then asked him, "Please tell me about *Mukteshwar.*" Padman took 7–8 months to slowly tell him about *Mukteshwar.* Now, he says, they pray in his home and read a Bible together, and he is slowly coming to faith. Interview with Padman, May 15, 2010.

30. The differences in peoples' perception of "*Yeshu*" clearly depend on their level of education and, relatedly, their caste. In contrast to Padman's experience with his highly educated friend, for example, Ravi shares a humorous example of how some people in local villages have never heard the word "*Yeshu*," let alone the phrase "*Yeshu Masih,*" which most Christians use. He says, "If we go to a village and ask them, 'Do you know *Yeshu Masih*?' Some people hear, 'usha machine.' 'Usha machine' is a thread, threading machine. Sewing machine [E]. Yeah, many people call Jesus, 'usha machine' because most of the people are not educated" [H]. Interview with Ravi, Jun 24, 2010.

pastor Sandeep and becoming discipled and acquainted with the *Yeshu satsang* approach, he began to change his opinion regarding the Sikh scriptures. For Navdeep, then, the centrality of the Bible and the restraint that belief brings to an understanding of revelation does not discount the possibility that the Sikh scriptures contain aspects of morality or truth. Thus, whereas the constraint of using the Bible is embraced and important to Navdeep and other *Yeshu satsang* leaders, they do not accept the extended constraint applied by many Christian leaders that gives no value to other scriptures or authority figures.

In addition to certain constraints, Christian CEPs also bring particular enablements. One such enablement is the ability of the *Yeshu satsang* leaders to relate to and bridge the *Yeshu satsangs* with the wider Christian community. Though the *Yeshu satsang* leaders are, for the most part, reacting against aspects of the Christian community, some also hope that their *satsang* approach will be embraced by other churches, and that others will pursue ministries that establish fewer barriers between the gospel and non-believers. Gaurav, for example, has had the opportunity to conduct various training seminars for church leaders and members regarding a *Yeshu satsang* approach. As a result he has identified several leaders, including Dinesh, who have decided to adopt a *Yeshu satsang* approach, and Gaurav has gathered these into a leadership team that meets periodically and collaborates on various projects. Ravi also shares a desire to have good relationships with local churches, and to influence them. He explains:

> We have good relations with different churches. And gradually our style that we are applying with the Bible is gradually making an influence (over other churches) . . . We have relations with different churches and denominations. And we are gradually telling these things to them also. We get into arguments with some people. Some people do not want to accept, but gradually this *satsang* style is coming in other churches as well. And they are influenced by it. [H][31]

Similarly, Pastor Sandeep regularly holds training seminars on evangelizing Jatt Sikhs. The focal point of his seminars is a *Yeshu satsang* approach, and several leaders, including Jagdeep and Manpreet, have been influenced by his ideas and adapted their house churches to a *Yeshu satsang* style. There is thus a desire to communicate and to maintain a

31. Ibid.

level of influence and relationship with the Christian community, which the CEPs allow them to do.

Padman has identified two enablements of biblical teaching important for his Arya Samaj community. First, he has identified a tendency among some in his community to reduce their spiritual devotion to a set of symbols. Though he uses the Arya Samaj symbols, such as the fire and *havan kund*, Padman promotes the biblical concept that God is not reduced to or in need of such symbols. Rituals, he explains, are ultimately for peoples' benefit, not for God. He explains:

> Some people who have some idea about this [Arya Samaj *sat-sangs*], they will say it, "Do it like that, that, that." I do say, I have a simple, I mean, answer: that this is not for God. It is for us because we are tuned to sit only around this. God don't need [the rituals]. He has ample fire, so many volcanoes [laughs]. He has ample scent, beautiful forest and scent of flowers. He don't need all these things. It is because of our mind is tuned like that. [E][32]

The other biblical teaching that Padman has identified regards the servant role of a religious leader. Leaders, including those of *Yeshu sat-sangs*, should not exploit people in the manner that he has seen from Hindu *pandits*. These, he alleges, often charge high amounts of money in order to perform *satsangs* and to pray for people. In contrast, part of Padman's desire is to, through his *satsang*, present a good example of a spiritual leader. He explains, "They need a *pandit* like me! [laughs]. Who never ask for money, and who pray for all, all of them and explain them in their own language. I have seen it. Yeah. That's [why] we have started this sort of program" [E].[33]

A final, and perhaps ultimate enablement of these CEPs, as perceived by the *Yeshu satsang* leaders, is their soteriological importance. Ultimately, for these leaders, it is the ideologies, or doctrine, that create the understanding and commitments needed to bring salvation. Ravi, for example, relativizes the importance of his *Yeshu satsang* approach in relation to soteriology by saying, "Looking at all these things (*satsang* practices) we do not think that culture and dress are going to take us to heaven. But they can be a medium in sharing the message of the Lord with people . . . God's word is the thing that changes peoples' hearts, but (the

---

32. Interview with Padman, Apr 19, 2010.
33. Interview with Padman, May 15, 2010.

satsang practices) helps us to keep relationships with people" [H].[34] As another typical example, Gaurav shares in the preparation for the Lord's Supper, which includes several of the Hindu symbols described above, "What is this [Lord's Supper] for the *Yeshu Bhakta*? Salvation. Jesus died for our sins on the cross . . . So we need to remember three things. That Jesus died for us on the cross. For the whole world. He took all the sins on him. He died and was buried and was resurrected on the third day" [H].[35] In this way, the leaders use Christian CEPs to help shape a proper allegiance to God and subservience to his will. As *satsangis* do so they will, according to the leaders, experience the salvation and blessings of God.

Though many of the practices that the *Yeshu satsang* leaders are incorporating and modifying occur within the *Yeshu satsang* gatherings, their *satsangis* regularly encounter other religious practices outside of the *Yeshu satsang*. Each of these practices contain their own SEPs and CEPs, and the *satsangis* must decide which practices they will engage, and which they will seek to avoid. It is to this issue that I turn next.

SEPARATING PRACTICE PROPERTIES BEYOND THE SATSANG: SUCCESSES AND CHALLENGES

As I have discussed at certain points, various practices of the *Yeshu satsang* leaders and *satsangis* extend beyond the *satsang* itself. As they do, the religio-structural properties of these practices impact the interaction that the *satsangis* have with others. In some cases, the types of interaction that these practices allow is desirable and, for the *satsangi*, quite predictable. Above, for example, I discussed Naveen's experiences and rationale for wearing a turban. As he wears it beyond the *Yeshu satsang* the properties it shares with the Sikh social structure allows him to sit "in the midst of them." The types of interaction it allows are desirable for him and his relationships and ministry. In addition, wearing the turban does not require of him to interact with or embrace any propositions or beliefs with which he disagrees. In other words, for Navdeep and Naveen and the other *satsangis* and leaders, there is little religio-cultural meaning in wearing a turban. When I asked one *satsangi* what meaning the turban now held for him he replied, "The importance of this is that people get upset (and would say), 'Oh, they have cut their hair.' And what they would do, yes, if you cut your hair, from this would oppose

34. Interview with Ravi, Jun 24, 2010.
35. From Gaurav *satsang*, Jan 17, 2010.

you a little" [P]. The opposition, similar to that posed by others in other contexts, would be that the *satsangi* had somehow changed community to become an Other. The *satsangi* thus interpreted my question in terms of the practice's religio-structural significance, rather than attributing any ideological importance to it. In this way, the leaders and *satsangis* have little trouble distinguishing between the SEPs and CEPs of this practice, even as it extends out beyond the confines of the *Yeshu satsang*.

Though people can separate religio-structural and religio-cultural properties of some practices, others blend together more tightly, making a separation difficult. One of the more difficult issues and examples of this tight association is that of taking the *prasad* (food offering) that comes from a Sikh *gurdwara* or a Hindu temple. Should a *Yeshu satsangi*, when attending a Sikh or Hindu function accept and eat *prasad* that has just been offered before an idol? Or, when at work, should a *Yeshu satsangi* take a *prasad* that is being offered by a co-worker who has just returned from a visit to a temple? Gaurav addresses this question regularly with his *satsangis*. At one point he counseled a *satsangi* who had just married a Christian woman. The new wife was reticent to take *prasad* at the marriage celebrations that the husband's family was hosting. Whereas the husband was comfortable with the practice, he struggled with how to help his wife understand the practice in light of their shared Christian beliefs. In response Gaurav counseled them to both read and study 1 Corinthians 8. There was ultimately freedom to take the *prasad*, said Gaurav, but he also emphasized that the husband should not pressure his wife to take it. "It doesn't make any difference," said Gaurav. "But she has a weak conscience so you have to (bear it) a little bit" [H].[36]

For his own part, Padman feels free to take *prasad* from people. He explains, "Actually it is not a big issue because generally people uh, they link it with religiosity. And if you don't take they feel offended. And if we are clear in our conscience then there is no problem. If we are not clear then we should not" [E].[37] Padman thus recognizes that there is a close association between cultural and structural properties in the practice of *prasad*, but senses freedom to take it as conscience allows.

Similarly, the Sikh *Yeshu satsang* leaders acknowledge the tight connection between properties with the practice of *prasad*. However, in contrast to Christian pastors who have not allowed the practice, the *Yeshu*

---

36. Discussion between Gaurav and G-10, Jan, 31, 2010.
37. Interview with Padman, Apr 19, 2010.

satsang leaders give room to their *satsangis* to decide what is appropriate, with an emphasis on preserving the relationships of the community. Navdeep expresses in this manner:

> Many people ask us about the *prasad*. Some people want to test us, because they know that we are pastors. They ask, "What do you say? Should we take the *prasad* of the *gurdwara* or not?" And our answer is . . . , "I would like to see [consider] the time, the place, and the circumstances there. I would like to assess these. I can't say anything about the situation, whether I should eat *prasad* or not at that time. And my Lord is with me. He has given me the wisdom. There, I mean, I have to make sure that I would not be a reason for anybody to stumble. If I take *prasad* there I will take this in the name of the Lord. If somebody gets benefit from you eating then you should take. And if there is no loss by not taking *prasad* then you should not take *prasad*." [P][38]

Despite the freedom that the leaders give to *satsangis* to discern their own choice on the matter, another association also makes the practice unacceptable to some *satsangis*. Above I discussed the connection made by some Christians between the Hindu/Sikh practices and the presence of demonic forces. Though Nandita, for example, is positive about using some Sikh practices in the *Yeshu satsang*, she is clearly against participating in practices that potentially have evil powers attached to them. Regarding the issue of *prasad*, she says that the *jadugars* or *jyoshi* (shamans) will sometimes advise someone afflicted with an evil spirit to prepare and bring the *ladoo* (*prasad* food) to the *gurdwara*. When the *prasad* is distributed among the people, the person's problems and the afflicting spirit will also be distributed among the people. For this reason, followers of Christ should not take *prasad* offered at the temple, since they could then be afflicted by an evil spirit. For Nandita, and other Christians who share this belief, the practice of taking *prasad* can bring a state of spiritual contamination to the practitioner. In this case the evil consequences that could come from taking the *prasad* supersede any potential structural association that could result from taking it.

The teachings by Christian pastors on matters related to *prasad* and its connection to evil forces are often drawn from Old Testament teaching regarding the worship of gods and idols. One *satsangi* describes the teaching that his previous pastor commonly gave on the subject saying:

38. Interview with Navdeep, May 2, 2010.

(The pastor said), "We have come [to Christ] leaving those things behind. So it is best for you to not do the same things [temple practices] again." So this is what [the pastor] used to tell us. As per [the pastor], it was related to *prasad*. Meaning, if we start following the Lord after forsaking our temple and gods and goddesses, we should not eat the things offered to these . . . A person should not eat the things that harm him. [H][39]

In response to this teaching, some *satsang* leaders address the problem of evil and its connection to *prasad* in two ways. First, they promote the practice of praying over the *prasad* in the name of Jesus in order to change its quality or property. Some *satsangis* confess that they would prefer to not take the *prasad* offered to them by others, but that they are sometimes compelled to do so out of a desire to not offend or preserve a relationship. In such cases prayer offers a way of taking the *prasad* while keeping relationship with others. One *satsangi*, for example, shares, "If someone gives us *prasad*, then we do not like eating it. (But) if we do not find anyone to whom I can give the *prasad*, then I pray over it and eat it" [P].[40] The practice of prayer thus transforms the perceived properties of the practice and allows them to take it and preserve the structural properties and importance of the practice.

Secondly, *satsang* leaders emphasize New Testament teaching over-and-against Old Testament teaching regarding food restrictions. Gaurav, as I have discussed, teaches his *satsangis* from Acts 10 and 1 Corinthians 8 that the *prasad* in itself is not wrong. He contrasts this with the Old Testament law, in that the New Testament gives *Yeshu Bhakta* freedom to eat it as food if his or her own conscience allows for it. The practice of prayer again is interlaced with this to help *satsangis* understand the transformed qualities of the *prasad* when it is taken in faith. One of Gaurav's *satsangis* shares, "The Bible says that we can eat everything. Whatever you like you eat. And eat with prayer. And the things you are eating will not harm you. And the thing that comes out from inside of you, everything, I mean, only that will give you problems" [H].[41]

Another practice that *satsang* leaders debate because of its tightly connected properties regards whether it is practically possible for *satsangis* to attend the *gurdwara*. Part of the controversy arises because this practice is often combined with the related practice of bowing before

39. Interview with G-8, Feb 22, 2010.
40. Interview with N-10, May 29, 2010.
41. Interview with G-8, Feb 22, 2010.

the *Guru Granth Sahib*. As Sikhs walk into the main worship hall, of the *gurdwara*, it is customary to walk up to the platform on which the *Guru Granth Sahib* is placed and to bow down before it. Some leaders, like Gaurav, make a differentiation between worship and honor, and use the example of the Indian practice of bowing before one's elders to touch their feet. In these cases, they argue, a person is not worshipping their elders, but simply honoring them. In the same way one could bow before the *Granth Sahib* and consider it as an act of honor but not worship.

Though this is possible in theory, most Sikh *Yeshu satsangis* are not convinced by this and are uncomfortable with the practice of bowing before the Sikh scriptures. Even Navdeep, who is the most positive of the leaders in his opinion of the Sikh scriptures, is not comfortable with and counsels against bowing before them. Nonetheless, Navdeep and Naveen maintain that *satsangis* should be allowed to attend the *gurdwara* and show respect and solidarity with the Sikh community structure without bowing down and showing devotion to the *Guru Granth Sahib*. Jasbir and Nandita, however, argue that the *gurdwara* attendees and leadership would surely take notice if a *satsangi* did not bow to the *Guru Granth Sahib*, and would take great offense at this. As Jasbir noted above, this is particularly the case in small village *gurdwaras* where everyone would notice if someone did not bow before the *Guru Granth Sahib* and would interpret it in an offensive way.

Thus, in this situation engaging one practice (attending the *gurdwara*) invokes the other (bowing down before the *Guru Granth Sahib*). Whereas *satsangis* may desire to retain structural, community relationships by attending the *gurdwara*, refusing to bow before the Sikh scriptures (because of its cultural property) would cause a rupture of relationship and undermine their original intent.

In general, Sikh *Yeshu satsang* leaders seem to encounter greater difficulties in separating structural from cultural properties in practices outside of the *satsang* than do Hindu *Yeshu satsang* leaders. Though the Sikh *Yeshu satsang* leaders have sought to re-embrace aspects of their Sikh religious structures within the *satsang*, the surrounding communities often continue to view them and scrutinize them as an Other, though perhaps a less offensive Other than Christian churches. One reason for this, according to Sikh *Yeshu satsang* leaders, is that Sikh leaders in some communities have sought to more carefully police practices in keeping with Sikh orthodoxy. This was seen in 2007 when a religious sect offended the region's Sikh community,[42] causing riots and prompting local Sikhs to look on all fringe and non-Sikh sects, including the *Yeshu satsangs*, with suspicion. Because of this, some leaders are mindful that Sikhs, and particularly the Sikh leadership in local towns and villages, would take offense to the *Yeshu satsang*'s use of Sikh worship and speech practices. For example, Jagdeep and Manpreet have tried offering a *halwa prasad* at the end of a large *Yeshu satsang*, but now only practice it occasionally and reticently for fear that Sikh leaders in their community would become angry at the *satsang* for copying Sikh practices. The Sikh community in some areas thus exerts a strong constraint on the ability of the *Yeshu satsang* community to embrace a practice and differentiate between its structural and cultural properties, particularly outside of the *satsang*.

Despite this, the Sikh *Yeshu satsang* leaders continue to utilize the various Sikh practices within their *satsangs* in the hope and belief that many Sikhs will find them attractive. In addition, the leaders seek to give their *satsangis* freedom to negotiate these practices according to their own consciences and in relation with their communities. This contrasts the approach of many Christian leaders who, perhaps because of the tight association between the CEPS and SEPs of certain practices, usually do not make a distinction, and counsel Christians to avoid the practices altogether.

CHAPTER SUMMARY

In this and the previous chapter I have analyzed the ways in which *Yeshu satsang* leaders are incorporating Hindu and Sikh practices within their *Yeshu satsangs* and their *satsangi*'s understanding of these. In Table 3 below I have summarized the various Hindu and Sikh practices that the *Yeshu satsang* leaders are incorporating.

---

42. The leader of the popular interfaith sect, Gurmeet Ram Rahim Singh, was allegedly shown in a poster or advertisement dressed as Sikh guru Gobind Singh, causing outrage among the Sikh community, and particularly more orthodox groups. In one village several families stopped attending the *Yeshu satsang* out of fear of local Sikhs.

Table 3
Summary Of *Yeshu Satsang* **Hindu/Sikh Practices**

Satsang Category	Worship Practices in Satsang	Speech Practices in Satsang	Acceptable Practices Outside Satsang
Yeshu Bhakti Satsang	*Bhajan* music Indian instruments Devotional dress No shoes Sitting on floor Religious objects (*diyas*, coconut, *shankh, rehal*)	Self-ascription as "Hindu," and/or "*Yeshu Bhakta*" (Jesus Devotee) "*Satguru Yeshu*" (True-Guru Jesus) "*Tatasthu*" (amen) "*Jal diksha/sanskar*" (baptism) "*Paramatma*" (Great Spirit/God) God as Father *and* Mother "*Prabhu*" (Lord)	Wearing *bindi* Taking *prasad* Attending Temple or functions
Arya Samaj Yeshu Satsangs	*Bhajan* music *Svaha* prayer Devotional dress No shoes Sitting on floor Religious objects (*havan, havan samagri*, Sanskrit text)	Self-ascription as "Hindu," and/or "*Yeshu Bhakta*" (Jesus Devotee) "*Satguru Yeshu*" (True-Guru Jesus) "*Tatasthu*" (amen) "*Paramatma*" (Great Spirit/God) "*Prabhu*" (Lord)	Taking *prasad*
Sikh Yeshu Satsangs	*Kirtan* music style Indian instruments Devotional dress No shoes Sitting on floor	Self-ascription as "Sikh" "*Sat Sri Akal*" (Greetings) "*Satguru Yeshu*" (True-Guru Jesus) "*Satbachan*" (amen) "*Naam Daan*" (baptism) "*Waheguru*" (Wonderful Guru/God) "*Dhan Satguru Yeshu*" (Blessed true-Guru Jesus) "*Prabhu*" (Lord)	Taking Sikh *Prasad* Attending Temple or functions

As can be seen in the table, the leaders have several practices in common. All the *Yeshu satsang* leaders utilize *bhajans* (or *kirtans*) and objects that reflect Hindu and Sikh devotional settings. In addition, all the *satsang* leaders use Indian instruments, encourage their *satsangis* to not wear shoes, to sit on the floor, and to use various speech practices reflecting the Hindu and Sikh social structures. When it comes to Hindu and Sikh practices that *satsangis* encounter outside of the *Yeshu satsang*, the leaders give their *satsangis* a level of freedom to make decisions that reflect their devotion to Jesus, but that also preserve harmonious relationships with Hindu and Sikh family members.

The *Yeshu satsang* leaders also diverge from each other in the details of certain practices. Dinesh includes speech practices regarding the importance of the low-caste Ravidas movement and Dalit leader B. R. Ambedkar, reflecting his own background in that movement. Gaurav reflects on and seeks to replicate inter-caste practices derived from the Hindu *bhakti* traditions, such as the Radha Soami, whereas Ravi uses caste-specific language in his desire to shape *satsangs* particularly agreeable to high-caste Hindus. Padman, in his Arya Samaj *Yeshu satsang*, utilizes a high degree of symbols and rituals that would be familiar to his family, including *bhajans*, the *havan kund*, and the use of Sanskrit prayer. The leaders of the Sikh *Yeshu satsangs* utilize less symbols than do the Hindu *Yeshu satsangs* to reflect the common worship practices of the Sikh *gurdwaras*.

Why do these leaders utilize these practices? These leaders attempt to accentuate the religio-structural properties of various Hindu and Sikh practices while redefining their religio-cultural properties. Though each practice has its own distinct history and property, they have similar Emergentist functions within the ecclesial setting. The practices that *Yeshu satsang* leaders use within the *satsang* help form a part of, and contribute to, the overall elaboration or identity of the *satsang*. Outside of the *Yeshu satsang*, the *satsangis* encounter various Hindu and Sikh religious practices and, aside from idol worship, the *Yeshu satsang* leaders give *satsangis* a level of freedom to make their own decisions on these practices. However, leaders often encourage *satsangis* to make their decision in light of the need to preserve harmonious relationships with Hindu family members. Thus, though the *Yeshu satsang* leaders exhibit some variance regarding practice, particularly as they relate to their specific Hindu or Sikh communities, they nonetheless all have a relatively positive understanding of Hindu/Sikh structure and culture, and the potential of God to reveal himself through this. They also critique some of the basis upon which Christian churches have separated themselves from the surrounding Hindu and Sikh communities.

However, the *Yeshu satsang* leaders see the need to form communities, or *satsangs*, with distinctive contours shaped by Christian beliefs. The primary aspects of this are Christological and soteriological. Christologically, the *satsangs* seek to distinguish the nature and work of Jesus from other views that would reduce Jesus to a guru among other gurus. A large part of this distinction is soteriological, where they recognize that Jesus' shame, suffering and death on the cross is critical for forgiveness from sin. The practices that the *Yeshu satsangs* share with the Hindu and Sikh communities thus provide a means for connection to those communities while also containing revelatory potential regarding the person and work of Jesus.

I have thus far focused on the *Yeshu satsangs'* use of Hindu and Sikh practices. In addition to these, however, the *Yeshu satsang* leaders also employ practices that originate from Christian traditions and churches. These are also highly important for the emerging ecclesial identities of these *Yeshu satsangs* and for the theological contours with which they shape the *satsangs'* ecclesial identities. I turn to these in the next chapter.

CHAPTER 7

Resisting and Reshaping Christian Practices

YESHU SATSANG LEADERS REFLECT much on the Hindu and Sikh practices that they incorporate into their *Yeshu satsangs* and those practices that they encounter outside of the *satsang*, and they also incorporate practices that are shared with Christian churches. *Yeshu satsangis* and leaders associate these with Christian structures to some degree, as do people outside of the *Yeshu satsang*. However, rather than rejecting these practices, the leaders instead hold onto them and in some ways attempt to disassociate the connection between the practice and the structure of the Christian church. Sometimes this is successful, and at other times it is not. In any case, these practices are adopted and retained in part because of their high level of importance for shaping the ecclesial identity of the *satsang* and *satsangis*. In addition to those practices that leaders seek to reshape, there are also practices that the leaders retain, with little modification. These, as I will describe below, tend to be practices that help facilitate what they see as "miraculous" power.

I will discuss four practices that the leaders are using and, in some ways, seeking to reshape: (1) the use of the Bible, (2) the Lord's Supper, (3) baptism, and (4) certain speech practices. Following this I will discuss practices of miraculous power, some of which are practiced in near-habitual ways. However, before exploring these specific practices, it is important to address some of the practices that Christian pastors use to shape ecclesial identities of their churches, and that *Yeshu satsang* leaders resist and regard as unhelpful.

RESISTING AND RESHAPING RULES

Though the *Yeshu satsangs* retain some practices that they share with churches, others are resisted. One example of these, as indicated in previous chapters, are various practices that, in the opinion of the *Yeshu satsang* leaders, add to the foreign and negative identity of Christian churches. Examples include loud pentecostal worship, non-Hindi or non-Punjabi religious words such as "hallelujah," Christian teaching that denounces Hinduism and Sikhism as evil and filled with demons, and traditional Christian ascriptions, such as "Christian" or "*Isai.*"

Another example that the *Yeshu satsang* leaders resist are the "rules" that some churches teach to their members, including practices associated with jewelry, dress, burial, and other behaviors. As an example, Navdeep refers to such rules and teachings in one sermon, explaining:

> What the preachers do when someone comes to Christ, the preachers make the people afraid. [They say], "Don't wear ornaments, don't take *prasad*, don't do this." This is also the thing. When a person dies, they say that they should be buried. But our culture [says] that the body should be burned . . . So these are the obstacles keeping people from coming to Christ. [P][1]

Though not all Christian churches foster such teachings, and not all restrict the same things (such as jewelry), many do.[2] For their part, churches may emphasize such external changes to reinforce and reflect the change of peoples' faith and allegiance to Christ. *Yeshu satsang* leaders, however, generally feel that such changes are not strictly biblical. In addition, many *satsangis* associate these rules with churches led by south Indian pastors, or in other ways originating from outside the *satsangis'* context. Because of this, the *Yeshu satsangis* and leaders see such rules as adding to the church's Otherness and creating unhelpful barriers between the church community and the Hindu and Sikh communities.

---

1. From Navdeep *satsang*, May 3, 2010.

2. Ruth, who was one of Gaurav's *satsangis* shares that her previous church was not as strict as some, saying, "Pentecostal churches are very, very strict in so many things . . . (But) I didn't find any such strictness in [previous church]. Because, one thing that could be, we didn't have any south Indian families in the church. So, they are different. They are very rigid" [E]. Though Ruth's previous church did not have the same "rigidness" as some, she ultimately left when her daughter married a Hindu man and the pastor ostracized her and her family for it. After coming to the *Yeshu satsang* her son-in-law became a follower of Jesus.

To counter the Otherness of these rules the *Yeshu satsangs* seek to correct what they see as an improper focus on outward change and instead emphasize changing the "inside" of the person. One of Gaurav's *satsangis* states, "The difference (between the *Yeshu satsang* and churches) is this . . . . They try to change themselves from the outside. But they can't change the heart they have inside. So that person will not reach the place where he is supposed to reach. So this is the difference between the *satsang* and churches" [H].[3]

The *Yeshu satsangs* have placed an emphasis on "changing the heart" as opposed to changing outward practices, particularly those that contribute to the religio-structural Otherness of the church. One of the strategies that the *Yeshu satsang* leaders employ to counteract the emphasis on rules and external change taught by some churches is to rhetorically use these as analogies for the heart. Another of Gaurav's *satsangis* reflects on this via his previous experience in a church led by a pentecostal south Indian pastor. He shares:

> Before coming to [Gaurav's *satsang*], like in my previous church . . . that south Indian pastor. [He taught] other teachings also, like not to wear like gold rings or not to wear costly clothes or not to keep, like, statues or idols in your home. Like these are their rules . . . So these things, these misconceptions . . . [Gaurav] teaches us that . . . if I wear gold, it's not a bad thing. But if I, if my mind indulges in gold and I start worshipping gold, so then it's bad. Then it becomes a devil. [E][4]

In this example Gaurav and the *satsang*i agree that it is important to teach about and be mindful of the possibility of greediness and worshipping money. However, they critique the outward practices that supposedly protects followers of Jesus from this. Instead, they say, wearing jewelry is acceptable, so long as the heart is changed. In this the leader reframes the teaching so as to create different emergent properties; ones that attempt to reshape the inner life of the person and to minimize the dissonance and signs of variance between his community and the Hindu and Sikh communities.

---

3. Interview with G-5, Feb 17, 2010.
4. Interview with G-14, Mar 4, 2010.

PRACTICE 1: THE USE OF THE BIBLE

The *Yeshu satsangs*, however, retain other practices that they learned from or that relate to Christian churches. One of the primary practices they have retained is reading and studying the Bible. Even where *Yeshu satsang* leaders have a level of openness to Hindu and Sikh scriptures, the Bible is emphasized as a higher and ultimate authority. Dinesh, as discussed above, sees the Vedas and Bhagavad Gita as containing certain truths. However, for him "the Bible is the conclusion of all" [H].[5]

The *Yeshu satsang* leaders use the Bible throughout their *satsang* meetings. In most meetings they read it openly, from common Hindi or Punjabi versions, and *satsangis* are encouraged to have their own copies that they can also read on their own. Some *Yeshu satsang* leaders, such as Dinesh, conduct responsive readings of biblical passages. In addition, many of the *bhajans* make biblical references. Finally, biblical passages are given a central role in sermons. Many sermons, though often topical, have several key passages on which the leader anchors his teaching.

Most of the *Yeshu satsang* leaders have a clear preference to teachings from the New Testament (NT). Miracle stories from the gospels feature prominently in the leaders' sermons, particularly among those leaders who strongly emphasize healing. As well, the leaders emphasize certain teachings from the epistles regarding dietary restrictions and other prohibitions of Old Testament (OT) law. For example, Gaurav, in a teaching series that he gave to one of his *Yeshu satsangs*, illustrates the freedom that the NT gives on OT dietary restrictions, and links this to the freedom that *Yeshu satsangis* can have for foods that may have been offered in *prasad*.

As will be seen with other Christian practices, some *Yeshu satsang* leaders modify the way a Christian object is used, or the way it is labeled to help associate it with the Hindu or Sikh communities. Most of the *Yeshu satsang* leaders, for example, are sensitive to the treatment of scriptures and do not agree with laying a Bible directly on the floor where someone's foot could touch it. Because the Bible is to be respected as scripture, it should be presented in a respectful way during the *Yeshu satsang*, including placing it on a *rehal* (wooden stand) and placing a cloth over it.

Another example regards the ways in which the Bible is referred to using Sikh or Hindu words. Though most *Yeshu satsangs* use the word "Bible," many also intersperse this with other words. The most prominent

---

5. Interview with Dinesh, Mar 22, 2010.

among the Sikh *Yeshu satsangs*, for example, is the use of the word *"bani"* (word). The *"bani"* commonly refers to the various writings and prayers within the *Guru Granth Sahib*. In the *Yeshu satsangs* this word is sometimes used on its own, and sometimes as *"Yeshu bani"* (Jesus' word) or *"Pavithra bani"* (holy word).

Though most *Yeshu satsangs* change the name of the Bible in various ways, all except one use the physical Bible quite openly in their *satsangs*. The one *Yeshu satsang* that does not do so is that of Padman, whose family associates the common Bible cover with past experiences in which Padman, in his opinion, insensitively rejected his family's beliefs and rituals in favor of a "Western" Christianity. Because of this Padman has translated various passages from the New Testament into Sanskrit, which he then reads and explains during the *Yeshu satsang*. Though he does not publicly ascribe these to the Bible, he often identifies the source as "the saying of 'Sant' (saint) Matthew." or others. In this case, then, Padman recognizes that his family makes structural associations with the Bible. In response Padman continues to incorporate the Bible, but in ways such that its meanings will be conveyed and its religio-structural associations de-emphasized.

PRACTICE 2: THE LORD'S SUPPER

The *Prabhu Bhoj* (Lord's Supper) is practiced periodically by the various *Yeshu satsangs*. When celebrating this, the leaders clearly explain the practice from biblical passages referring to the Lord's Supper. For example, on one occasion Gaurav preached on the Lord's Supper, using Matthew 26:26–28; Mark 14:22–26; Luke 22:19–20; and 1 Corinthians 11:22–26. In addition, he talked about the Festival of Passover and how Jesus transformed the festival and its practices to focus on him and his sacrifice. The main emphasis of the Lord's Supper, says Gaurav, is to remember Christ and his suffering. He explains: "So when you see Jesus' body and blood, don't you feel pain? When we see his blood, we feel pain. So Jesus wants us to have communion, to share that suffering that he went through. So this *Prabhu Bhoj* reminds us that we have to face suffering when we follow Christ" [H].[6]

Gaurav continues by giving an example of the recent persecutions and killings of Christians (or *Yeshu Bhakta*) in Orissa, emphasizing that people will persecute the *Yeshu Bhakta* for following Christ. In addition

6. From Gaurav *satsang*, Feb 7, 2010.

131

to this emphasis, however, Gaurav also talks about how Jesus carried the sin of the world on the cross, and that followers of Christ should "judge themselves" and their hearts before taking it. Though he does not restrict anybody from taking the Lord's Supper, he encourages only those who "understand" to do so. He explains, "If you don't understand and still take it its okay, but it will not be good for you, because you are not understanding what you are doing. That's why I want you to understand it. Only then come before the Lord and take it" [H].[7]

Though Gaurav encourages people who "understand" to take, he does not strongly restrict the practice. This contrasts the approach of some churches, particularly the local Roman Catholic churches regarding this practice. Padman reflects on the practice of a local Catholic church that refused to give him the Lord's Supper. When he went to the priest to discuss the matter, the priest gave him some literature on the Catholic view of communion, which failed to convince Padman. He returned to the priest and explained:

> "This is not my idea, I am just, because so many people around you, they need your love . . . If you give this to everybody, so many people will come here. Huh? So many people can come here. Because so many, they don't come, because you don't give them this." Yeah, this is, this is general perception. The common person, if he goes there and in the middle of prayer the priest says, "You stand up. You make a queue." And everybody moves there. They will make a queue. And we in India knows that this is *prasad*. It is free for all. Everyone should be given it. But their, because this is their tradition, we cannot change it. They have some authoritarian rule, that you have to do it like that only. I was offended by that. I tried to convince them but I thought they will change. But they said, "No, no. Each and every thing will be changed by the Pope. Uh, so he's the authority." [E][8]

As Padman's example shows, the Hindu and Sikh cultures of the northwest readily interpret the Lord's Supper as a type of *prasad*, the blessings of which should be freely offered to any who come for it. In response some *Yeshu satsangs*, like Gaurav's allows for a semi-open Lord's Supper, where people can participate if they like, even if they are new to the *satsang*. Other *Yeshu satsangs*, however, reflect a more exclusive view of the Lord's Supper. Manpreet, for example, conducted the Lord's Supper

7. From Gaurav *satsang*, Feb 7, 2010.
8. Interview with Padman, May 16, 2010.

during one *Yeshu satsang*. On that day several Hindu and Sikh friends who were not yet followers of Christ visited the *satsang*. In her explanation of the Lord's Supper, Manpreet read from 1 Corinthians 10 and said:

> Whoever comes to the Lord's table with a sinful heart and takes the bread and drink will be guilty in the sight of God. The person has to judge himself before taking part in Holy Communion. If we are not fulfilling these demands then we become guilty ourselves. That person becomes guilty. That is why so many people among you are sick and some have slept. Because they are guilty for the blood of Jesus Christ. We can't judge ourselves but we can ask the Holy Spirit so that he can judge us, check us and make us correct. And we can ask, "Lord have mercy on me, forgive my sins." Let's commit ourselves to the Lord and those who want to take the Holy Communion can stand and the others can remain sitting. [P][9]

Manpreet offered pieces of *roti* (flat bread) and juice. On this occasion, Manpreet had sufficiently distinguished the Lord's Supper from a *prasad*, and none of the visitors stood up to take communion.

Thus, in retaining the practice of the Lord's Supper the *Yeshu satsangs* vary in the level of openness they give for participation. However, as the examples above have indicated, all teach from standard passages in the NT regarding the significance of this practice for remembering the death of Jesus, the forgiveness of sin, and Jesus' and our suffering. In these ways the *Yeshu satsangs* share with Christian churches many of the propositional properties of the practice.

In addition, some *satsangs* also retain the symbols and names of the practice, such as using bread and juice, calling it *Prabhu Bhoj*. However, some leaders such as Ravi and Gaurav also change aspects of the practice. For example, these leaders sometimes use the coconut, a symbol common in Hindu temple worship. However, the *Yeshu satsang* leaders are careful not to attribute too much importance to the symbols themselves, reflecting some of the protestant teaching that they received through their work with Christian churches or mission organizations. Gaurav, for example, discusses the danger of attributing power to the symbols themselves. He clarifies:

> So we don't have to break coconut. Of course it is symbolizing. When we go into Hindu houses we can do it. In our *satsang*

---

9. From Manpreet *satsang*, Apr 4, 2010.

> that's why we made it. We can do it with the coconut . . . [But]
> just make it sure that nobody gets stuck. The early Christian's
> thinking, you know, that the elements got the power . . . There's
> no power in it. Its just element. It doesn't . . . its not a problem,
> its just your faith in Christ and the remembrance of Christ. [E][10]

Gaurav continues by explaining that when he has tried to force some in his *satsang* to use the coconut, they did not feel good about it. His conclusion is that it is perhaps better in any case to alternate symbols so that anything he starts will not end up becoming a tradition devoid of significance and that those from Hindu backgrounds will not attribute too much power to the symbol itself.

Another aspect of the practice that the *Yeshu satsang* leaders sometimes change is its name. Though most leaders use the common Christian phrase, *Prabhu Bhoj*, some also use *"mahaprasad"* (great *prasad*). This term is used by different temples and groups in varying ways, but generally refers to a special, occasional *prasad* presented to a deity. When the *Yeshu satsang* leaders use this term, they tend to use it in close proximity in their discourse to *"Prabhu bhoj."* Ravi prefers to use *"mahaprasad"* but indicates that, because many people in his area and *satsang* know about the Christian practice of *"Prabhu Bhoj,"* he also calls it that. Gaurav prefers not to call the practice *"mahaprasad,"* but does so because it might sound better to some Hindus. Nandita has yet to start the practice of the Lord's Supper in her small *satsang*. When I asked how she would call it and practice it, she said that she would not give it a title, but simply describe that they are doing something to remember Christ's death. However, because some people in her *satsang* have been to local churches, she says that they will probably know it as *"Prabhu Bhoj."*

Thus some *Yeshu satsang* leaders make subtle changes to aspects of the practice of the Lord's Supper to make it understandable and somewhat open to Hindus and Sikhs. On the whole, however, the religio-cultural aspects of the practice are retained. In addition, the leaders do not in their discourses exhibit the level of concern over the Christian religio-structural associations of this practice that they have with other practices.

PRACTICE 3: BAPTISM

In the history of the Church in India there is perhaps no single ecclesial practice as defining and as widely discussed as baptism. Scholars

---

10. Interview with Gaurav, Mar 6, 2010.

have long noted that the ways in which baptism has been practiced and its relationship to the institutional church has made it an important focal point signifying conversion to Christianity and providing membership for churches.[11] In such cases, from the standpoint of Archer and Emergentist theory, many churches use baptism to strengthen the religio-structure of the church. In my own experience with churches in various parts of India, baptism often forms a central place in the testimony discourses of Christians, particularly of those who "converted" from other religious communities, and is an important ritual signifying their entrance into a new community structure. As an example, *Yeshu Bhakta* in New Delhi, with whom I conducted pilot interviews, refused to take baptism because it would require radical religio-structural change with which they were not comfortable.

According to discussions with *Yeshu satsang* leaders, Christian churches in the northwest also use baptism as a ritual indicating a change of religious community. In contrast, the *Yeshu satsang* leaders and *satsangis* de-emphasize the socio-structural interpretation of baptism by lessening its importance in the overall discipleship of believers. For example, rarely did *satsangis* discuss baptism without solicitation, even if they had taken it. Whereas baptism is sometimes a pivotal experience for Indian Christians, for most *Yeshu satsangis* the pivotal experience was instead a healing or miracle that prompted their turn to Jesus and regular participation in the *satsang*.

Despite this lower emphasis, however, *Yeshu satsang* leaders do practice baptism and, according to them, these events do form an important part of their ecclesial lives. Of the *Yeshu satsang* leaders, Gaurav has the most experience with baptism and its place in the *satsang*. For him and his *satsang*, baptism is an indication of commitment to God, with an implied but de-emphasized commitment to the *satsang* itself.[12]

One of the reasons that leaders de-emphasize the relationship between baptism and community is because of its possible structural associations with the Christian church. To help with this leaders make small

---

11. The Thomas-Newbigin debates referenced in Chapter 1 are an important and relatively recent example of way in which baptism is closely and sometimes problematically tied to the Otherness of the Christian community and institutions.

12. None of the *satsangs* yet had a system of "membership," though Gaurav was just initiating one. His proposed system was to first teach through a set of *satsang* "values" and to then have *satsangis* sign a form indicating their commitment and "membership" to the *satsang*. However, baptism was not directly tied to this.

changes that seek to in some way de-emphasize the structural associations with the Christian church, and to minimize dissonance between Hindu and Christian structures. The leaders do two things to achieve this. The first is that leaders take steps to reduce the public profile of the practice. Gaurav takes his *satsangis* to a small lake on private land whose owner will give him permission for different social events. No one aside from the *satsangis* are therefore present at the baptism. Ravi gives baptism in a canal outside of the city. Though he does it "openly," they also take the precaution of not singing and loitering much in the area, but instead conducting worship at his house.

Another way leaders alleviate religio-structural association and conflict is by changing the name of the practice to "*jal diksha*" (water initiation), *jal sanskar* (water immersion), "*pavithra ishnaan*" (Sikh holy initiation), or "*naam daan*" (name-taking).[13] These names reflect Hindu and Sikh rituals of initiation of disciples by their guru. Leaders hope that such renaming might minimize the structural dissonance that these Christian practices can create between Hindu, or Sikh, and Christian communities. One of Gaurav's *satsangis* prefers this way of referring to baptism, though he admits that the word *jal diksha* was new to him when it was introduced in the *Yeshu satsang*. When I asked, "What is the difference between *jal diksha* and baptism?" he replied: "'*Jal diksha*' is spoken according to Hindi language . . . It is good to say '*jal diksha*.' It is right. But whoever does not know this as '*jal diksha*,' then we should say 'baptism' to him . . . [But] I think '*jal diksha*' is better. If you are born in India or you are living in India, '*jal diksha*' is good" [H].[14]

Despite the inclusion of these new words, however, leaders often juxtaposed these with "baptism;" sometimes using them close together. For example, when Navdeep preached on Philip's ministry and the baptisms he gave in Acts 8:12, he says, "So when the people listened to these kinds of things the women and people came there. They also took *pavithra ishnaan*. So when the sorcerer saw that everyone was gone, he also went

13. In Hindu practice *jal diksha* and *jal sanskar* express commitment to God through the guru's instruction and presence. In Sikh practice *pavithra ishnaan* forms part of the ritual of initiation into the Sikh *khalsa*, or orthodox Sikh community. Sikhs, Hindus and various sects use *naam daan* as an initiation into a particular sect where the initiate takes the name of, or shows commitment to, the guru. Whereas many of these rituals express devotion to a leader or mediator, *Yeshu satsang* leaders try to deflect any mediatory role that *satsangis* may try to ascribe to them by focusing the ritual on the *Satguru*, or ultimate guru, of Jesus.

14. Interview with G-8, Feb 22, 2010.

there and took *baptisma*" (From Navdeep *satsang*, May 2, 2010). Gaurav and Dinesh also often juxtaposed the terms together.

Yeshu satsang leaders thus conduct baptism, similar to other practices with Christian tradition, in ways that accentuate the propositional cultural properties of the practice and that strengthen peoples' faith. In addition, baptism is part of an ongoing growth in spiritual maturity and commitment to God.

PRACTICE 4: SPEECH PRACTICES

Though, as seen above, *Yeshu satsang* leaders often try to adopt self-ascriptions that do not have structural associations with the Christian church, some leaders and their *satsangis* continue to use certain Christian self-ascriptions. For example, and as mentioned above, Dinesh prefers to use the self-ascription "*Masihi*." Dinesh readily acknowledges the association that this word has with the Christian community. However, in his own use, particularly when combined with *Yeshu Bhakta*, Dinesh seeks to define this word as a revival *bhakti* sect of Christians. Dinesh explains in one conversation:

> I believe in Christ. I am a *Yeshu Bhakta*. I am a *Masihi* but I am not an *Isai* [Christian]. I am not Christian. Because I believe in the Lord Jesus and he is my father, and I am his son, you can call me *Masihi*, call me *Yeshu Bhakta* or whatever. I tell these people only that I am a *Yeshu Bhakta*. Yes, *Masihi* people are there [in the *Yeshu satsang*]. We are not Christians, we are not Hindus, not Sikhs. [H][15]

Though, as he says in other conversations, "*Masihi*" is closely connected to the Christian community, Dinesh differentiates his group and term from "Christians" and "*Isais*." The latter groups, he explains at various times, are associated with marginal spirituality, drunkenness, and questionable character. The *Masihi*s are a "branch" of the overall Christian group, but one that has more spiritual integrity. In addition, Dinesh combines this with the *bhakti* tradition, readily associating himself with the devotion of *bhakti*, as well as the critique that some *bhakti* groups have made of high-caste power. In all of this Dinesh seeks to frame the *Masihi*s, and particularly his *Yeshu satsang*, as a breakaway Christian *bhakti* sect.[16] He identifies with the Christian community to a certain de-

15. Interview with Dinesh, Mar 22, 2010.

16. Dinesh uses the example of various *bhakti* sects to illustrate what he envisions.

gree in his speech practices, but invokes the *bhakti* tradition and utilizes Hindu worship practices so as to distinguish himself from the Christian churches of his area.

PENTECOSTAL PRACTICES AND PRACTICES OF MIRACULOUS POWER

A final set of practices that the *Yeshu satsang* leaders share with Christian churches is what I call practices of miraculous power, often related with various pentecostal practices. Practices of miraculous power are those that leaders use, often along with prayer, to help facilitate miracles or healing from God. One example of such a practice is that of putting oil on a person's forehead. Dinesh, for example, uses oil quite prominently in his prayers for healing and places a small bowl of oil next to his Bible on the platform in his *Yeshu satsangs*. When someone needs prayer for healing he applies the oil on the person's temples and on the forehead in the form of a cross while praying loudly. In explaining this practice, Dinesh admits that he saw his original pastor bring back anointed oil from Brother Dinakaran, a south Indian pastor known for his television broadcasts and large healing crusades. However, he claims his main inspiration as James 5:14, which provides "the authority that we have." He also shares that he has adapted this practice by praying over peoples' own oil and water containers. He explains: "I give them this water and I tell them that you go to your house and sprinkle this water. All the demons will flee [laughing], and they get this belief. And in the same way I give them oil, and tell them make a cross [with oil], and you get up in the morning and make a cross and no demon, or evil spirit will touch you" [H].[17]

The adaptation, Dinesh says, reflects the common ways in which many Hindus in his area seek healing. In this, many go to temples or sacred sites and will drink water from there or bring back some symbol that supposedly carries spiritual energy for healing. Dinesh says, "People have faith in temples, that they go there and bring the water. They go to the temple and bring flowers or threads. And (when) people come to us they have this same belief, so we give them this oil and this so that they

He explains, "As Radha Soami came out of the Hindu religion, Nirankari came out, Sikhs have come out. In the same way we have come out of Christians" [H]. Interview with Dinesh, Mar 22, 2010.

17. Interview with Dinesh, Mar 22, 2010.

will feel, 'See? Here also is something of God'" [H].[18] Dinesh's practice thus reflects in some way the local practices of healing, though he has found and adapted scripture, and the example of Christian pastors, to shape his practices according to a scriptural model.

The use of oil and water are related to an overall practice of prayer that Dinesh and most of the other *Yeshu satsang* leaders actively embrace. Prayer for healing and other miracles formed an important part of the *satsangs* of Dinesh, Manpreet/Jagdeep, and Navdeep/Naveen. In addition, Gaurav, Padman and Ravi all also emphasized the power of God to heal and do miracles. Though there were often references to and prayers for healing in the midst of the *Yeshu satsangs*, most prayers for miracles occur after the *satsang* or in special prayer meetings during the week.[19] The manner in which leaders prayed for healing usually included laying hands on the sick person and praying forcefully over them. In addition, Dinesh and Naveen also used oil, as described above.

The point of such practices was to ask God to change a situation and display his power miraculously. *Satsangis* would regularly share about God's answers to those prayers during testimony-sharing times in the midst of *Yeshu satsangs*.[20] Such testimonies were often central, thematically and temporally, in the *satsang*, and normally regarded an answer to prayer, such as the provision of a job, a change in a family member, or healing.[21]

Related to these practices, in many instances, were practices that leaders and *satsangis* identified as originating from evangelical and pentecostal churches. Common among these practices were shouting

---

18. Ibid.

19. Manpreet was an exception, in that she would take time in a *Yeshu satsang* to pray for someone's specific healing.

20. The exception to this was again Padman's *Yeshu satsang*. Padman regularly prayed for the healing of family and community members, but did not have times for testimony in his *satsang*.

21. In one of Dinesh's *Yeshu satsangs* a person stood and said, "Greetings in Christ. My husband went for a test. At nighttime the Lord said to me, 'He has passed.' When I called him he said, 'I am in second division.' I was very happy because at nighttime God already told me that everything would be okay. *Tataastu* (amen)." Another woman shared, "Greetings in Christ. I want to thank the Lord that he uses me to share a testimony (begins to cry). For the last two-to-three months my mother has been very sick and I want her to be able to walk. She was very sick but the Lord helped us and touched her and healed her. So she walked and came here to this *satsang*. I want to thank the Lord, you helped me so much. I want to thank him [people applaud]" [H]. From Dinesh *satsang*, Mar 23, 2010.

"hallelujah," raising hands and shaking during worship, and praying for healing with loud prayers using themes common in pentecostal churches (against Satan, proclaiming healing loudly in Jesus' name).

As previously discussed, two *Yeshu satsang* leaders—Dinesh and Manpreet—make healing prayer and associated practices a central theme in their prayers and ministry among their *satsangis*. During the time of this study, for example, Dinesh finished a long fast during which he asked God to heal more people through him. He and his wife shared that, as a result of this, he had seen a marked increase in the number of people that were experiencing healings and other miracles through his prayers. I also noted that several of his *satsangis* spoke about how God had recently healed them or their relatives of various ailments as a result of Dinesh's prayers. Though Dinesh regularly visits people to pray for them, a prima-ry place for healing prayer, and other pentecostal expressions of worship, is in his own home during *Yeshu satsang* and evening prayer meetings. Whereas in the *satsang* such practices and prayers are interlaced with Hindu worship and speech practices, the evening prayer meetings are simple and (sometimes) short meetings that consist only of prayer.[22]

For Manpreet, it was the healing and deliverance of her brother in a local church that attracted her to the church and, ultimately, to following Jesus. Healing prayer and other pentecostal practices continued to be im-portant parts of the subsequent churches she attended, and thus became important for her and Jagdeep when they began their own house church. Even after transitioning to a *Yeshu satsang*, healings and the prayer and worship practices that often accompanied it in her past churches re-mained an important aspect of her ministry, and often a primary factor in the testimony of her *satsangis*. Similar to Dinesh, though Manpreet often visits and prays for people in their houses, it is in her and Jagdeep's *Yeshu satsang* that she takes particular time for this. Manpreet sometimes takes twenty-to-thirty minutes during the *satsang* for everyone to stand and raise hands while singing short Christian choruses and praying out loud for healing and other needs. Curiously, she was aware that such wor-ship can be confusing for Sikhs visiting the *satsang*, and perhaps needed

---

22. The typical structure of Dinesh's evening prayer meetings begins with everyone praying to and praising God out loud at the same time. This continues for approxi-mately five minutes. Towards the end of this time the *satsangis* begin to finish their prayers while Dinesh then continues for another fifteen or twenty minutes, praying for a variety of needs and sicknesses.

to be modified further or practiced carefully. Nonetheless, for her, such worship was important for showing God's power.

Two of my consultants, Jasbir and Nandita, also retain a strong emphasis on healing, miracles and related pentecostal-style practices. As mentioned above, each currently leads a church group in a highly pentecostal style despite their inclination towards a *Yeshu satsang* style, and their sensitivity to Sikh practices. Jasbir, for example, discussed the importance of subdued, reflective worship in a Sikh style as well as the recent experience he had in shouting "hallelujah" and praying loudly over two sisters that were demon-possessed. Though he is partially aware of a disparity between these two sets of practices, he explains that both are important for different situations and that he is able to move between both "communities" as appropriate.

Some leaders see the structural associations that such practices have with Christian churches and try to communicate and pray for God's power in ways that minimize some of these associations. Navdeep and Naveen, for example, have refrained from the use of loud pentecostal practices in their *Yeshu satsangs*, while continuing to preach, pray for and encourage the experience of God's power through miracles and healings. This can be seen in prayer times that occur spontaneously after the *satsang*, where Navdeep will quietly apply oil to peoples' foreheads and pray for healing, as well as in the frequent references during sermons to the power of God to heal and to fulfill peoples' needs. In addition, healing and miracles are the dominant theme about which *satsangis* share during testimony time in the *Yeshu satsangs*.

Gaurav and Ravi, in a similar way, also seek to minimize certain pentecostal practices while retaining an emphasis on the power of God. In their cases, and particularly Gaurav, prayer for healing occurs more often outside of the *satsang* in special prayer meetings or house visits. In these cases, and when the *satsangis* involved are themselves familiar with pentecostal practices, Gaurav will initiate or allow for prayers that are quite loud, using pentecostal speech practices. In this way he is able to retain an emphasis on God's power, along with related practices, in places and amongst people where such feels appropriate, while minimizing these practices in *Yeshu satsangs* where Hindus and those not familiar with such practices may be present.

Despite Gaurav, Ravi, Navdeep and Naveen's efforts to minimize pentecostal and other socially identifiable Christian practices in their *Yeshu satsangs*, some *satsangis* who have previously attended Christian churches nonetheless continue to intermittently use certain pentecostal and Christian speech practices, such as certain spontaneous acts of praise. The *Yeshu satsang* leaders are aware and quite reflexive about these practices, and sometimes even lament the ways in which they are used by *satsangis*; but, nonetheless do not want to "force" *satsangis* to refrain from those practices. The *satsangis* that use such practices are, in many cases, not highly reflexive about them and indicate that they are continuing with practices they had learned prior to the *satsang*'s transition from a pentecostal-style church; or, that they had learned at other churches or Christian rallies that they visited.[23] When asked, some indicated that the practices of raising hands or saying "hallelujah" simply felt good in the context of prayer and worship. In Chapter 9 I will return to the ways this indicates the presence of a possible *habitus*.

Some *satsangis* were quite aware of the differences between the Hindu or Sikh *satsang* and the pentecostal practices they had previously learned. This was particularly evident among some *satsangis* in Navdeep and Naveen's *Yeshu satsang*. For example, as mentioned briefly above, one *satsangi* discussed the changes that had been made about two years prior, and expressed his preference for pentecostal-style worship and prayer. These, he said, were important for helping people to experience God's healing. He shares, for example, "The thing is, our main thing is power. And that main power is nothing else other than you ask and He (God) will give to you . . . . But if we change our words, our dress and think we will win souls then I think it is wrong" [P].[24] He continues by relating how some pastors have told them to clap during worship and not to allow Satan to "bind our hands." Such clapping was thus an expression of freedom from Satan's bondage, and clapping would help bring more power.

Though not every *Yeshu satsang* exhibits practices of power or pentecostal practices to the same degree, nor in every meeting, such practices are nonetheless widely evident. In Chapter 9 I will again return to the question of these practices, their persistence, and their importance as it relates to the past experiences of *Yeshu satsangis* and their leaders.

---

23. Some had also watched the God Channel, a Christian cable television channel available throughout the region that often broadcasts the programs of south Indian pentecostal pastors and healers, as well as international speakers such as Benny Hinn. It was not clear, however, to what degree *satsangis* based their practices on these programs.

24. Interview with N-5, May, 20, 2010.

CHAPTER SUMMARY

In this chapter I have analyzed the Christian practices that *Yeshu satsang* leaders seek to resist, as well as those that they modify and use. Table 4 summarized the Christian church practices that the *Yeshu satsang* leaders resist in their *satsangs*.

Table 4
Yeshu Satsang **Christian Practices Resisted**

Satsang Category	Worship Practices in Satsang	Speech Practices in Satsang	Practices Outside Satsang	Teachings
Yeshu Bhakti Satsangs	Loud pentecostal style	Self-Ascription as "Christian," "*Isai*" "Hallelujah" "*Jai Masih ki*" (greeting)	- Rigidity in rules regarding dress, jewelry, prasad, bindi, and attendance of Hindu/Sikh functions - Name change	Hinduism/ Sikhism is evil.
Arya Samaj Yeshu Satsang	Loud pentecostal style	Self-Ascription as "Christian," "*Isai*" "Hallelujah" "*Jai Masih ki*" (greeting)	- Rigidity in rules such as *prasad*. - "Immoral" practices like drinking and sexuality - Name change	- Change yourself quickly. - Hinduism/ Sikhism is evil.
Sikh Yeshu Satsangs	Loud pentecostal style Not respecting the Bible	Self-Ascription as "Christian," "*Isai*" "Hallelujah" (sometimes) "*Jai Masih di*" (greeting)	- Rigidity in rules regarding attendance of Sikh functions	Sikhism is evil

In their worship practices the leaders generally resist the loud pentecostal styles of worship, including standing, shouting, clapping, shaking, and loud singing. In their speech practices they try to avoid the use of various titles and words that they feel are ascribed as the vocabulary of the Christian community. For some of these they have introduced or adapted phrases from the Sikh and Hindu communities and use them in a way similar to the pentecostal churches. Thus, for example, instead of saying "Hallelujah," the Sikh *Yeshu satsangs* say "*Dhan Satguru Yeshu.*" The *Yeshu satsang* leaders also resist Christian teachings that establish strong rules against certain Hindu or Sikh practices, such as wearing the *bindi,* and teachings that regard Hindu or Sikh beliefs and practices as demonic and evil. The *Yeshu satsang* leaders generally resist these various teachings because, in their opinion, their structural emergent properties (SEPs) emphasize an identity that is Other to the Hindu and Sikh community. To counter these, the *Yeshu satsang* leaders either resist the practices or introduce teaching that affirms the need for personal change, but identifies this as non-structural, internal qualities.

In addition to resisting certain practices and teachings, the *Yeshu satsang* leaders also modify and use other Christian practices. Table 5 summarizes some of the common practices that the leaders have embraced, including the use of the Bible, the Lord's Supper, and baptism; as well as various teachings regarding sin, the centrality of Jesus and the need for forgiveness.

Table 5
Yeshu Satsang **Christian Practices Embraced**

Satsang Category	Worship Practices in Satsang	Speech Practices in Satsang	Teachings
Yeshu Bhakti Satsangs	- Some Christian *geets* (songs) - Modified pentecostal prayer style - Baptism - Communion	"Church" "Amen" "*Vishwasi*" (believer) "*Masihi*" (Christ-follower)	- Centrality of Jesus - Sin and need for forgiveness - Heaven and Hell - God's power, healing & miracles
Arya Samaj Yeshu Satsang	- Use of Scripture		- Forgiveness - God's love - Godl's power
Sikh Yeshu Satsangs	- Some Christian songs - Modified pentecostal prayer style (Manpreet) - The Lord's Prayer - Baptism - Communion	"Church" "*Bandagi*" "Amen" "*Vishwasi*" (believer) "*Masihi*" (Christ-follower) "pastor"	- Centrality of Jesus - Sin and need for forgiveness - Heaven and Hell - God's power, healing & miracles

The leaders feel that these practices and teachings have cultural emergent properties (CEPs) that are essential for gaining salvation and growing in devotion to Jesus. In general the leaders are mindful that these practices also have (SEPs) that link the practices to Christian churches, and they sometimes employ various strategies to minimize these. I found, however, that such strategies were not always consistent. For example, though the leaders resist certain loud pentecostal worship practices, they continue to use some pentecostal prayer practices in modified ways. One of the reasons for this is that the leaders value what they see as miraculous power stemming from particular ways of praying and eliciting God's power.

Thus, though the *Yeshu satsang* leaders try to accentuate practices that relate them to the Hindu or Sikh communities, they also retain and reshape Christian practices that clearly distinguish their *satsangs* from the surrounding Hindu or Sikh communities. However, the *Yeshu satsang* leaders tend to make these distinctions according to different criteria than some of the Christian churches around them. Though they embrace the Bible, for example, they de-emphasize passages and interpretations that condemn other religions or establish external rules. In addition, the leaders interpret practices such as baptism and the Lord's Supper not as rituals for Christian or community membership, but as *bhakti*-like opportunities for *satsangis* to display their deepening devotion to Jesus, and to join with others that are doing the same. Thus, while these practices are not used to create strongly structural associations, such as church membership, the leaders do emphasize their Christocentric nature as practices that show devotion to Jesus.

In Chapters 5 through 7 I have discussed the ways in which leaders and *satsangis* use and understand various practices within their *Yeshu satsangs*. In terms of Emergentist theory of identity formation, I have described how the *Yeshu satsang* leaders are strategically shaping practices in order to give expression to their "project" of a *Yeshu satsang* and create an appropriate *modus vivendi*. I have thus addressed and answered the research question: How do *Yeshu satsang* leaders in northwest India use, modify and resist various practices to shape their ecclesial identities? In addition, these chapters have begun to indicate some of the themes that characterize these identities. What, then, are the particular ecclesial identity markers, or theological themes, that these practices suggest?

CHAPTER 8

Ecclesial Identity Markers of the *Yeshu Satsangs*

EMERGENTIST THEORY SUGGESTS THAT people choose and utilize practices to give shape and expression to those "projects" that they value. Relatedly, the *Yeshu satsang* leaders, in their quest to create a new ecclesial community and identity, have chosen and adapted various practices whose properties have important associations to them. What do these practices, and the meanings given to them indicate regarding the *Yeshu satsangs'* ecclesial identity? My coded analysis of the data suggests that there are four prominent and often interrelated themes: (1) a *bhakti*-influenced devotion to Jesus, (2) experience of God's blessing and power, (3) carefully discerning evil, and (4) witness. When these theological themes, or markers, are publicly expressed and shared through their corresponding practices, they become important facets of their ecclesial identity. In this chapter I will describe the four markers and the ways in which the practices and narratives shape these, thus addressing my third research question (What are the ecclesial identity markers of six Hindu and Sikh *Yeshu satsangs* in northwest India?).

THEME 1: BHAKTI-INFLUENCED DEVOTION TO JESUS

Through various practices, the *Yeshu satsang* leaders have sought to incorporate and invoke aspects of the Hindu and Sikh *bhakti* traditions. Such *bhakti* traditions have characteristically focused on cultivating devotion towards particular deities as a path towards salvation. Relatedly, a crucial aspect of *bhakti* and its practices, as per the *Yeshu satsang* leaders, is the emphasis on devotion, which leaders direct towards Jesus. Leaders expressed this emphasis on devotion in two ways.

First, leaders sought to shape the *Yeshu satsang* as a space where *bhakti* could be experienced and incorporated practices that provide an affective experience of God and that help maintain *satsangis'* relationship with the Hindu or Sikh structures. Important practices for this included the use of *bhajans* and *bhakti* self-ascriptions, but also encompassed prayer and teachings on devotion to Jesus.

Bhajans and prayers typically convey a quality important in the *bhakti* tradition—its internal, personal experience.[1] For example, *bhajans* often use the imagery of Hindu worship and devotion to illustrate an inner devotion. One common *bhajan* sung by the Hindu and Arya Samaj *Yeshu satsangs* states:

> Keep the lamp burning so the Lord's name will remain.
> Remain in my (inner) temple, remain in my temple.
> In the morning and in the evening my soul sings your name, Jesus.
> Lord Jesus, your name,
> Let your name remain in my soul.[2]

Following such *bhajans, Yeshu satsang* leaders and *satsangis* often pray prayers that re-emphasize the importance of inner devotion. On one occasion Gaurav followed the above *bhajan* with a prayer, saying, "Jesus we give that (passion) to you. Your lamp lights in our heart-temple. Light is among us. Your light shows us the way in every situation. Your light helps us in every difficult decision."[3] The *bhajan*, and Gaurav's prayer, thus drew on typical Hindu *bhakti* imagery of light, hearts and temples to express devotion to Jesus.

In addition to the use of *bhajans, Yeshu satsang* leaders use practices whose qualities facilitate respect and reverence, including a more quiet and reverent atmosphere, properly handling the scriptures, sitting on the floor, and using various symbols when appropriate. The leaders contrast this devotional atmosphere with the loud, sometimes irreverent-sounding pentecostal style prevalent in their region. Jasbir, as discussed above, sees the reverence evident in Sikh *satsangs* as a proper approach to God, and one that contrasts the informality implied by many pentecostal approaches. Relatedly, leaders avoid certain practices that displayed irreverence, such as not having a turban or wearing inappropriate clothes.

---

1. Lipner, *Hindus*, 178.
2. Dev, *Deep Jale*.
3. From Gaurav *satsang*, Jan 17, 2010.

The *bhakti* devotion of the *Yeshu satsangs* was reflected in another theme that several *satsangis* and leaders repeated. Some *Yeshu satsang* leaders change and internalize the rules of Christian churches regarding external appearances. For example, while some Christians teach that followers of Christ should distinguish themselves through a change of dress, not wearing the Hindu *bindi* and other outward actions, the *Yeshu satsang* leaders emphasize changes that reflect the inner, personal qualities of the follower of Jesus. This reflects the *bhakti* emphasis on cultivating the interior state through practices that enhance that state, versus the actions that create social distinctions.

Some *satsangis*, reflecting this emphasis, discussed how they had not changed their religion, but had instead changed their heart. One of Gaurav's *satsangis* expresses this idea when he describes his message to Hindus, saying, "And you also don't need to change your religion. You only have to change your heart. You don't need to change your religion. Your name will remain the same after coming to the Lord Jesus Christ. Whatever you have, that will remain the same" [H].[4] Such an assertion represents a *bhakti* spirituality that emphasizes the internal aspects of change and devotion.

The marker of a *bhakti*-influenced devotion to Jesus is thus expressed in various ways in the life of the *Yeshu satsangs*. However, the leaders' main concern is to create a space and gathering that expresses the feelings of reverence and devotion that *satsangis* experienced in prior Hindu or Sikh *satsangs* and other worship settings, and to place emphasis on inward change versus social community change. Theologically, the leaders understand the corporate gathering as a way to orient individuals towards Jesus and to help guide them as they continue living in their Hindu and Sikh communities. In this the *Yeshu satsangs* critique the ecclesiocentric identities of Christian churches that strongly counter the surrounding structures. As will be seen below, such countering strategies have, in the experience of the *Yeshu satsang* leaders, caused the Christian churches to differentiate themselves from others for the wrong reasons.

Rather than countering the Hindu/Sikh communities in terms of structure, the leaders instead rely on a strong Christocentric focus for the *satsangs*. The role of Christ, however, is seen as a primarily personal matter that transforms the internal character of a person. The leaders acknowledge that the external behaviors of followers of Christ will

4. Interview with G-4, Feb 17, 2010.

certainly change, but that these external manifestations will be different than the rule-oriented behaviors that distinguish some Christian churches. Changes should not be evidenced through practices such as dress and family rituals. Rather, changes will be seen in character and in the miraculous work and blessings of God in the lives of *satsangis*. Thus, whereas some Christian churches may seek to embody and express their Christology by being a clearly set-apart community, the *satsangs* seek to support the individual's ongoing re-orientation and devotion to Christ, and to encourage transformations that reflect this.

THEME 2: EXPERIENCE OF GOD'S BLESSING AND POWER

Most *Yeshu satsang* leaders are mindful that people of any religion can easily display devotion without experiencing a personal connection and relationship with God. For example, reflecting on how she used to follow Sikh devotional practices, Manpreet says, "The people who follow the *Guru Granth Sahib*, how they worship it! They get up early at 4:00 in the morning. How much devotion they have according to their faith! But still they are empty of the power of God. Empty of the power of God! Right? There is no peace. There is no joy in them."[5]

Thus equally important, if not more important than devotion for some leaders, is the presence, blessings and power of God. This is expressed and practiced in a variety of ways, reflecting the hybrid of Hindu/Sikh and pentecostal practices that leaders use in their *Yeshu satsangs*.

One way this is seen is through the prayers of the leaders and *satsangis*, which often begin with, and return again and again to the theme of God's presence and the work of the Holy Spirit. Such prayers communicate that, though God's presence is everywhere, it is particularly strong and efficacious in the *satsang* itself. For example, when talking about his vision for the *satsang*, Naveen shared about his desire to bring Sikhs into the *Yeshu satsang* as "into the presence of God."[6] In a similar way other *Yeshu satsang* leaders indicate that the *satsang* creates a space wherein the presence and blessing of God can be experienced. The blessings that people experience are often recounted and discussed through the practices of testimony, which often talk about God's healing, deliverance from evil, acceptance and forgiveness from sin, and other answers to prayer.

5. Interview with Manpreet, Apr 4, 2010.
6. Interview with Naveen, May 2, 2010.

The importance and marker of God's blessing and power can also be seen in the teachings surrounding the issue of *prasad*. When *satsangis* pray for and eat *prasad* in the context of a *Yeshu satsang*, the *prasad* is considered to be blessed by God and able to convey some blessing to those that eat it. However, when *Yeshu satsangis* are given *prasad* in the context of a Hindu or Sikh temple or event, they sometimes experience a dilemma of whether or not to eat something that has been presented to an idol or temple. In cases where the *satsangi* wants to preserve relationship with the Hindu or Sikh family or friend that has offered it, some find comfort in praying for God's power to cover and bless the *prasad*.

Thus, integral to the ecclesial identity of the *satsangs* is the blessing and power that God can have on peoples' material world through the practices of the community, particularly prayer and other practices conveying God's power. Importantly, and similar to the previous marker, this one does not emphasize or require a religio-structural change. However, some leaders have retained some pentecostal practices that invoke God's power, and that also carry some associations with the Christian church. In these cases the leaders seem to hold the practice in tension with their desire to relate to the Hindu or Sikh communities because of the importance of their desire to have public displays of the presence of God. I will return to this tension in Chapter 9.

THEME 3: CAREFULLY DISCERNING EVIL

The presence of evil is readily, and regularly discussed. The testimonies of *Yeshu satsangis* often refer to this, with some having experienced deliverance from demonic spirits. Leaders acknowledge that this power exists and address it in their prayers and discourses. However the leaders do not usually locate the power in Hindu/Sikh structures. This careful move to not demonize the beliefs or structures of the Hindu or Sikh community contrasts the practices of some Christian pastors, and seeks to avoid the barriers that such a belief would cause between the *satsang* and the local Hindu or Sikh communities. Rather than locating it in these structures, the *satsangis* sometimes claim that it relates to the work of a *jagudar* (shaman) or a Muslim *pir* (spirit). These shamans and spirits, at the fringe of the Hindu and Sikh religious structures, are popular among the folk beliefs of many Hindus and Sikhs, but are not viewed as central to their communities, as the priests and respective temples are.

Another aspect of evil sometimes discussed by leaders is the issue of persecution. Though the leaders do not themselves attribute this to personal beings, such as demons, it is nonetheless an evil that they seek to nuance carefully. In more than one instance *Yeshu satsang* leaders made a link between the harsh criticism of Christians and the persecution that they sometimes receive. Navdeep talks about a pastor who, several years ago, wrote a booklet condemning Hinduism and Sikhism. Other pastors also spoke inappropriately, such that the Shiv Sena, a local Hindu fundamentalist group, beat them up and caused a lot of tension. Navdeep explains: "And the reality behind this was that these are the pastors who directly attack (condemn other religions). That should not happen. And we have good news. And if here is a person who from the beginning has faith (in some other religion), and if you hurt him, then what will happen?" [P].[7]

In a similar way, Gaurav and Padman suggest that sometimes it is the Christians' approach to other religious communities that provokes persecution and attacks. According to Padman, if followers of Jesus could remove the "cultural hindrances" between them and Hindus, then the "hate campaigns" of the latter, including the violence they inflict, would not ensue. Thus, though not condoning the evil violence of Hindu and Sikh fundamentalist groups, these leaders nonetheless place some blame and burden on the harsh way Christian pastors have talked about the other religions.

Another aspect of persecution that Christians sometimes attribute as evil, and even Satanic, is the persecution that new believers sometimes face from Hindu or Sikh family members. The *Yeshu satsang* leaders try to counsel their *satsangis* to make choices that, where possible, allow them to retain relationships with their family members. Ravi reflects on this:

> Most of the time when people come to know about Jesus, usually they are taught that when you accept Christ your family will oppose you . . . . And all of a sudden they start thinking by themselves, "Yes, because of the Lord Jesus this is happening to me." But its not happening because of Jesus, but because of the wrong teaching that has come into their minds. I teach them that we have to love. You stay in touch with the family, then only you can win them. You do not have to tell about Jesus, show him through your lifestyle, and then slowly you can win them. [H][8]

7. Interview with Navdeep, May 2, 2010.
8. Interview with Ravi, Jun 24, 2010.

In a similar way, Ravi critiques Christians who accuse Hindus of being evil. Thus, in various ways the *Yeshu satsang* leaders are seeking to be sensitive to issues of evil as it impacts *satsangis*, but to also nuance some of the common Christian views of evil. In this they suggest that the Hindu or Sikh communities, or practices, are not always the source of demonic evil power. In cases of persecution, the leaders do not condone the violence, but neither do they completely accept the standard Christian rhetoric regarding the violence. Instead they suggest that the insensitive actions of Christians, including their harsh critiques of Hindus and Sikhs, sometimes help to antagonize and fuel such persecution.

Theologically, this theme reflects the high view that the *satsangs'* theology gives to cultures and structures. Whereas evil certainly exists and needs to be countered, the *Yeshu satsang* leaders do not view the Hindu or Sikh cultures and structures as primary venues through which it comes. Rather, these cultures and structures can actually contain some level of truth that God uses to direct people towards the complete revelation of Jesus through the Bible. Once people have received that revelation and become followers of Jesus, the Hindu/Sikh cultures and structures continue to be valuable places for the work of God.

THEME 4: WITNESS

One of the ecclesial identity markers that leaders and *satsangis* discussed the most is the desire to be an evangelistic witness to the Hindu and Sikh communities. At the heart of this witness is the need for relationship with Hindu and Sikh family members and communities, and conducting the *satsang* and their lifestyles in ways that communicate a sustained connection with those community structures.

Many *satsangis* and leaders reflected on the *satsang* style and related it to the need for witness. One of Navdeep's *satsangis*, for example, reflects on the change that was made from a Christian church to a *satsang* style about three years ago. She recounts:

> Then when (Pastor Sandeep Singh) came from Singapore, he sat us all together and talked with us. Then they told, they shared the verse where Paul said, "I became Jew for Jews and Greek for Greeks so that I can pull some in to God." Then I felt it is a way. It is a resource so that we do not look different than people. So that people would not say, "He is the Guru of foreigners or someone else." But we will go among the people by being like them. Then they might accept us more easily. Because I used to think that

only an ant can understand the language of an ant. Only birds can understand the language of birds. Then I thought and it came to my mind that if we will go among them by being like them then they will consider us their own. But if we will look different then them, then we will stay different. I like this system now because through this now we can put a cassette of a *kirtan* on a high volume and people come and they feel happy. They listen to them also. Earlier the worship songs, in English or some others, people used to ignore them and they do not understand them at all, and (say), "You have become foreign and started believing in the Guru of foreigners." But now the other people, the neighbors also take interest. And all like this also. This is the same as our culture. They are not different than us. [P][9]

Like the reflections of other *satsangis* and leaders, this person suggests that one of the major markers of the *satsang* identity is witness, and the *satsang's* practices are understood through this aspect of their identity. This would include, in the case of the Sikh *satsang*, Sikh language practices, as well as the *bhajans* and other changes that are made to the worship setting. In the Hindu *satsangs* this includes objects such as the *diya*, *shankh*, and some of those that are used in the Lord's Supper. For Ravi, one of the main goals of the *satsang* is to foster an open atmosphere of love for people. Beyond the actual practices, he says, is the importance of communicating God's love to Hindus. He says:

We won't forsake loving humanity, being with humanity. If a person is an idol worshiper then it is okay, because his eyes are closed. But we can make him understand through love, by having relationship with him . . . Looking at all these things (practices) we do not think that culture and dress are going to take us to heaven. But they can be a medium in sharing the message of the Lord with people. And I don't say that our *satsang* style is the only style. The Holy Spirit works and everything depends on the Holy Spirit. God's word is the thing that changes peoples' hearts, but (the *satsang* style) helps us to keep relationship with people. [H][10]

The witness of the *satsangs* is also reflected in the types of identifications that the leaders encourage the *satsangis* to retain outside of the *satsang*. Above I have periodically discussed how *satsangis* and leaders

9. Interview with N-1, May 1, 2010.

10. Interview with Ravi, Jun 24, 2010.

were able to retain a level of relationship with their families because of the practices and identity of the *satsang*. Relatedly, *Yeshu satsang* leaders encourage their *satsangis* to maintain practices and relationships that do not compromise their faith in Christ but that also allows them to relate to and be witnesses to their family. Ravi, for example, encouraged a new member to stay a part of a dera to retain his relationships with that community.[11]

A final way that this witness is conveyed relates to what I discussed above regarding the change of hearts versus the change of religion. *Satsangis* and leaders, responding to the accusation that following Jesus is a conversion of religious community and "religion," assert in various ways that the change they have made represents an internal devotion and change of character. In terms of Analytical Dualism, they have embraced different religio-cultural properties, but have not changed their association with their religious structures of community.

Nuanced Differences in Witness

Though all *Yeshu satsangs* share the ecclesial identity marker of being a witness, they nuance and express this differently. I will discuss two of the prominent ways in which the leaders differ: (1) the question of motivation for the *satsang* style and identity, and (2) the long-term identity that they hope the *satsangs* to hold.

Difference 1: Motivation and Depth of Identification

All *satsang* leaders share a desire to relate more closely to the Hindu and Sikh communities. In addition, all share a desire that this relationship would create better opportunities for witnessing to them. Some, however, also view the *satsang* as a means for more deeply expressing their own

---

11. As another example, a few years ago Ruth's son, who was not a follower of Jesus, married a Hindu woman. Before he brought her to Ruth's home to meet her, Ruth bought a small *mandir* (temple) to place on a shelf in her front room. Inside this she placed a Bible instead of a Hindu scripture, along with a small plaque saying, "Christ is the head of this house, the unseen guest at every meal, the silent listener to every conversation." When her son and new daughter-in-law arrived, Rebecca brought them straight over to the *mandir* and offered a prayer of blessing for their marriage. Ruth continued to have daily prayers with them at the *mandir* and talked about Jesus. Ruth shares that her daughter-in-law did not seem impressed by it, but neither was she put off by it. It was, Ruth felt, a way of expressing her faith in Jesus that did not communicate the foreignness or Otherness of Christian churches.

identity. Amongst them, I suggest, there is a continuum of levels of Hindu or Sikh identification. On one end of the continuum are leaders for whom a close Hindu or Sikh identity is intrinsic to their ecclesial identity. On the other end are leaders who show little affinity for the Hindu or Sikh community on a personal level and use the *satsang* style as a means of reaching Hindus and Sikhs. In between these poles are leaders who view the *satsang* style as an important way to relate to and reach-out to Hindus and Sikhs, and who show a bi-cultural and structural affinity to both Christian and Hindu or Sikh communities.

Ravi and Gaurav perhaps comes closest to the first pole of the continuum, adopting a Hindu *satsang* style and identity both for its ability to relate to Hindus as well as their desire to identify closely with their own Hindu community. Gaurav, who is familiar with western "church-growth" missiology critiques some of the missiology and its emergent properties that try to make *satsangs* an outreach tool. In particular he critiques what he calls the "cult of the high-caste," or mission strategy calling for contextual outreach focused on single castes. This, he says, is simply fueled by a western focus on numbers rather than process. In contrast, he highlights the *bhakti* culture of the northwest that has promoted cross-caste communities, or *deras*, focused on devotion to God. A *satsang* identity that truly reflects the *bhakti* religious traditions of the northwest, he believes, will be one that is caste inclusive. In this regard he does not view the *satsang* simply as an outreach effort. In terms of his identity, Gaurav identifies with the Hindu community. However, he also retains close ties with the Christian community as well. He does not mind being called "pastor," though he does not encourage it. Also, while he encourages his *satsangis* to embrace Hindu culture, he "does not force it." Because of his urban context there are, he notes, numerous *satsangis* who are from Christian or Dalit backgrounds who are uncomfortable calling themselves "Hindu" or adopting certain Hindu practices.

Ravi shows a similar attitude towards the *satsang* and his identity. He embraces a Hindu identity while clearly being comfortable with the Christian community. The *satsang* also has a mix of people, including Hindus and Christians, and exhibits a mix of influence that he is comfortable with. However, while he talks about the Hindu elements of the *satsang* in terms of outreach, they also represent for him aspects of a culture that he embraces for its own sake.

Padman follows Ravi and Gaurav closely on the continuum. He identifies closely with his Hindu Arya Samaj family. When talking about the Hindu Arya Samaj community, for example he often uses the inclusive word "we." The marked exception to this is his distaste, and even anger, over Hindu *pandits* and gurus (religious leaders) whom, he claims, mislead and exploit people. What the people need, he says, are religious leaders like him who will not charge high amounts of money to conduct a *satsang* and will not lead his people into false beliefs. His *satsang*, he feels, gives witness to Jesus as well as gives value to his people. However, as seen above, he also views the symbolism of the *satsang* as a means of helping to introduce people to Jesus.

In the middle of the spectrum are Navdeep and Naveen who have re-adopted aspects of the Sikh community identity, but for whom the Sikhs, and particularly the Jatt Sikh community, clearly remain as an Other. This is evident when Navdeep and Naveen talk about their desire to witness to and bring the Sikhs to faith in Jesus. One of the most often discussed reasons for adopting a Sikh *satsang* style is the hope that they will create a movement of *satsangs* throughout the Punjab, comprised particularly of the upper-class/caste Jatt Sikhs. In these discussions the Sikh style of the *satsang*, and the practices they have adopted, serve as a bridge for relationship. For example one of Naveen's rationales for wearing a turban was that it provided a "bridge" through which he could sit and talk "in the midst of them."

Two of my consultants, Jasbir and Nandita, though not presently leaders of *Yeshu satsangs*, lean towards the other side of the continuum. On the one hand, both have strong Jatt Sikh family identities. For Jasbir this identity has fluctuated in importance. He explains:

> Yeah, there came a time in my life when I didn't want to think of myself as a Sikh. But now I think I do. Some things have changed. Especially like I can go to any big [Christian] leader's function now. I can go to a *gurdwara* now. Not bowing before there, but I can still, uh, show as I'm not, uh, I'm not really being very critical towards what they are doing. [E][12]

Part of Jasbir and Nandita's move back towards their community has come through the experience of certain life events. As Jasbir considers his children and the community to which they will relate, and as Nandita looks for a husband that will be acceptable to her and her wider family, both are drawn to re-engage their Jatt Sikh identities. However, though they maintain or ponder some connections with their Sikh communities,

---

12. Interview with Jasbir, May 29, 2010.

the Sikh-style *satsang* remains mainly an outreach tool, and both have some questions about its effectiveness. Jasbir says that, though he wants to continue developing *Yeshu satsangs*, the *satsangs* he has seen thus far have not been as effective for reaching Sikhs as had been hoped. Nandita is intrigued by the style, particularly following the *satsang* that Jasbir helped lead at her house as a memorial to her grandfather, but still attends a pentecostal-style church, and conducts her house-church in a pentecostal style.

At the other end of the continuum would fall Dinesh, Jagdeep and Manpreet. For these the Hindu and Sikh identities are tenuous. They occasionally call themselves or identify themselves with these communities, but not in a consistent way. Dinesh, as described above, most clearly and consistently identifies with a renewed *Masihi* community or sect, distinct from the Christian community, but not highly integrated with the Hindus. Jagdeep identifies himself with the Sikh community in name and in dress, including keeping uncut hair and a turban. Whereas this has some importance for him on a personal level, it is also important in part because through it he retains his caste-reservation and job. His wife, Manpreet, retains little identification with the Sikh community in name or practice. They do, however, critique the way Christians have separated themselves from the Sikh community and believe they should follow Paul's example in 1 Corinthians 9 so that, as Manpreet paraphrases, "when you go to the Greeks speak like the Greeks, and if you go to the Hebrews then be like the Hebrews" [P].[13] This, for them, is mainly evident in the ways they relate to and teach about the Sikh and Hindu practices and community.

DIFFERENCE 2: LENGTH OF IDENTIFICATION

The other way in which the *Yeshu satsangs* differ from each other in the witness marker regards the long-term identities that they envision for their *satsangs*. Not all leaders commented or reflected on this, but those that did matched their responses and position on the continuum above. Gaurav, Ravi, Navdeep and Naveen, for example, have hopes for a "movement" of *satsangs* that would closely connect with the Hindu and Sikh communities, and that continue to reflect the practices and identities that they have begun in their present *satsangs*.

Others, however, view the *satsang* as a temporary strategy, necessary to help young believers build their faith. Padman, as described above,

13. Interview with Manpreet, Apr 4, 2010.

says that the Arya Samaj *satsang* and its symbols, such as the *havan* and fire, are temporary and only useful until people have matured in their spiritual understanding. Thus, while Padman expresses a strong connection to his community, he is ambiguous about the ways mature *satsangis* will relate to the community in practice in the future.

Dinesh expresses something similar. Hindu symbols are, he says, helpful for a time, but simply as a way to introduce people to Christ and bring them to the *satsang*. They are, he says, only necessary for the first stage of their growth, and perhaps only for six months. After that the people are able to move beyond this and do not need the symbols. Here again, for Dinesh the symbolic connections of his *satsang* to the Hindu community serve only as a bridge that, once crossed, can be dispelled with.

Witness Summary

The *Yeshu satsang* leaders have a common, shared focus on the importance of being witnesses to their Hindu and Sikh communities. They critique the ways in which certain practices and identities of the Christian church have impeded this witness, particularly among non-Dalit Hindus and Sikhs. In response, the leaders shape *Yeshu satsangs* with practices that form bridges to the Hindu and Sikh communities. The motivation for some leaders stops with this, and *satsang* practices are in some ways temporary tools to help bring Hindus and Sikhs to faith in Jesus. For others, however, the *satsang* practices express a personal connection to the Hindu and Sikh communities and will, they hope, form the basis for an ongoing movement of such *satsangs*.

Theologically, some Christian churches accept and even promote the sense of being a set-apart community, and seek to draw others to join that community. The *Yeshu satsang* leaders also focus on drawing people from Hindu and Sikh communities to their *satsangs*. However, the *Yeshu satsangs* would place less emphasis than some Christian churches on the value of a witness that counters and contrasts the wider society in culture and structure. Indeed, the *satsangs* indicate that it is the structural contrast of the Christian church that has hurt the witness of Christ-followers in northwest India, and much more emphasis needs to be placed on structural solidarity coupled with internal and personal change of devotion. The *Yeshu satsangs* would thus strongly critique the barriers that, they believe, Christian churches have erected and that make it difficult for others to become followers of Jesus.

CHAPTER SUMMARY

In this chapter, as well as Chapters 5 through 7, I have inductively explored, through Emergentist theory, the ways in which leaders and *satsangis* are using various Hindu or Sikh and Christian practices to shape particular ecclesial identities. These, I have suggested, highlight four important markers of ecclesial identity shared by the *Yeshu satsangs* and directly relate to the purpose for this research.

With these markers and their theological significance in view, it is now helpful to look backwards retroductively to consider some of the systems and processes that have contributed to their emergence. In the following chapter I will address my fourth research question: How did the *Yeshu satsang* leaders' Hindu and Sikh backgrounds and interaction with Christian churches help shape the ecclesial identity markers of their *Yeshu satsangs*? To do so I turn to the testimonies of the *Yeshu satsang* leaders themselves and consider how their interaction with the identities of the Christian church, as well as their particular experiences and contexts, have contributed to the emergence of the *Yeshu satsangs* and their ecclesial identity markers.

CHAPTER 9

The Emergence of the *Yeshu Satsang*'s Ecclesial Identities

As COVERED IN CHAPTER 2, Emergentist theory is a temporal theory in that it emphasizes causation and emergence over time.[1] I have described the present practices and ecclesial identity markers of the *Yeshu satsangs*. The ecclesial identities that these represent are, in the process of the Morphogenetic cycle, the T4 or present elaboration, comprised of the sets of practices that currently give expression to the leaders' desired identity. However, prior to this were a myriad of processes and interactions into which the Yeshu satang leaders were born and with which they interacted as they grew in maturity. One of the major elaborations with which *Yeshu satsang* leaders have interacted is the existing ecclesial identities of the churches in northwest India. Chapter 4 described the various identities of the Christian church and some of the situational logics that have helped to shape this.

This chapter I will retroductively analyze the processes and interactions that have influenced and enabled the *Yeshu satsang* leaders to develop the ecclesial identity markers described above. In particular I analyze the testimonies of the *Yeshu satsang* leaders to understand their own particular influences, as well as how they interacted with the Christian ecclesial identities as they has developed in northwest India. I begin by discussing the way in which I use Emergentist theory of identity formation to understand the testimonies of the *Yeshu satsang* leaders.

---

1. Archer, *Realist Social Theory*, 66.

EMERGENTIST THEORY OF IDENTITY FORMATION AND TESTIMONIES

One of the emphases and strengths of an Emergentist theory of identity formation is its focus on the agential abilities of people to reflect upon their context, survey projects, and make choices from among these. Though such ability may seem self-evident, Archer shows that many social theories do not allow for the possibility that people really are doing what they think they are doing—subjectively reflecting on themselves in relation to their objective circumstances. Instead these theories seek to account for peoples' actions through various accounts of cultural conditioning or discourse.[2]

To sustain this argument, however, and to rescue reflexivity from various conflationary accounts, Archer tends to sidestep the place of unconscious, non-reflexive action, such as the *habitus* proposed by Bourdieu.[3] In response, rather than posing reflexivity and *habitus* as two conflicting accounts of agency, I suggested that they exist on a continuum. The place an action and its underlying thought has on the continuum at any one time depends in part on the "field" that is being traversed or crossed (Bourdieu), or the morphogenetic process in which a person is engaged (Archer).

Critical Realism theorist Roy Bhaskar, in his influential statement on agency says that, "the causal power of social forms is mediated through social agency."[4] This, as Archer has discussed, is an essential theorem that seeks to avoid reifying social structures while showing that "structural and cultural factors ultimately emerge from people and are efficacious only through people."[5] In Chapters 5 through 8 I discussed the ways in which the *Yeshu satsang* leaders are using particular religious practices to create particular outcomes and ecclesial identities for their *Yeshu sat-*

2. Archer, *Structure, Agency, and the Internal Conversation*, 13.

3. The closest Archer seems to get in acknowledging the place of the unconscious is in a statement of delimitation where she says, "In stressing that our inner thoughts are matters of conscious awareness, I do not exclude matters of which we can become aware through self-examination but obviously do not include those of which we remain unconscious" (ibid., 25). She goes on to say that she does not focus on these because "non-conscious features may play a part in the depiction of the passive agent, to whom things happen, but by definition can play no part in the conscious, *reflexive deliberations* of the active agent" (ibid.).

4. Bhaskar, *The Possibility of Naturalism*, 26.

5. Archer, *Structure, Agency, and the Internal Conversation*, 2.

sangs. In Bhaskar's terms, the *Yeshu satsang* leaders are seeking to mediate the causal powers of Hindu/Sikh cultural and structural systems. In this chapter I look more closely at the religio-structural and religio-cultural systems that have helped shaped the leaders, including the competitive contradictions of the Christian church, and how these have constrained and enabled particular choices and projects. I will discuss how these systems, and the *Yeshu satsang* leaders' interactions with them, have profoundly shaped their choices and provided the practices and resources for the ecclesial identity markers that their *satsangs* embody.

The methodology used in this section is primarily narrative analysis. I follow an approach that gives attention to both the "historical" identity that the narrative points to, as well as the identity constructed through the narrative itself. Such life stories, when properly used, provide insight into both of these, though it is important to recognize that the life story given in the interview is "but one instance of the life story."[6]

I analyzed the testimonies of the eight *Yeshu satsang* leaders, and also included in this two of my Sikh *satsang*i consultants, Jasbir and Nandita. Though they are not currently leading *satsangs*, their knowledge of and sensitivity to the *satsang* approach, along with the similarities of their journey helped to enrich the data set. In general the testimony narratives of the leaders display six stages, and each demonstrates an interplay between agency, *habitus*, and the various systems engaged by the leaders. The six stages are demonstrated in Figure 2. I will discuss each stage in turn, noting the general commonalities as well as nuanced differences between leaders.

6. Lieblich, Tuval-Machiach, and Zilber, *Narrative Research,* 8. As Lieblich et al discuss, the actual life story of a person can never be fully accessed through research because, 1) it changes and develops through time, and 2) it is impacted by the interview context. "Hence the particular life story is one (or more) instance of the polyphonic versions of the possible constructions or presentations of people's selves and lives, which they use according to specific momentary influences. Ibid., 8. Despite this, however, the life story does transmit important meanings. People "construct their identities and self-narratives from building blocks available in their common culture, above and beyond their individual experiences" (ibid., 9).

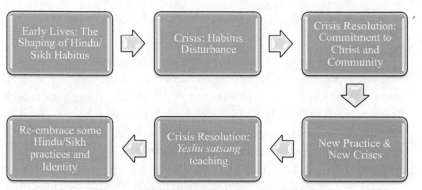

Figure 2: Life Stages Of *Yeshu Satsang* Leaders

EARLY LIVES: MORPHOSTASIS AND THE SHAPING OF HINDU AND SIKH HABITUS

To begin with, each of the leaders of these *Yeshu satsangs* was born into Hindu and Sikh families. Though this is of temporal importance, I was interested to note that in their testimonies, none of the leaders focused on their family's religious placement and background without prompting. Three of the leaders chose not to begin their narratives with any discussion of religious background and instead began at the point of a crisis, only referring to their families' religious communities at a later point in the narrative. Only four leaders briefly discussed religious backgrounds at the beginning of their narrative. Even this, however, was normally presented only briefly and as a backdrop to the crisis that followed.[7] For example, Dinesh begins one of his testimony discourses recounting:

> I, we were from a Hindu family. We were, according to our understanding we used to read (in) marriages, used to read the *Gita, Shatru Maraya*. We used to do this. My father still does those things. When I came here, after I came here, we, after my marriage, we were okay till my marriage. We had no problems

7. Of the leaders, Dinesh, Jasbir, Manpreet, and Nandita gave some brief religious background. In contrast, Jagdeep, Navdeep, and Ravi begin with a point of crisis. Naveen began with his background as a stage performer and rarely refers to his Sikh family background. Padman begins his testimony recounting his early memories of conflict between Hindus and Christians. Gaurav's testimony narrative at this stage was broken up by dialogue between he and I, obscuring his own structural departure point.

till my marriage. After marriage when our first child was born, she died. [H].[8]

These sections of the narratives and their compressed chronologies form what could be called a "cold chronology," where large periods of time are skipped or given brief summary.[9] While most came back to and discussed further their socio-religious background at a later point, this information was often used to discuss tensions that eventually moved them towards Christ, as will be discussed further below.

Initially I was surprised by the leaders' lack of emphasis on their socio-religious background, particularly in light of the way in which they were seeking to reintegrate aspects of their socio-religious practices into their *Yeshu satsangs*. Several explanations are possible, including the influence of common testimony discourse structures as modeled in churches and ministries, and assumptions respondents may have had regarding my expectations as a foreign Christian. However, an additional explanation, discussed by Archer, suggests that this also reflects a phenomenon common in the process of identity formation. In this case, when *Yeshu satsang* leaders minimize the details of their "pre-crisis" socio-religious Hindu or Sikh life, it reflects the perspective of the new life to which they dedicated themselves following the crisis. As Archer describes, "Retrospectively, the dedicated life takes up an increasingly distanced stance from his or her previous first-order emotions and their commentaries, for the past itself becomes transvalued. The person may actually view this in 'before and after' terms . . . ."[10]

The word "transvalued" is appropriate here in that most of the leaders, with the exception of Manpreet and Jasbir, are careful to not devalue their socio-religious background. Even those leaders who admit to at one time devaluing this background can describe a process where they recognized this as a faulty response and took steps to correct this, as will be discussed below. The concept and process of transvaluation is important since the refusal of the leaders to neither value nor devalue the socio-religious background in the initial stages of their narratives foreshadows the types of nuance they are attempting to give their socio-religious identity in their practices and discourses.

8. Interview with Dinesh, Mar 22, 2010.

9. This is in contrast to Franzosi's "hot chronologies," where days and weeks are expanded upon. Franzosi, "Narrative Analysis."

10. Archer, *Being Human*, 243. Emphasis in original.

Though many of the leaders did not begin or initially elaborate on their socio-religious placements, these were discussed at other times both through their own initiative, and at my prompting. The picture that emerges from this stage of the leaders' lives is one of morphostasis, or general stability—except for Ravi, who had early instability with the death of his father; and Padman, who rarely discussed his early life.[11] Most leaders readily recalled various practices in which they or their parents engaged. Dinesh's father, for example, was a *pandit* (priest) in their Ravidasi community. As a family they regularly attended religious functions for families in the community while his father led the ceremonies and explained the Ravidas and Hindu scriptures. Though the Ravidasis have traditionally been against idol worship, Dinesh's father and community did not adhere to this strictly. Within his family home, for example, were various Hindu idols such as Shiva and Durga that his father directed the family to worship. Dinesh admits that this formed a contradiction, but says, "Among us this thing happens, right? (We are) Ravidasi but we believe in all the gods . . . We have many gods and goddesses here."[12] In Dinesh's family and community the cultural emergent properties (CEPs) of the Ravidas community and teaching were in some ways superseded by those emergent properties of the wider Hindu community, though they became important for Dinesh later in life. In addition, the effect of his father's work, and their belief in gods and offering prayers in community events shaped an early *habitus* for Dinesh which was displayed in a clear way when he and his wife later went through the crisis of two miscarriages and two infant deaths.

Other leaders remember and reflect on similar *habitus*-forming experiences. Though the relative strength of these *habitus*' and their make-up differed slightly from individual to individual, most discussed the practices that they participated in or observed, their importance for expressing their or their families' devotion to Hindu or Sikh deities, and their importance for showing respect to the family. However, though these parts of their narratives gave some indication regarding the shape

---

11. Though there were most certainly various tensions and changes in the early lives of the leaders, none of these, in the retrospective view of the leaders, created morphogenetic changes significant for what eventually transpired in their lives. The relative morphostasis of their early lives gave way to change, however, in the crisis narratives.

12. Interview with Dinesh, Mar 22, 2010.

of the *habitus*, it was in the crisis narratives that the *habitus* as formed during this stage could be more clearly seen.

CRISIS: HABITUS DISTURBANCE

As mentioned above, in their testimonies leaders usually began with or moved quickly to the circumstances of a crisis, whether their own or that of someone close to them. In this crisis stage, most leaders experienced some physical or moral dilemma that their normal resources could not sufficiently solve. The early placement of crisis narratives in the leaders' testimonies reflects the importance of these events to the leaders and provides an interpretive key for what follows.[13]

The crises are particularly important in light of the leaders' later relationship with their Hindu or Sikh communities, and the way in which these communities contributed to or did not help relieve the crises. In many cases the crisis caused the leaders to feel disillusionment with aspects of their Hindu or Sikh beliefs. In addition, though the crises form crucial parts of the narrative trajectory towards Christ, they were often not caused through the introduction of a new religious idea, such as an evangelistic message about Jesus. In the few cases where it was, the narratives often discuss ways in which they had already begun to question or become disassociated from their previous religious beliefs.

I will in this section discuss the various ways in which the crises faced by these leaders interfaced with their Hindu or Sikh beliefs and communities. First, however, it is important to frame the way a theory of *habitus* can help us interpret this phase. The *Yeshu satsang* leaders' crisis narratives all highlight a point of disruption in the course of life events that then led to the adoption of a new course. These disruptions, when viewed through the function of *habitus*, create what Bourdieu called the "hysteresis effect." This concept, taken from the scientific description of the time-lag between magnetic effects and their causes, describes the disruption and change that occurs in peoples' *habitus* when they encounter

---

13. The emphasis is indicated in at least two ways. First, the placement toward the beginning indicates that leaders regard the crisis narratives as highly important in their "narrative strategy." Chase, "Narrative Inquiry," 663. Secondly, the crisis narratives usually formed one of the "hot chronologies" of the overall discourse, where days, events, and characters were described in more expansive detail than other periods of time. The choice of facts, particularly those of the "hot" periods of such narratives often serve a "fundamental ideological function" in the overall discourse. Franzosi, "Narrative Analysis," 530.

a significant change in their social field.[14] When people encounter social conditions different from those in which their *habitus* were originally created, they attempt to respond to the new situation through their old *habitus*. However, because the new situation requires cultural tools not a part of their present *habitus* tool-kit, people experience tension.

This tension, according to Bourdieu's main body of work, causes people to adjust their practices, but rarely causes them to engage in reflexivity. However, as Mesny has discussed, late in his life Bourdieu seemed to acknowledge that increasingly rapid changes of society may cause increased levels of hysteresis and more reflexivity.[15] Talking about Bourdieu's *sens pratique*, or "feel for the game," Mesny summarizes, " . . . it is indeed possible to argue that lay people routinely develop theoretical and reflexive postures in the course of their day-to-day lives which extend far beyond the realm of *sens pratique*."[16]

In addition to raising peoples' levels of reflexivity, I suggest that a crisis and *habitus* disruption initiates a renewed process of evaluation; or what Archer calls a survey of their "ineluctable concerns."[17] According to Archer, as people survey their concerns they prioritize them "in terms of what they care about most."[18] However, Archer does not discuss when such prioritizing occurs, except as a general process resulting in maturation. In light of this discussion, I suggest that such prioritizing, and re-prioritizing, is one of the effects of *habitus* disruption. In this a crisis brings to consciousness the practices that no longer mesh and that instead cause tension with a current situation, prompting a reflexive survey of priorities and the practices that will relieve the tension.

14. Bourdieu, *Outline of a Theory of Practice*, 83; Bourdieu, *The Logic of Practice*: 63. Bourdieu describes it thus, "But the specific efficacy of *habitus* can be clearly seen in all the situations in which it is not the product of the conditions of its actualization (increasingly frequent as societies become differentiated): this is the case when agents formed in a precapitalist economy run up, in some disarray, against the demands of a capitalist cosmos, or when old people quixotically cling to dispositions that are out of place and out of time; or when the dispositions of an agent rising, or falling, in the social structure—a *nouveau riche*, a *parvenu* or a *declasse*—are at odds with the position that agent occupies. Such effects of hysteresis, of a lag in adaptation and counter-adaptive mismatch, can be explained by the relatively persistent, though not entirely unchangeable, character of *habitus*." Bourdieu, *The Social Structures of the Economy*, 214.

15. Mesny, "A View on Bourdieu's Legacy," 66.

16. Ibid.

17. Archer, *Structure, Agency, and the Internal Conversation*, 138.

18. Ibid., 139.

The source of the tension impacts the nature of the reflexivity and the types of practices that are adopted to relieve the tension. Some crises caused direct tension with the peoples' Hindu or Sikh beliefs and practices, while others did not, from their vantage point, create direct conflict with these. I will discuss each of these in turn.

Crises Causing Tension with Religious Beliefs and Practices

Five leaders—Dinesh, Manpreet, Jagdeep, Nandita and Jasbir—experienced crises for which they turned to their Hindu or Sikh beliefs for resolution. However, when the crises persisted they experienced tension with these, prompting a survey of priorities and a change of practices and beliefs. Dinesh, for example, discusses two crises; both involving children. The first occurred following two miscarriages and two infant deaths. In the midst of these he and his wife went to various temples to seek-out healing. When these were obviously not helping to save their children they went to a doctor who told them, "You may never be able to have a child." In response Dinesh became disillusioned with religious practices focused on idols and temples. As he reflexively engaged his situation he says, "We shut the idols inside the room. We put them in a locker. (We said), 'There is no God. This is a lie.' We started thinking like this."[19]

Shortly after this, in 1990 Dinesh joined the Ambedkar mission, an organization named after Dalit politician B. R. Ambedkar, dedicated to promoting Dalit rights. He also joined a new political party, the Bahujan Samaj Party (BSP) that was becoming popular among the Dalit Scheduled Castes, Scheduled Tribes and Other Backwards Castes. Dinesh ran for and was elected to local political office through the BSP which, founded on the teachings of Ambedkar, promoted lower-caste groups and rejected Hindu idol worship. For Dinesh this agreed with the Ravidas teaching that his family was exposed to, but did not follow completely, and also affirmed the disillusionment he felt when Hindu practices and gods did not save their children. The crisis at this point in his life thus prompted Dinesh to reject the temples and the cultural emergent properties of Hindu beliefs while affirming the Ravidas cultural emergent properties of his community. The choice of these agreed with a new (or renewed) set of practices that affirmed a new set of priorities, expressed through the Ambedkar mission and BSP.

19. Interview with Dinesh, Mar 22, 2010.

In 1999, however, he and his wife had a daughter who, when 1 ½ years old, developed a kidney disease and was subsequently hospitalized. When Dinesh's lack of finances precluded more advanced care, a new crisis situation ensued. He began to drink alcohol and fell despondent when, one day, he met a local pastor who offered to pray for Dinesh and his family. After three months his daughter was completely healed, and they began attending the pastor's church, became followers of Christ, and experienced a turn-around in their lives.

In addition to Dinesh, Manpreet, Jagdeep, Nandita, Jasbir and Ravi experienced crises that they in various ways associated with their religious beliefs. In each case their religious practices and beliefs were, in their estimation, unable to relieve the tension they were experiencing, thus causing them to distance themselves from those beliefs. In each of these cases the crisis was a key point where their religious *habitus* was brought along the continuum towards greater and greater levels of reflexivity. In Dinesh's case, he and his wife moved increasingly away from one set of religious practices (*habitus* resources) with which they were familiar. They eventually discarded these in favor of a set of practices (affirming Dalit activism) that eased a level of tension. The second crisis, formed around their sick daughter and their inability to pay for higher levels of medical care, caused another crisis, and again raised to consciousness the inadequacy of their present practices.

The narratives of Dinesh and the other leaders in this category illustrate a crisis that was in some ways attributed to or associated with the person's religious beliefs. One of the strategies that people can and sometimes do adopt, as in Dinesh's case, is to reflect on the practices of their religious *habitus* and modify these in ways that make them more receptive to the beliefs and practices presented by a follower of Christ.[20]

20. This is not unlike a process noted by Andrew Walls where some who convert from one religion to another often move through an "agnostic" phase. As Walls says, when people and societies face various environmental, religious, or other changes, they "may enter a period of disillusionment and re-evaluation which might be described in religious terms as agnosticism." Walls asserts that this may be an "essential precondition" for major religious change. Walls, The Missionary Movement in Christian History, 126.

Crises Not Directly Causing Tension with Religious Beliefs and Practices

Whereas crises caused these leaders to experience tension with their Hindu or Sikh beliefs and practices, other leaders, from their present vantage point, do not narrate any tension with their Hindu or Sikh beliefs or practices. That is, though they experienced physical, moral and spiritual crises and were eventually prompted to survey new priorities presented by the gospel, these leaders did not narrate a direct turning away or separation from their Hindu or Sikh beliefs. Though all later separated themselves from Hindu/Sikh beliefs and practices through the discipleship of a church or organization, they do not presently frame Hindu/Sikh beliefs, practices or community as deficient; only that Christ and the gospel was that which provided the solution to their crisis.

For Navdeep, for example, the first crisis was a life-threatening injury sustained while he was in the police service, and the second a gradual economic and emotional slide that damaged his relationship with his wife, family and community. A theme prominent throughout Navdeep's crisis narrative is the injustice that he faced and the shame he experienced in relation to his family and a community system that he valued. Of significance, and in contrast to those leaders' story in the above section, the breaks are not attributed to "Sikhs" or Sikh beliefs, nor did they result in him distancing himself from Sikh practices right away. Rather, they came from others who have corrupt motives, from his own vices such as bribery, drinking, and bad company, and from a spiritual attack. These things were, in his later estimation, like a punishment from God. In reflection he says, "In Romans Chapter 1, when we know God and we did not give him glory for that which he is worthy, God handed us over to our own minds. And that bad wisdom came into me. And [because of that] I lost everything" [P].[21]

In addition to Navdeep, Padman also experienced a crisis that he did not directly attribute to his Hindu beliefs. When his only child became sick Padman and his wife went to medical experts and then various Hindu temples and Muslim *pirs*. At this time Padman met Indian missionaries whose lifestyles and concern for the poor deeply impressed him. He also worked for a Christian hospital as a physician where he had numerous conversations with a foreign missionary team whose teachings and lifestyles again impressed him. When medicine, temples and shrines

21. Interview with Navdeep, Mar 2, 2010.

did not heal their daughter, Padman and his wife took her to a local pastor for prayer. She was subsequently healed and Padman continued attending his church.

Unique among the *Yeshu satsang* leaders, Gaurav frames his crisis as related to the introduction of Christian beliefs through others. However, even in this, Gaurav indicates that he had already begun distancing himself from his religious community's beliefs. Even before he encountered people talking about Christian beliefs Gaurav had a "rebellious nature" that caused him to follow Marxism and to travel with Marxist drama and poetry groups. One night, however, he had a bad dream where, he says, "I was dying and going to some dark hole somewhere."[22] The dream sufficiently caught his attention and reflected a growing dis-ease with his current commitments.

Concurrently he met some foreign missionaries who began to share about Jesus. Interested in practicing his English, and enjoying the chance to debate foreigners, Gaurav began to meet and offer counter-arguments based on his Hindu beliefs. Throughout this time Gaurav grew more and more interested in Jesus, but was reluctant to fully embrace Christian beliefs. However, Gaurav experienced a turning point one evening while on a train. Afraid that someone would steal his luggage, Gaurav prayed to Shiva, Krishna and Jesus, saying, "Whoever [is] the God, take care of my luggage" [E]. In his sleep he saw a dramatic vision of Jesus and a voice that told him, "This is my son. Follow him." When he woke up and found his luggage was still safe, he says, "I personally ask the Lord [to] forgive me. 'Cleanse me from my sin, all the idol worship, everything. I follow you'" [E].[23]

Through his narrative Gaurav portrays a period of time where he disassociated himself to a certain degree from some Hindu beliefs through his embrace of Marxism. However, the dreams of a black hole began to disrupt him and cause him to start re-evaluating priorities. Even though his Hindu beliefs and practices were less important, they still came to the forefront when faced with Christian teachings. The introduction of these teachings created a crisis of belief that caused Gaurav to examine and call into question beliefs and practices that had previously formed an appropriate *habitus*. The process of doing so formed a crisis, necessitating a re-evaluation of available responses. The experience of a

22. Interview with Gaurav, Mar 6, 2010.

23. Ibid.

dream and miracle then confirmed to Gaurav that Jesus was the right and appropriate direction through which to resolve the tension. Of interest is that, though Gaurav narrates a contrast between and a degree of separation from his Hindu beliefs, he is careful to narrate that he still viewed himself as a Hindu throughout this time.

Similar to Dinesh and leaders like him, the crises encountered by Naveen, Navdeep, Padman and Gaurav helped them listen to people who prayed for and told them about Jesus; and eventually leading them to become followers of Jesus. In contrast to Dinesh and others, however, the leaders of this section did not directly fault their Sikh/Hindu practices and communities. Thus, in social terms, the crises that these leaders encountered again created a hysteresis effect in their *habitus*, though one not directly attributed to the Sikh/Hindu communities and practices. As will be seen below, this has important implications for how they later relate to their Sikh and Hindu practices and identity.

CRISIS RESOLUTION: TURNING TO CHRIST

The next stage of the narratives, already alluded to above, involved the process in which the crisis was eventually resolved through commitment to Christ and the initial involvement in local Christian churches. From a narrative perspective, at this stage an important feature is noticeable in most of the leaders' testimonies. Whereas the leaders often speak about and acknowledge the role of others in introducing them to Jesus, many strongly affirm God's action in combination with their own agency in making the final choice for Christ. Gaurav demonstrates this in his testimony when he describes the way his friends wrongly interpreted his initial "confession." He says, "But . . . they did not know. They thought, 'This guy truly believes.' And that's the thing, you know? Just confess prayer doesn't help believing in Christ. They haven't seen my heart. Because they asked me to pray, I prayed with them. So they believed that I believed in Christ" [E].[24]

Despite the prayers and activities of his friends, it was only when Gaurav experienced the dream described above that he made a "true" commitment to Christ. Thus, Gaurav and the other leaders[25] find it im-

24. Ibid.

25. This is particularly strong for Gaurav who in his discourses is often concerned to demonstrate his relationship with but independence from foreign missionaries. In addition, however, Ravi demonstrates his agency through his decision to more fully follow Christ following a miraculous reunion with displaced family members.

portant to, as Archer says, demonstrate that they themselves surveyed the practices and beliefs available to them and made choices that reflected their own concerns, and that provided a resolution to the crises they were facing.

The other feature of this stage of the testimonies is their Christocentric nature. Each leader identified particular encounters with Jesus, either through dreams, miracles, or deeply personal reflections that emphasized a combination of Jesus' power and imminence. It was this experience that prompted or affirmed a change of religious practices. Nandita, for example, experienced a dream one night after her parents told her that they wanted to pray with a pastor to Jesus for her mother's healing. Nandita was wary of this because she had heard in college that Christian pastors "want to make us Christian." However, she had also been vexed with the question, Who is God and why does he not answer? Because of this, before going to sleep she prayed, "If you are God I want to see you and I want to talk with you. Because so many times I, I call to gurus, I call to God but nobody talks with me. But I want to talk with you and I want to see you" [E].[26] That night she had a dream in which a person came down out of the sky in the midst of lightening. She says,

> He came, uh, he sat outside. Jesus sat outside. And when he sit, I sit down. And I ask, "Who are you?" And he said, "I am Jesus. I am God, uh, which you are searching." And I said, "Okay. Uh, so, Jesus, how [did] you made, uh, stars and moons?" I ask the question. So, he laughed. [laughs]. And, uh, afterwards what happened, uh, my mother [was] also sitting there and, uh, he prayed for my mother and said, "One day I will remove the satanic power from you. One day." [E] (Interview with Nandita, Jan 29, 2010)

The deeply personal experience with the person of Jesus gave Nandita, as it did for other leaders, a focal point from which to consider new practices. As I will describe more fully below, the practices that they considered were usually chosen from those that had been presented to them by the friends or pastors with whom they interacted. One practice

---

Navdeep discusses the caring attention and teaching he received from a pastor but then talks about his decision to enter a three-month time of isolation where he studied the scriptures and prayed alone. Naveen talks about the financially difficult decision he made to follow Christ and not sing at parties any longer. Shortly after this a series of miracles and music-ministry opportunities provided money for he and his family.

26. Interview with Nandita, Jan 29, 2010.

that some people immediately engaged was prayer (often for forgiveness), as well as Bible study. In addition, an overall practice engaged in by everyone was immediate attendance of a church or various churches. I will elaborate on the nature and impact of this phase on the lives of these leaders in the following section. Here, though, I emphasize that in each case the practices, and particularly the practice of attending a local church and becoming part of a Christian community, was one presented to them by Christians who were with them during or right after the crises. As such, the Christians played an important role in suggesting new practices that would alleviate the tension and *habitus* hysteresis that these people experienced.

EMBRACING CHRISTIAN BELIEF AND COMMUNITY

Prior to their commitments to Jesus, many of the *Yeshu satsang* leaders had negative impressions of Christians and Christian churches. For example, Navdeep describes the impressions he had of local Christians in and around his village, saying:

> I had bitterness towards them [Christians]. [A pastor], whose village we were talking about, the Christians of that village were very bad. There was no preaching on Christianity at that time. They used to drink liquor and sing and dance and shout on Christmas. And, I mean, we saw only those things. And this was the reason to be bitter about Christianity . . . I mean, those who were Christians, they were very low in the sight of other people because of their deeds. Because they did not have any [credible] reputation. [P][27]

Importantly, while the leaders had negative feelings for the Christian community, their feelings toward Jesus were more benign, allowing for more openness to approach Jesus as a solution to the crises that they faced. As each leader approached pastors or other Christians for prayer, or as mediators to Jesus, they experienced Jesus' power in their lives and a

---

27. Interview with Navdeep, Mar 2, 2010. Padman shares a similar impression of Christians, saying, "My perception about the Christian people was that they . . . eat drink and be merry [and] wear less clothes. And all these villains in our movies wearing cross and all these, uh, night girls, eh? [laughs]. Wearing cross and, and uh, these bar girls and they used to wear clothes . . . This was, this was my perception, really, about Christianity. Because, because I have seen the wearing-cross girls naked and, and dancing and enjoying. So I thought this was their religion" [E]. Interview with Padman, Apr 19, 2010.

‚resolution to their situation. However, because the experience was mediated through Christians and Christian practices (primarily of prayer, but sometimes also in the context of a worship service), the *Yeshu satsang* leaders began a process of "transvaluing" their past emotional commentaries regarding the Christian community, supplementing and supplanting these with new understandings based on their new experiences.

As they embraced new socio-religious beliefs, and practices shaped by these beliefs, an Emergentist process can be detected. First, the leaders initiated a new morphogenetic process. As discussed above, the processes that normally occurred within their Hindu/Sikh communities often produced morphostasis and the outcome of which affirms the social roles, beliefs and structures in such communities. With the introduction of Christian beliefs and practices, however, a new process was initiated that had morphogenetic outcomes. In particular, they experienced new CEPs in the form of teachings and interpretations of God's work in the context of a new structure, the Christian church. The second process that can be seen through the narratives of the leaders was the establishment of new pentecostal practices that *Yeshu satsang* leaders continue to use in ways that suggest a type of *habitus*. I will discuss these two processes in turn.

The New Morphogenesis and Situational Logics

As the *Yeshu satsang* leaders began embracing various Christian beliefs and practices, particularly reading the Bible and attending Christian churches, they encountered various challenges from their families and surrounding communities. These encounters represent the morphogenetic processes that were occurring as they sought to engage the systems of Christian beliefs and practices, Christian social community, and their own Hindu/Sikh beliefs and structure. As a result certain situational logics began to surface, with many acknowledging the presence of a type of constraining contradiction—where one idea invokes another contradictory idea. The tensions that they felt were initially constrained through the presence of, and desire to maintain, a cohesive socio-cultural context.

As one example, Jasbir's narrative regarding the first year of following Christ demonstrates the presence of a constraining contradiction. Aware that his embrace of Christ was directly opposed to his father's will, Jasbir hid the fact that he was meeting with a pastor for discipleship and reading Christian literature. In addition, through this process and the teaching of his pastor, he became increasingly uncomfortable with Sikh practices, particularly attending the *gurdwara*. Though his father had observed him reading Christian literature, he thought, "it is just reading." However, when Jasbir began refusing to attend the *gurdwara*, the social situation began to shift. He recounts:

> Jasbir (J): I never told my father [about faith in Jesus]. My father happened to know it.
>
> Darren: How did he find out?
>
> J: Actually what happened was that uh, this *gurdwara* thing was always prevalent in our family. So, I kind of started finding ways of not going to *gurdwara*. I didn't want to offend my dad but I at the same time didn't want to go to *gurdwara*. And, uh, I knew its idol worshipping. So I didn't want to be a partaker of that. But I did go to *gurdwara* many times. But then I didn't want to bow before that book. And then that was another struggle. So then one day my grandmother said, "Can you take me to my sister's home?" . . . .So I took my grandmother to her home. But on the way was this *gurdwara* which our family had been. So she wanted to go to *gurdwara*. I said, "Okay, please go." She said, "Oh you come." I said, "I don't want to come. You go." Then she got so upset. And she went and talked with my dad. She said, "Oh what has crossed the head. He doesn't want to go to *gurdwara*. Means, he's out of our clutches." So then my father happened to know that I had become a follower of Jesus. [E][28]

For Jasbir and his family the constraining contradiction began to develop that said that following Jesus contradicted the socio-religious practices of his family. This was emphasized by his pastor, about whom Jasbir explains:

> Jasbir (J): He, I think he never knew much about Sikhism. So, what he usually talked was about moral issues and stuff like that. So, I used to ask him questions. So, I always had questions. But he wanted me to get rid of Sikhism completely. And uh, he wanted me to embrace the Christian world . . . [for instance] he saw, okay, I'm wearing the [Sikh] bracelet. He said, "Oh, this, my friend . . . has put it in the toilet and he uses it to pull the toilet chain." And . . . he would talk about some other things. He would mock Sikhism things. And embracing the Christian world he would say, "Oh you are supposed to be member of one church. You are supposed to be . . . you are supposed to pay your

28. Interview with Jasbir, May 20, 2010.

tithes here and you are supposed to come under the banner of this particular church." And he always taught churchianity more that Christianity.

Darren: Hmm. How did you feel about that?

J: I was VERY uncomfortable. I asked him very hard questions and he always get, got [angry] from the pulpit. My father never allowed me to come to church on Sundays because Sunday was a holiday. So I just cannot come to church. So . . . my pastor used to persuade me, used to just get hard on me to come to church. He thought if a Christian does not come to church on Sunday that means he's not a Christian. [E][29]

Other leaders experienced similar constraining contradictions. Over a period of time, however, the constraining contradiction gave way to a competitive contradiction. This was in most cases built-in from the beginning of their interaction with churches and church leaders. Though some attempted to maintain a level of relationship with their families, the contradiction in religious beliefs and practices moved them to embrace the separate community of the Christian church.

As discussed in Chapters 2 and 4, in its starkest form the situational logic of the competitive contradiction is elimination. In this the different socio-cultural communities battle each other for the supremacy of their own beliefs and for the elimination of the contrasting beliefs, if not the community that holds to it. Normally, however, the actual outcome is a form of "ideational pluralism," or sustained differentiation. This was the situational logic that emerged from the historic interplay between missionary Christianity and the regional religious communities. The same logic was mirrored in the lives of the *Yeshu satsang* leaders, to varying degrees. Most often, in order to "sustain" the differentiation, the new believers separated from their families and communities.

Jasbir, for example, left his family and began to stay with various pastors and churches. Padman, after being thrown out from his family home, moved to a nearby city and had minimal connections with his family.[30] Others, such as Nandita and Manpreet, started following Christ

---

29. Ibid.

30. Gaurav is unique among the *Yeshu satsang* leaders in this regard. In his case, when he received criticism from a local priest and from an uncle, Gaurav's father defended his choice to follow Jesus, saying, "He's not doing anything wrong. He's following God. Hinduism believes all gods are same so what is wrong he is doing? He has not changed his religion" [E]. Ibid.

at about the same time as other members of their immediate family, and thus experienced a competitive contradiction as a group in relation to their wider family and community.

Nandita, for example, says she and her parents soon received criticism from their relatives for going to a church and following Jesus and the impact this would have on Nandita's marriage prospects. According to Nandita they said, "Where are you going? How you will get married? They are, they are low-caste people who are, uh, accepting Lord. And, uh, it's a very bad thing . . . It's a foreign, foreign religion. Uh, you are, you are becoming a Christian . . . You are doing wrong things" [E].[31] The result of this tension was a distancing of relations between Nandita's family and her community. When her grandfather died, for example, her family invited the other Jatt Sikh families of the community to attend the memorial service that they hosted in their home. Though some came, others were reticent to come because of the possible Christian content of the service. Thus a competitive contradiction emerged with a situational logic of pluralistic beliefs and a difference sustained by a social split.

For Navdeep, while he found a meaningful role and identity within the Christian organization and church, tensions began to develop between he and parts of the Sikh community, represented by his village and his father-in-law. Before his problems, Navdeep had regularly practiced Sikh rituals, and his father had made him a "religious kind of person" by teaching him to recite the Sikh morning and evening prayers. However, the ministry that he joined following his conversion spoke harshly about Sikhism. He began to emulate the approach of his leaders, causing tension within his local village. The tension with the village was, in his later reflection, the main reason why he became open to a Sikh-style *Yeshu satsang*. He describes an early confrontation he had with Sikhs in his village and his initial response:

> In the beginning [the Sikh villagers] tried to stop the church from running saying, "There is no Christian in this village." They put pressure [on us]. Then the thing was that my behavior was not good. I also stood against them. Because of that I preached with more anger. I even started speaking lots of other things. They were saying, "This is the Guru of the English people." Then I spoke in anger, "You like foreigner's ties. You imitate, wearing coat and pant in their style. You like the foreigner's dollars but you don't like their Guru." I mean, my words were in anger. And

31. Interview with Nandita, Jan 29, 2010.

when I was preaching, I used to say, "You like their [foreigner's] standard. You feel proud to send your sons and daughters in the foreign [place] for study but this foreign Guru creates pain in your stomach." And, I mean, this is how [because of my preaching] they opposed me . . . And now, I came to know that what I was doing in those days was wrong. [P][32]

The bold approach of he and his organization also caused increased tension with his father-in-law, who was a leader in one of the Sikh political parties of the region. This was exacerbated on one occasion when his pastor, on being asked to speak at a rally hosted by Navdeep's father-in-law, publicly and strongly disagreed with the father-in-law, causing deep offense. Such experiences served to further create a competitive contradiction between Navdeep and his Sikh family.

Though not all *Yeshu satsang* leaders experienced constraining contradictions in the same ways, or to the same degree, each became more and more aware of the contradictions that their new faith in Jesus and association with Christian churches posed in the wider social context of northwest India. I will return to this awareness and the eventual responses to this contradiction when I discuss the next phase. First, though, I will discuss the impact of Christian and pentecostal practices in the early discipleship of the *Yeshu satsang* leaders.

The New Christian and Pentecostal Practices

While the beliefs and practices of the Christian churches initiated new morphogenetic processes and situational logics in the social milieu of the leaders, the leaders also began to be socialized into the church's practices. Some of these were Other to their culture, but were eventually accepted. Jasbir, for example, talks about replicating what he was taught by south Indian pastors, saying,

> Jasbir (J): What I did, I saw my pastor doing. Shouting "hallelujah" for giving a punch. So, I was knowing all that stuff. [But] I think things need to change. We have a bad DNA somewhere.
>
> Darren: Bad DNA?
>
> J: Yeah, I would say. I can dare that to say. Because south Indians came to north India. They spoke in a different . . . way, because they didn't KNOW the language. So they, they just

32. Interview with Navdeep, Mar 2, 2010.

> came to Punjab and they said, "Ah, *khuda hai*" [in south India accent]. And we started saying, "*khuda hai*" [repeating same accent]. "Praise the Lord, praise the Lord." Even if you meet an illiterate people (Christian) in a village in Gurdaspur, he knows what "praise the Lord" is all about. But, does a Sikh knows what "praise the Lord" is? He doesn't know anything. He doesn't know the ABC of "praise the Lord," "hallelujah." [E].[33]

The practices of saying or shouting "hallelujah" are often coupled with emphases on healing and deliverance of evil spirits. Though people and leaders from many different Sikh, Hindu and related groups value miraculous healing and promote practices designed to elicit healing, the Christian churches of the northwest have distinct pentecostal healing practices derived, directly or indirectly, from south Indian and foreign missionaries. The experiences of healing were, as seen above, very instrumental in relieving the crises that several of the *Yeshu satsang* leaders initially faced. In addition to helping them come to Jesus, however, experiences of healing and deliverance, and the practices associated with these, continued to be important in their ongoing discipleship and the beginning of their own ministries.

Around 2003, for example, Dinesh experienced conflict with the pastor and other Christian leaders in the area when they started to say hurtful things about Dinesh. Through the prompting of a dream, Dinesh left the church and began his own house church. It was also around this time that he received his "God-gift" of healing. Dinesh explains the night that he received this gift:

> So at that time [one woman] was about to die. She was from the Radha Soami [Hindu *bhakti* sect]. Those people said [to me], "Pray at our home for her to get healed." . . . I received the anointing of the Holy Spirit there. It was the first God-gift [E] that I received. And when I received the Holy Spirit I was shouting out loud. I did not know [what this was], and the whole community gathered at her home [asking], "What is happening here?" I was unable to control myself. I was feeling as if I have been lifted up from that home . . . After that I saw that that lady got completely healed. She is still, she is still (healed). [H][34]

Dinesh continued to use his gift of healing, and people continued to come to him for healing in their own lives.

33. Interview with Jasbir, May 20, 2010.

34. Interview with Dinesh, Mar 22, 2010.

As another example, Navdeep describes the way he first experienced his sister and brother-in-law's pentecostal church, which he would continue to attend and in which he would be discipled. He explains:

> Then [my brother-in-law] started taking me to the church. My sister had taken baptism. And the atmosphere of that church was this, that they, I mean, they did not do slow worship. They used to do worship with a lot of excitement. Uh, when I went for the first time, I wore a turban on my head. And I was feeling very embarrassed about this. It seemed to me that everybody was looking at me though, I mean, in fact it was nothing like that. And my sister, she was clapping like this. I asked her, "What are you doing?" She said, "You will not understand now. This is the Holy Spirit." I told her, "If you have to do this then you are creating a scene!" [P][35]

Despite his initial confusion, Navdeep continued to attend the church, even cutting his hair and removing his turban to be similar to the Christians. The pastor, he reflects, had the gift of healing but did not give very clear teaching. After some months he was introduced to another pastor whose preaching was "full of passion" and who also had the gift healing. Through his influence Navdeep began taking steps to preach and to pray for healing for others. Similar to his pastor, Navdeep sometimes had people apply oil to their forehead in the midst of prayer. Through his prayers various people experienced healing.

The experience and gift of healing, often coupled with an emphasis on the Holy Spirit and prayer, were important aspects of most *Yeshu satsang* leader testimonies. As was illustrated above, these narratives often provided substantiation for the presence and favor of God on their lives and their new ministries, and an affirmation regarding the new priorities they were beginning to survey and adopt. In addition, the pentecostal speech practices and the miracles that were a part of the Christian church settings where such practices were performed, over the course of time, began to shape a new *habitus* regarding the appropriate ways to invoke the power of God in corporate settings.

Ironically, while miraculous power and its associated practices were important for these leaders and their growing church ministries, the practices added to the competitive contradiction that their church communities faced in relation to the wider Hindu and Sikh communities. The foreignness, or Other, of the practices not only created further tension in

35. Interview with Navdeep, Mar 3, 2010.

some cases, but also impacted the church's relationship with and ability to evangelize particular parts of the Hindu/Sikh communities. The implications of the situational logic in which the leaders found themselves immersed set the stage for an eventual re-evaluation of aspects of the Christian church approach.

YESHU SATSANGS: ATTEMPTING A DIFFERENT SITUATIONAL LOGIC

In the last and most recent stage narrated in these leaders' testimonies, the *Yeshu satsang* leaders began to question aspects of the Christian community which, when combined with particular influences, led them to re-adopt various Hindu/Sikh practices. In most cases the main influence, direct or indirect, were seminars that various Christian ministries began to host from 2005 onwards. Included in these seminars were teachings on "contextualization" which provided the leaders models and rationale for implementing new practices and changing the ecclesial identities of their gatherings.

Prior to this, as I mentioned in the above section on embracing Christian beliefs and community, many of the leaders had begun questioning the Otherness of their faith and ecclesial identities. The competitive contradiction that this Otherness had created had two different but inter-related effects on the leaders. One was a sense that the churches they were forming were foreign or Other, and in various ways not authentic expressions of them and their communities. The other was the sense that the competitive contradiction created by the sense of Otherness was hindering some Hindus and Sikhs, particularly from higher castes, from becoming followers of Christ. Most leaders were sensitive to both of these, though emphasizing one more than another.

For Navdeep and Naveen, the sense of Otherness and the competitive contradiction, though felt, was not questioned until their leader, Pastor Sandeep Singh, started to talk to them about his new ideas for a Sikh *Yeshu satsang*. Navdeep began working with Pastor Sandeep Singh around 2004, conducting ministry in a style similar to the other pentecostal churches that he had worked with. However, around 2005 Pastor Sandeep attended a Christian conference on contextualization. Though the main focus of the conference was on Hindu *Yeshu satsangs*, the ideas and approach resonated with those that Pastor Sandeep had already been considering. After this he made a major change in his approach towards a Sikh-style *satsang*. Navdeep at first was not convinced of this approach, but slowly became convinced through discussions with Sandeep. Gradually he accepted that a change of approach and style was necessary.

At that time Sandeep and he went to visit Navdeep's father-in-law who had become bitter towards Christianity as Navdeep was practicing it. However, when Navdeep and Sandeep conducted a Sikh-style *Yeshu satsang* for the family, he and others in the family started changing their minds about Navdeep. Now, says Navdeep, "There is no wrong question in their minds" regarding what he does. In fact, he has now gained his father-in-law's respect.

While valuing the relationship that the *satsang* style has again given him with his family and Sikh community, Navdeep also values the evangelistic potential of the approach. The main aim of the various practices, he says, is to be able to "preach among the Sikhs." The "Sikhs" that Navdeep references, according to he and Pastor Sandeep, is specifically the upper-caste Jatt Sikh community. Thus, the *satsang* style has provided Navdeep with a renewed connection to his own lower-caste Majhabi Sikh community, as well as an evangelistic approach with which to reach out to the Jatt Sikh community.

In his discussion, Naveen tends to more strongly emphasize the evangelistic potential of the *Yeshu satsang*. Naveen, as will be recalled, was also serving Pastor Sandeep's churches when the latter made a shift towards a Sikh *Yeshu satsang*. Naveen recalls that, once Pastor Sandeep explained the new approach in terms of evangelism, he saw the logic of it and embraced it. He recounted:

> Naveen (N): He taught us all these things [about Sikh contextualization] in a very good manner. That we are living with those [Jatt Sikh] people, right? We have repented. And we are following everything. We are in the light now. Now who will bring those who are not in the light into the light? Let's make such a system that those people also could come in the light. As earlier in Punjabi there was a notion that these foreigners convert [peoples'] religion. He gave us so many reasons to stop this notion. And he started here after making us understand lots of things . . . . I feel now as if I was, I mean, very backward [thinking]. And now I came into my sense. Now, I mean, I feel good.
>
> Darren: What does "backward" mean?
>
> N: Yes, yes. We used to say "hallelujah," "amen" with great passion at that time. Though Sikhs came to . . . the *bandagi*

> [Christian prayer meeting] and even repented and did every-
> thing, still 2–4 months later they again used to go back [away
> from the *satsang*]. But [Sandeep Singh] shared that truly follow-
> ing Christ means that the Sikh, the real Sikh, would also do what
> Christ has said in weddings and marriages and all. And now we
> have understood that [till then] the Sikhs have not been told
> how to follow Christ [in their community]. [P][36]

At the same time, Naveen talks about the disjuncture that the
church members felt in terms of identity. He explains, "We used to tell
[Sikhs], 'Repent and take baptism.' Then about 'hallelujah.' Then we used
to say 'amen.' And they became happy for some time. They also used to
get saved. But when they went outside and said our language, 'hallelujah,
amen,' [others said], 'They make Muslims.' Some say, 'They make foreigners'" [P].[37] The ecclesial identity, in the eyes of the wider Sikh community,
was an Other that did not agree with what the leaders desired.

Similar to Navdeep and Naveen, Ravi embraced a *Yeshu satsang* style
after receiving teaching on it. In his case, while receiving training from
his mission organization, Ravi heard teaching explaining the evangelistic
need for contextualization. As he listened, he says, he realized:

> The message that came here [to northwest India] did not come
> in this culture but [the missionaries] brought the other culture
> here. If south Indians came they presented Jesus in a totally
> south Indian style. The north has not understood this: Out of 10
> people only one person was able to grasp it. The remaining 9 just
> stay like that. Then slowly I understood, and I started looking
> from a cultural point of view. [H][38]

As was discussed above, some *Yeshu satsang* leaders, while emphasizing the community relationships and the evangelism that the *Yeshu
satsangs* create, also suggest that the use of the *satsang* practices may be
temporary. Dinesh, for example, first discusses both the way the *satsang*
style has reconnected him with his parents and Hindu community, while
also clearly stating that he sees this style as instrumental for outreach. After his decision to follow Christ, Dinesh began to experience conflict with
his family in part because of some of the church teachings and practices
he and his wife had adopted. One such example regarded the *bindi*, which

36. Interview with Naveen, Mar 3, 2010.

37. Ibid.

38. Interview with Ravi, Jun 24, 2010.

Dinesh's wife stopped wearing.[39] As a result of the changes in Dinesh and his wife, his family stayed separate from them for three years. In addition, the neighbors began to voice their disapproval with the loud "hallelujah-style" worship that would come from Dinesh's house during his church services.

In response Dinesh took two steps. First he began to study Hindu scriptures, making a comparative study to know, as he says, "Am I coming to the right road or the wrong road?" In addition, however, Dinesh wanted to know how to "teach the people" and his family regarding the comparative truths of Christianity. This step seemed to instill two values in Dinesh. On the one hand, it strengthened his conviction regarding the superiority of Christianity over-and-against Hindu beliefs. In addition, however, Dinesh also found "truths" in the Hindu scriptures that agreed with the truths of the Bible.

Dinesh took a second step around 2007 when he came into contact with Gaurav and his teachings on *satsang* style ministry. At this time Dinesh studied the Bible on the subject and found, "Nowhere was it written, 'Do not put a bindi on (your forehead). Do not do this do not do that.' It is not written anywhere" [H].[40] Through this Dinesh altered his teaching on Hindu religious practices, such as allowing women to wear the bindi and not requiring *satsangis* to stop idol worship immediately. He also made changes to his church service, calling it a *Yeshu satsang*, adopting Hindu symbols, speech practices and *bhajans*.

One of the results of these changes was a positive response from his family and the local Hindu community. His father felt that now he was going "in the right way," and some of his family members became followers of Christ. Local Hindus too were in favor the difference in worship style and identity, advising Dinesh to "stay away from the Christians."

However, while Dinesh reflects positively on the ways in which the *satsang* style has helped to reconnect him to his Hindu family and community, he also maintains that the style is only really important for a person's first few months as a believer. After a person has been a believer for a period of time, the Hindu symbols should become less important, and could even be done away with. Their importance, Dinesh says, is in

---

39. Culturally wearing a *bindi* is also a sign of marriage, and to not wear a *bindi* often means that the woman's husband has died. Because of this Dinesh's family used to ask, "Who is the one who has died?," causing Dinesh to feel some shame.

40. Interview with Dinesh, Mar 21, 2010.

helping people feel comfortable with the *satsang* gathering, to learn about Jesus, and to become his followers.

As described in Chapter 8, several other leaders display a similar opinion regarding the important-but-temporary nature of their *satsang* practices. Jagdeep retains the Sikh self-ascription and some practices in part to retain his job, which is reserved for lower-caste Sikhs. However, according to Jagdeep, the eventual ideal is for he and his family to become openly "Christian." As he expresses it, "So I cannot declare it openly now. Uh, I think in my future when my children will get married in Christian families automatically we purely become the Christians [smiles broadly]" [E].[41] At the same time, however, Jagdeep is quite clear and committed to the new *Yeshu satsang* style that he and Manpreet have adopted for their group. Through this, he says, "We can win the Sikh people by adopting their habits" [E].[42]

As another example, Nandita highly values the way a Sikh *Yeshu satsang* memorial service for her grandfather decreased barriers between her family and the local Sikh community and the opportunities it provided for people to hear about Christ. She also values the way certain practices in *satsangs* will help Sikhs hear about and become followers of Jesus. However, after a period of time, she says that the believers will learn and use the "other" words spoken by the Christian community, such as "*Parmeshwar*."

Similarly, Padman has adopted the *satsang* style as both a connection point and an evangelistic opportunity in regards to his family and community. As mentioned previously, after the death of his brother Padman was able to more freely go to his family home. As he did so, he says, "I saw all these things and there was lot of [relational] distance going on and [court] cases were going on. People are fighting. So I then start praying [with them]. And then they, they felt, 'Okay, it is a good thing'" [E].[43] His prayers, he says, were simple but in the Christian style that he had previously learned. However, also at this same time Padman attended a

---

41. Interview with Jagdeep, Apr 25, 2010.

42. His wife, Manpreet, also expresses this point of view, saying, "We also need to see Sikh people in heaven. Let's bring them along with us. Then, how can we take them along with us? First we need to reach them. We will reach them. Only then can we share with them, I mean, only when we speak their language. If they don't understand our language they don't come to us. Then how can we take them towards Jesus? How can we help them to walk on his path?" [P]. Interview with Manpreet, Apr 4, 2010.

43. Interview with Padman, Apr 19, 2010.

conference on contextualization hosted by a Christian organization. At that conference he learned about various ways to express the Christian faith in a Hindu community. Following this, in 2008, he developed his Arya Samaj *Yeshu satsang* for his family.

On the one hand, according to Padman, the *satsang* style and practices have helped him reconnect his faith with his family. He can provide spiritual leadership to his family, give them hope through prayer, and begin introducing them to the truths of the Bible and Jesus in a way that is not foreign to them. On the other hand, and similar to Dinesh, Padman views the *satsang* rituals as a temporary necessity to bring people towards faith in Christ. He shares about the change that new believers will encounter as they grow in spiritual maturity:

> Padman (P): After some time hopefully, definitely! It is a must! They will change. It is going to happen!
>
> Darren (D): What is the change, meaning, that they will . . . .
>
> P: Change, meaning, that they, that they will know the real God . . . That once a person is knowing that he's your god, so why he waste his time burning all this firewood and everything? [laughs] . . . .
>
> D: So if your family, by God's grace, all become believers, say in the next 2 years or something, 2–3 years, like this. What would, what would you do different on Sundays?
>
> P: Ah yeah. This fire will go away from in between. Cause, this has no relevancy with our prayer. Then, to sit together we don't need any fire. It is good in Winter season but not in such a hot climate! [laughs]. So by that time hopefully they will realize, but by this uh, uh definitely this will vanish and the real prayer will dawn on some. [laughs]. [E][44]

As this narrative suggests, Padman values the *satsang* practices both for the relationship it creates with his family and community, but also for their utilitarian function of bringing people towards faith in Christ. However, once people have become sufficiently strong in their faith, Padman feels that the practices and symbols will have served their purpose and could be disposed of.

Thus, in the view of Dinesh, Nandita, Jagdeep, Manpreet and Padman, the *satsang* practices help to temporarily ease the competitive

44. Interview with Padman, Apr 19, 2010.

contradiction regarding the feeling of Otherness in following Christ. Such practices, they contend, are important to ease the tension new believers may feel during the initial, vulnerable stages of their journey towards Christ. However, once they have become strong in their faith, the *satsang* practices are no longer important and, having served their purpose, can be put aside or de-emphasized.

This, they express, is a view of the practices from the standpoint of growth in understanding of Jesus. However, when they discuss their own or other *satsangi*'s relationship with their Hindu or Sikh families, the importance is not as temporary. Padman, for example, emphasizes the ongoing cultivation and attention to relationship that is necessary to be a witness among his people. He says, "So, if it is a life-long process, so all my people, and I have to BE in touch with them. It is my duty to visit all my relatives and to pray for them. I can pray! This is, I have been, uh, assigned this duty to, uh, to preach them the word of God. To plant the good news in, into their hearts and to nurture it and to, uh, and to remain there. To look after it" [E].[45] One of the means for maintaining relationship, particularly over the long-term, is to maintain practices that are helpful and communicative to the community. The hope is to create a loving community that is open to Hindus and, in the course of time, that minister's Christ's love to them.

Whether temporary or ongoing, the common theme between the *Yeshu satsang* leaders has been the desire to address the competitive contradiction created by their former ecclesial identity. In order to do so, as discussed in previous chapters, the leaders have surveyed various practices that matched with their concerns to help form a new ecclesial identity and a modus vivendi.

ONGOING HABITUS

Chapter 8 highlighted some of the pentecostal practices of miraculous power that some *Yeshu satsangis* and leaders continue to use. Most leaders have retained a strong emphasis on the miraculous power of God, reflecting their own experiences of healing and miracles during the early years of their commitment to Christ. Five leaders have explicitly retained in their *satsang* services associated practices that they learned during these years, and two leaders have relegated such practices to prayer

45. Ibid.

meetings outside of the *satsang*.[46] I was at first baffled by the presence of these practices. Most leaders indicated, as seen above, that they have modified the practices so as to make them less Other, and tried to counsel *satsangis* to refrain from the practices often associated with pentecostal churches, such as shouting "hallelujah." Why, in light of their desire to resist practices seen as Christian and their attempt to avoid a competitive contradiction, were they retaining or allowing certain practices of miraculous power, including those reflecting a pentecostal influence or origin?

First, in the course of interviews and discussions it became apparent that these practices were often not used in a particularly reflexive way. For example, when asked about such practices, *satsangis* indicated that they used these because it "felt right." As such, the practices often operate on the agency continuum at the level of a *habitus*. Second, interviews indicated that the *habitus* of these practices were linked not only to pentecostal church experiences, as I initially thought because of the associations with those churches, but also to practices from the peoples' Hindu or Sikh communities. In other words, on the one hand the particular form of practice reflects those that the *satsangis* reflexively surveyed in the midst and wake of the crises leading them to Christ or that they learned to value and practice in the early days of their Christian discipleship. In addition, however, such practices resonated with, and were also in various ways connected with the general repertoire of healing practices used by various religious authorities and centers in their contexts.

Regarding the latter, and when looking at the wider traditions of healing in India, it is apparent that the very emphasis on healing itself reflects an openness to and experience with those longstanding traditions. Despite the prevalence of western medicinal practices and resources, people continue to turn to alternative methods for healing, many of which have alleged roots in various ayurvedic, vedic, and local shamanic

---

46. Only one leader, Padman, does not retain any noticeable Christian or pentecostal practices. This is because, as has been discussed, no *satsangis* are yet followers of Jesus and have not attended churches. In addition to this, Padman very clearly resists practices associated with Christian social structures, reflecting a strong transition and reflexive process that Padman himself engaged around the time of his brother's death regarding the ways in which he had come to worship, pray and express his faith in Jesus. This process culminated following the seminar that he attended on contextualization, after which Padman began to resist Christian practices that were creating a competitive contradiction in relation to his family and to instead incorporate and redefine Arya Samaji practices in the context of a *Yeshu satsang*.

traditions and practices.[47] In addition, though these traditions sometimes highlight certain practices, it is the healing practitioners themselves, whether *jadugars* (shamans), gurus, or pastors, to which people give particular attention. This, as Sudhir Kakar has discussed in his survey of Indian healing traditions, reflects a general tendency for people to go to those whom they have heard have power and abilities for healing. As he states, "The belief that it is the person of the healer and not his conceptual system or his particular techniques that are of decisive importance for the healing process is also an unquestioned article of faith for most Indian patients."[48]

Because people readily long for healing and go to those leaders that purportedly can offer it, various Hindu, Sikh and Christian leaders often use healing powers to gain a hearing and to influence devotees towards their philosophy. Kakar, for example, studied various Indian gurus and their healing practices and found that most people that became devotees of particular gurus did so at least in part because of the promise of healing. Though such healing practices were not central to the teaching of the gurus, Kakar summarizes, "The gurus themselves would look at healing of sickness as a necessary bait for their proper task of leading a person towards self-realization."[49] Thus it is common for people to go to gurus for healing and subsequently become devoted and connected to them and their specific teachings. Similarly, the *Yeshu satsang* leaders' own experience of and implementation of healing practices reflects an underlying logic, a *habitus*, regarding the way healing practices can be used to gain peoples' attention and allegiance.

As previously discussed, for example, Dinesh continues to make healing prayer and associated practices a central theme in his prayers and ministry among their *satsangis*. As his testimony reveals, he and his wife sought out healing from all the people that were available to them before receiving prayer from a Christian pastor. Belief in healing power and rituals was thus an important component of Dinesh's experience, and the people and repertoire of various healing practices were well known to them. When he and his wife experienced healing through a pastor in the name of Jesus, they gave that pastor their attention and heard messages regarding the need to follow Jesus.

47. Sudhir Kakar, *Shamans, Mystics, and Doctors*.

48. Ibid., 39.

49. Ibid., 205.

Such experiences, as I have indicated, resonated with a wider cultural value on seeking out various forms of healing and giving attention to the person through whom such healing is given. In addition, the practices themselves were a mix of those familiar to them and others that were from outside their context. For example, practices such as applying oil to peoples' heads and asking them to drink or wash in water that had been blessed, were commonly used by other Hindu healers of the area, while others such as shouting "hallelujah" were unique and learned from the pastor and church.

Numerous *satsangis* spoke about and displayed a similar mix of practices. Some indicated that they were familiar with the various rituals of healing while other practices were more clearly originating from Christian churches. In such cases the *habitus* of these practices again reflects two interlinking sources of prior healing "toolkits," including those of Hindu and pentecostal healers. The ongoing use of these practices in the *Yeshu satsangs* thus continues to reflect a complex *habitus* shaped by aspects of both Christian and Hindu/Sikh healing and miracle practices. Their use in the *satsang* demonstrates that, for the *satsangis*, such practices continue to feel appropriate and congruent with the social space of the *Yeshu satsang*.

Despite the Hindu and Sikh orientation of some practices, however, it is still apparent that some of the particular practices that leaders and *satsangis* use are distinctly non-Hindu/Sikh or Other, and that leaders and *satsangis* recognize them as such. In these cases, the importance of displaying and conveying God's miraculous power through associated practices transcends the association that such practices may have with the Christian social structure and the dissonance they may create with the Hindu or Sikh communities. In addition, these are often leaders for whom healing was particularly important in the resolution of crises. For example, healing or the promise of healing was what initially caused both Manpreet and Nandita to attend a church. Though the practices seemed strange at first, pentecostal-style healing prayers and experiences soon became a part of their ministries. Jasbir experienced miraculous power early in his Christian experience, and continues to pray prayers of healing and deliverance for people. In addition, as seen above, the experience of healing through Jesus was a crucial experience for Dinesh, helping to relieve his crisis and later providing him with significant experiences that gave him notoriety in his early ministry. Throughout his ministry, and in the midst of his transition to a *Yeshu satsang*, such experiences have continued to be important for he and his wife. For these leaders, the experience of healing in their lives and the particular practices through which it was acquired are crucial for their practice and understanding of ministry.

Some leaders are reflexive about the ways pentecostal practices reflect Christian community associations and add to a competitive contradiction. Though these leaders seek to retain an emphasis on God's miraculous power, they more carefully try to communicate this through Hindu/Sikh practices. Navdeep, Naveen, Gaurav and Ravi seek to minimize certain pentecostal practices while retaining an emphasis on the power of God. However, despite their efforts to minimize pentecostal and other socially identifiable Christian practices in their *Yeshu satsangs*, some *satsangis* nonetheless continue to intermittingly use certain pentecostal and Christian speech practices, such as Christian greetings and identifiers. In these cases the practices again function at a level of a *habitus*, reflecting those responses to a social situation that the *satsangis* feel remain appropriate and important for worship and prayer.

In summary, the continued use of certain Christian and pentecostal practices by some leaders and *satsangis* suggests that, in many cases, these people continue to find previously acquired *habitus* practices appropriate in the *Yeshu satsang* social setting. Thus, in this present stage of their own spiritual journey and their *Yeshu satsang* development, the *Yeshu satsang* leaders, as well as their *satsangis*, have retained varying amounts and types of pentecostal and Christian practices that have in turn related to and resonated with prior repertoire sets of healing practices. Some leaders and their *satsangis* have reflected on and changed many of these practices in line with the new ecclesial identity that the leaders are attempting to establish. Others, however, continue to retain such practices through varying levels of reflexivity and *habitus*.

CHAPTER SUMMARY

Why have the *Yeshu satsang* leaders sought to create and shape new ecclesial identities in their *satsangs*? What of their own life contexts and journeys have influenced their decisions? In this chapter I have engaged a process of retroduction to trace the various interactions in the lives of the *Yeshu satsang* leaders and how these caused them to survey old and new concerns. This included the ways in which leaders and their *habitus* were shaped by and responded to various systems, the ecclesial identities of the churches they eventually joined, and the ways in which the leaders began to question aspects of their church's ecclesial identities and began forming new *Yeshu satsangs*. In what ways do these processes enrich our understanding of the ecclesial identity markers identified in Chapter 8?

A prominent theme in the early stages of the leaders' discourses were the roles of crises, and the quest for healing, blessing, or other miracles that would relieve the crises. In most cases the resources for alleviating the crises provided by their Hindu and Sikh communities did not work, and the crises were strong and prolonged enough to cause them to be open to the prayers from a Christian pastor or missionary. In some cases the leaders narrated a break with their Hindu/Sikh beliefs even before experiencing a miracle through Jesus, whereas others did not narrate such a break. In all cases, after experiencing a miracle, the leaders joined a church and became a follower of Jesus identified with that church. In each case, these churches had been established in the last ten-to-twenty years and were a part of the recent wave of pentecostal-influenced churches that emphasize enthusiastic worship, healing and other miracles. Importantly, then, these churches and pastors facilitated a miraculous experience of God's power that prompted the *Yeshu satsang* leaders to survey their concerns, follow Jesus and join a church. Though they encountered Christian structures, the spiritual power or authority of the pastors or missionaries strongly attracted them.

This experience was also reflected in many *satsangi* testimonies, which indicated that it was not the Hindu or Sikh practices of the *satsang* that initially attracted them to the *satsang*. Rather it was often the possibility of receiving prayer, or their response of gratitude after receiving a miraculous answer to prayer. Thus, for leaders and *satsangis* alike, the experience of God's miraculous power and blessing were defining experiences that motivated their interest in Jesus and their attendance of the *satsangs*.

In the case of the leaders, this experience was strong enough to allow them to join the structural Other of the church. Some of the practices that they experienced, such as healing oil or water, related to those with which they were familiar. Others, such as shouting "hallelujah" and praying and worshiping in particular ways, were not as familiar but were accepted and embraced because of their connection to the experience of God's miraculous power. In this way the *habitus* of the leaders and *satsangis* were reinforced but also modified to accept more pentecostal-looking practices.

This retroduction relates closely to the marker of experiencing God's blessing and power. Prayers and messages for God's blessing, healing, deliverance, and other imminent experiences of his presence are prominent in *satsangs* because these have been foundationally important for the leaders' and *satsangis'* faith. In addition, for the leaders, it is the miraculous power of God that has, and continues to compel new people to come to faith in Jesus and join the *satsang*.

However, in addition to relating to the marker of God's blessing, this data also nuances the marker of a *bhakti*-influenced devotion to Jesus. Though the leaders make distinctions between the way they and local churches worship and express devotion, an important question is: What draws *satsangis* to be devoted to Jesus in the first place? It is evident, from the testimonies of leaders and *satsangis*, that a primary reason that people begin to be devoted to Jesus is because of the miraculous power that they experienced in their lives and the crises that were alleviated because of that power. Thus, though the *Yeshu satsang* leaders critique some of the ways in which pastors counsel new Christians, the worship practices that pastors use, and the structural changes that this counsel and worship leads to, they nonetheless emphasize similar attributes of God as it regards miraculous power.

As the leaders grew in their understanding and leadership of churches, they became more and more involved in the situational logics of Otherness of the church. These situational logics, I sought to demonstrate, did not arise out of intentional design, but through the interaction between missionaries, Hindu/Sikh leaders, and new converts. This interaction corresponded with structural changes that were occurring throughout the late nineteenth and early twentieth centuries, resulting in competitive contradictions between the Hindu/Sikh communities and the Christian community. The *Yeshu satsang* leaders experienced the criticism of family and community that they had joined a cultural and structural Other that was "foreign" or "Dalit." Those from Dalit backgrounds experienced this Otherness, though not as acutely as did those from non-Dalit backgrounds; such as Padman, Jasbir and Nandita.

However, as these particular leaders came into recent contact with "contextualization" teaching, they considered new options that might alter the situational logics that they had experienced. In particular, they considered how modifying or changing this logic could enhance their witness and allow for more Hindus and Sikhs to become followers of Christ. This process, then, informs the ecclesial identity marker of witness. In addition, the crisis experience of the leaders gives further insight into the nuances between leaders. On one hand, Gaurav, Ravi, Padman and Navdeep in their discourses did not attribute their crises directly to the Hindu/Sikh system itself. These leaders also tend to be those who embrace the *satsang* style as a part of their identity, in addition to its importance for witness. On the other hand, Dinesh, Manpreet and Jagdeep more strongly place some fault or blame on Hindu/Sikh cultures/structures as contributing to their crisis, and also tend to be those who view *satsangs* as important for evangelism but not expressing any particular Hindu/Sikh identity that is personal to them.

Theologically, this process of retroduction further accentuates the importance of the personal and miraculous work of God, along with its Christological focus. In this the *Yeshu satsang* leaders' experience and emphasis points to an ecclesial identity that is strongly theocentric and Christocentric, calling people to orient themselves towards the God who manifests himself in power. The ecclesial structures, which have historically supported competitive contradictions and thus created barriers to people following Jesus, are de-emphasized in favor of an internal devotion to Jesus initiated and sustained by experiences of his imminent presence.

I have thus far in this study identified the ecclesial identity markers of the *Yeshu satsangs* and the means by which they have emerged. A final step in this study is to discuss the ecclesial identities of the *Yeshu satsangs* in critical correlation with a biblical resource. How does a biblical text, when read in light of the *Yeshu satsangs'* experiences and ecclesial identities, shed further light on those identities? For this I turn to the Book of Acts to further enrich the understanding of how ecclesial identities are shaped and emerge.

PART III

A Critical Correlation of *Yeshu Satsang* and Biblical Ecclesial Identities

CHAPTER 10

Ecclesial Identity Emergence in the Book of Acts

HAVING INDUCTIVELY IDENTIFIED THE ecclesial identity markers of the *Yeshu satsangs* and retroductively identified the processes and agency that helped shape these markers, I now turn to the final aspect of this study: to analyze the ecclesial identity markers that I have highlighted in comparison with those revealed in the Book of Acts. I choose Acts for the way its narrative displays the development, or emergence, of the early church and the insight this could provide to *Yeshu satsangs* as they pursue ecclesial identities in the midst of their religiously plural context. As I analyze the Acts I will be using narrative and reader-response methodologies[1] that utilize literary and historical data to illuminate the message "in front of the text."[2] In particular, this approach focuses on the

1. From a critical literary perspective "narrative" represents diverse meanings and methodologies. Initial work utilizing Narrative criticism tended to approach the text as "an interpretable entity independent of both author and interpreter." Gunn, "Narrative Criticism," 201. This approach denied the text any ability to speak to, transform or challenge the interpreter. To correct this, and drawing from developments in Reader-Response criticism, more recent work has given attention to the role and response of the reader and the historical and cultural context in which the text was produced. McKnight, "Reader-Response Criticism," 240.

2. Green, "The Challenge of Hearing the New Testament," 7–8. Using Green's typologies regarding biblical interpretation, a combination of Narrative and Reader-Response uses the insights of historical-cultural studies to allow the text "speak" more clearly, but does not seek to uncover the "true" historical situation "behind the text." This approach focuses "in the text" of the narrative, but does not treat the text as a unit insulated from its culture of production or from the reader. Rather, this approach is mindful of the reader "in front of the text" and the horizon and related questions that the reader brings to the text, while also allowing the text the power and ability to challenge and critique the reader's horizon.

"Model reader," or the way in which the text seeks to model or shape the reader or reading community.[3] Ultimately the focus on the Model Reader in theological interpretation concerns " . . . the formation of persons and communities who embody and put into play, who perform, the narrative of Scripture."[4]

I will first briefly discuss the structure of Acts and the emergence of ecclesial identities in the text. Following this, I will focus on the four *Yeshu satsang* ecclesial identity markers: (1) *Bhakti*-influenced devotion to Jesus, (2) experience of God's blessing and power, (3) carefully discerning evil, and (4) witness. I will consider how a reading of Acts guides and shapes an understanding of each marker, and then critically correlate insights from the text with those from the *Yeshu satsangs*.

AN EMERGENTIST READING OF ECCLESIAL IDENTITIES IN ACTS

In what ways do ecclesial identities emerge in Acts, and how does the structure of Acts reflect this? To briefly review, Emergentist theory involves the formation of wholes that are constituted by, but irreducible to the sum of the parts. However, the project of cultural sociologists such as Archer, which I have taken up here, has sought to describe and analyze the causal processes that lead to a particular social structure. Without reducing the structure to its parts, Emergentist theory nonetheless seeks to describe some of the ways in which the interaction between people,

---

3. In scriptural interpretation, the Model Reader approach looks not only for the type of audience and its knowledge presumed by the text, but also considers the type of audience that the text wants to produce. Green, "Learning Theological Interpretation from Luke," 60. The Model reader approach has two important components. The first is to identify the range of competencies that the text assumes of the readers by understanding the history and culture in which the text was produced. In the case of the Book of Acts, the text indicates that its readers are somewhat familiar with eastern Mediterranean geography, Roman politics and public figures, pagan religions and culture, and aspects of the Hebrew scriptures. Tyson, *Images of Judaism in Luke-Acts*, 35–36.. The second component is to identify the identity and story that the text calls its readers to embody and inhabit. This moves our analysis from a historical query to a quest for the identity and story to which the text calls *us*. Thus the Book of Acts, while generally assuming a Greco-Roman-oriented readership, also reminds its readers of their place within the story of God's revelation and work within the people of Israel. The identity of the readers, including our own, is expanded beyond national and ethnic categories of identity and embraces God's wider project of creating a people from all nations, the foundations of which were laid in Israel's history.

4. Green, "Learning Theological Interpretation from Luke," 61.

cultures, and structures lead to particular outcomes. In terms of ecclesial identity, I am applying this theory to give greater precision to the ways in which various structural and cultural properties interact, often through the use of practices, to shape a particular ecclesial identity.

As I turn to Acts, it is helpful to similarly consider the ways in which ecclesial identities emerge throughout the text in response to various practices, cultural beliefs, and structural associations. Such emergence can be seen in the structure of the text itself. There are, of course, various suggestions regarding how the Acts text is structured. One well-known structure uses the geographic categories of Acts 1:8 (Jerusalem, Judea/ Samaria, and "ends of the earth"). This three-part structure, particularly popular in missiology, emphasizes and facilitates the theme of the gospel's growth and expansion.

However, though numerical and geographic growth are no doubt important to the Acts narrative, the text gives clues that a more fundamental, and perhaps more important type of growth is also occurring. One of the textual indications of this is the phrase "the word of God grew," found in the summary statements of 6:7; 12:24; and 19:20.[5] This phrase has thematic similarities to the parable that Jesus narrated in Luke 8:4–15,[6] where the word-as-seed is sown onto various types of soil such that everyone "hears" the word. Even so, it is only within those who "hold it fast in an honest and good heart" that the word successfully takes root and bears fruit (8:15). Thus, after finding the right "soil" or quality of heart in which to take root, the word proceeds to grow and create "fruit" which, as Luke's gospel suggests, are "behaviors consistent with the word of God."[7]

---

5. Green, *The Acts of the Apostles*; Twelftree, *People of the Spirit*, 41. These statements are unique in their use of the phrase "the word of God grew," but show similarities with five other summary statements found in Acts 2:42–47; 4:32–35; 9:31; 16:5; and 28:30–31. Together these summary statements share several common characteristics, including descriptions of the actions of the believers (healing, prayer, teaching, etc.), characteristics of their community (unity, sharing, peace) and growth in numbers and devotion. They also transition narratives, emphasize the expanse of the God's work, and remind the readers of God's initiative and role in the story. Rosner, "The Progress of the Word," 221.

6. In this study I concur with scholars regarding the common authorship of Luke and Acts. See Marshall, "How Does One Write on the Theology of Acts," 16; Twelftree, *People of the Spirit*, 6.

7. Green, *The Gospel of Luke*, 329.

The word, and the behaviors that it creates, also form a new and distinct identity within those who have received it. In Luke 8:21, Jesus expresses this through the redefined image and concept of family, saying that those who "hear the word of God and do it" also enjoy bonds and relationships that can be likened to a family. Thus, for Luke the word of God calls for a response that, when positive, is evidenced through the fruit of new practices and behaviors, and through membership in the new people or family of God that Jesus proclaimed.[8]

The "word of God grew" summary statements in Acts delineate four sections (1:1—6:7; 6:8—12:25; 13:1—19:20; and 19:21—28:31). To draw on an Emergentist theory of identity formation, I contend that these sections describe particular stages in the emergence of the church's ecclesial identity as seen through the interaction between God, various people, cultures, and structures. A comprehensive discussion of the emergence of the ecclesial identities in each of these sections is beyond the scope of the present study. However, I will here consider particular narratives and stages of growth as they critically correlate with the ecclesial identity markers of the *Yeshu satsangs*.

YESHU SATSANG MARKER 1: BHAKTI-INFLUENCED DEVOTION TO JESUS

The first ecclesial identity marker that I identified is the *bhakti*-influenced devotion to Jesus emphasized by the *Yeshu satsangs*. As I discussed, the *bhakti* tradition is a resource from which *Yeshu satsang* leaders draw practices and shape a worship space that creates a particular affect within *satsangis*. I will discuss the ways in which the Acts text speaks to and sheds light on the use of a tradition such as *bhakti*, and then critically correlate this with the particular experiences of the *Yeshu satsangs*.

Ecclesial Identities and Cultural Traditions in Acts

How does Acts help us understand the ways in which a religious tradition such as the *bhakti* tradition, along with its practices and emphasis on reverent and personal devotion, shapes the ecclesial identity of a disciple

---

8. As Gaventa summarizes, "although Acts uses the 'word of God' to refer to the content of the gospel (8:14; 11:1; 13:5, 7), the text also uses it (in the summary statements) for the general flourishing of the community generated by that gospel." Gaventa, *The Acts of the Apostles*, 116.

community?[9] I argue that Acts gives input and guidance in two ways. First, it gives guidance regarding the presence and critical incorporation of socio-cultural traditions. In this, the text suggests ways in which the disciple community was shaped by and identified with the traditions of its context. Second, the Acts text models ways in which the disciple communities' Christocentric focus caused them to form identities that were distinct from and resisted aspects of their surrounding contexts. I will address each of these themes in turn, focusing in particular on the Jewish disciple community in Acts.

Ecclesial Identity and the Critical Incorporation of Jewish Traditions

The Jewish disciple community provides an important case study regarding the ways in which cultural traditions can enable and constrain a church or disciple community. In the first section of Acts (1:1–6:7), the Jewish disciple community displays a high level of structural and cultural association with its Jerusalem context. One way this is demonstrated is through the worship practices of the Jewish disciple community, many of which were held in common with the wider Jewish community. At the beginning of Acts 2, for example, the disciples gather together to celebrate the Feast of Weeks, or Pentecost. Though the text does not give details, it indicates that the disciples are gathered together with the rest of the Jews of Jerusalem to listen to recitations regarding the loving kindness of God, to confess sin, and to ask for God's wisdom.[10] The text, in this case, presents the disciple community as faithful Jews joining with their community structure.

As another example, in 2:46 the disciple community meets for worship, among other places, in the Jerusalem temple. While the community distinguished themselves from the wider Jewish community in a number of ways, meeting in the temple allowed the Jewish believers to continue

---

9. Though the concept of *bhakti* has at various times been raised as a potential philosophical category for theology, the main biblical correlation and study of *bhakti* was that of A. J. Appasamy in 1930. Appasamy particularly embraced the mysticism evident in many strains of *bhakti* and analyzed the book of John for its correlations in this. His work continues to be consulted as an important Christology formulated through language and categories of particular *bhakti* traditions. Appasamy, *Christianity as Bhakti Marga*. See also Alphonse, "The Gospel and Hindu Bhakti"; Selvanayagam, "Waters of life and Indian cups."

10. Twelftree, *People of the Spirit*, 128.

to affirm the Jewish origins of the faith and their own solidarity with the wider Jewish community. As Twelftree maintains, "The strongest impression Luke has left on his readers is that he does not consider that the followers of Jesus were, at least initially, isolated from the worship life of the (other) Jews. Rather, in his narrative, the followers of Jesus were faithful and thoroughly committed Jews in their prayer habits, in worshipping as devout Jews and, in so far as they were able, in being part of the twice-daily Tamid services in the temple."[11]

In addition to worshipping in the temple, the disciple community also worshipped together in homes. Acts 2:42–47 gives a brief description of these gatherings, including the practices of meeting together, teaching, fellowship, breaking of bread, prayer, and generosity.[12] This list of practices, together with the house setting in which they were shared, corroborate with the practices and setting of Jewish house synagogues of the time.[13] The home, as Bradley Blue has pointed out, was a common location for synagogues that was easily adapted by Christians for their own meetings.[14]

The disciple community thus actively incorporated and was shaped by the practices of the Jewish tradition that in turn allowed the disciple community to maintain a structural relationship with the surrounding Jewish community. In addition, this section shows that the "word of God" was growing and developing a community that was theologically a part of God's historic work, particularly as demonstrated through Israel. This is demonstrated, among other things, through the disciples' references to the prophets, and how Jesus, the coming of the Holy Spirit, and the present disciple community were all in continuity with God's historic work.[15]

11. Ibid., 138.

12. Though sometimes interpreted as an order of liturgy for the early church, this list is more likely a general depiction of the types of worship practices in which they engaged when gathered together at various times, including practices of service and care within the community. Peterson, "The Worship of the New Community," 389; Twelftree, *People of the Spirit*, 129.

13. Ibid., 131.

14. In addition, locating their gatherings in a home gave access to a kitchen, allowing for them to prepare the common meals that were an important part of their worship gatherings. Blue, "Acts and the House Church," 121.

15. Another way this is emphasized is found at the conclusion of this section in Acts 6:1–7, where the disciple-community addresses and resolves the conflict regarding the neglected widows. In this the disciple community reaffirms the overall importance of service in the community, an emphasis made by Jesus and the Jewish

However, in addition to the enablements their structural and cultural tradition gave them, this section also hints at a constraint that this identity created for the disciple community in regards to their witness. It is curious, as some scholars have pointed out, that the Jewish disciple community does not move beyond Jerusalem in its witness and only does so when persecution later materializes. As such, this lack of movement appears to be at odds with Jesus' instructions to the disciples and with Jesus' own movement towards the marginalized, like the Samaritans. Though the disciple's actions are incongruent with the call and example of Jesus, this is not the only time in Luke-Acts that the disciples are slow to fully grasp and respond to the work of God.[16] Thus, though Jerusalem and the Jewish tradition enable an important theological marker regarding the continuity of the disciple community with Israel, it also in some ways restrains the community from developing its witness and identity further.

Thus, in the first section of Acts the ecclesial identity of the Jewish disciple community is "growing" close to and within the Jewish cultural and structural context. However, in the second and third sections (6:7–12:25 and 13:1–19:20) the Jewish disciple community's identity begins a type of morphogenesis. In particular, the disciple community begins to conflict with the wider Jewish community over how to understand and interpret its common tradition.[17] This occurs in a dramatic way in 6:8–7:60 when Stephen critiques the centrality of the temple cult in the faith and worship of the Jews and the Jews' rejection of Jesus.[18] In do-

---

prophetic tradition (Luke 4:16–20). As they do so, the narrative introduces the first "word of God grew" summary statement. The "word of God" has found good soil and the disciple community's identity is marked by its continuity with a crucial component of its Jewish tradition.

16. Green, "Doing Repentance," 18,19.

17. The disciple community has come into conflict with the Jewish structures prior to this, particularly in 4:1–21 and 5:17–42. In these instances, however, the Jewish priests initiate the conflict and the disciple community continually asserts its Christocentric focus while defending its continuity with the Jewish tradition.

18. God was present with the patriarchs despite the lack of a temple, according to Stephen, and their later desire to build a temple signaled a "deviation from the pattern of worship established by Moses." Hertig, "Dynamics in Hellenism," 80. In addition, Stephen's reference to "human hands" in 7:48 subtly implies that Israel's devotion to the Temple is not only misplaced, but has begun to approach idolatry. Flemming, *Contextualization in the New Testament*, 33. Stephen broadens his focus beyond the temple to also critique Israel's understanding and interpretation of the Promised Land. In this, as John B. Polhill observes, "all God's special acts of deliverance in Stephen's historical

ing so Stephen seeks to reconfigure the story of God's people "in order to reshape his hearers' understanding and identity."[19] The narrative thus begins a series of instances where structural associations were, according to the text, appropriately disrupted for the sake of bringing critique and correction to peoples' cultural understanding of their worship practices. In this, the disciple community's critique of cultural beliefs regarding the temple creates a constraining contradiction that quickly turns into a competitive contradiction. As Stephen declares the exalted status of Jesus as the Messiah, he also criticizes those who had rejected him and critiques the central role of the temple in the worship of Jerusalem Jews. The situational logic becomes one of elimination, and the wider Jewish community soon persecutes the disciple community.

As the conflict surrounding the temple also indicates, one of the tensions and debates regards the role and importance of the Law. Though the disciple community begins to re-interpret the Law and its significance for its identity, it does not do so easily or quickly. Rather, the text shows instances where the Jewish disciple community's value for the Law created challenges in its identity and relationship with Gentile disciple communities. The two narratives most significant for this are Peter's encounter with Cornelius, and the Jerusalem council.

One of the purposes of the Cornelius and Peter narrative (10:1–11:18) is to encourage the disciple community to embrace and include Gentiles and others that are marginalized into the disciple community. In this regard it depicts the two complimentary "conversions" of Peter and Cornelius.[20] However, in emphasizing this, the narrative also continues to relativize the importance of the Jewish Law and its cultural and structural importance for ecclesial identity.

A key part of the Law, and particularly circumcision, regarded the maintenance of holiness. Jewish tradition, particularly as interpreted by its leaders during Jesus' time, taught that holiness was achieved in-part by observing practices and behaviors that separated the people of God

---

sketch take place outside the borders of Israel." Polhill, *Acts*, 192. Thus Stephen seeks to transform the concept of the presence of God and the worship of God from one that is controlled by people in a particular place, or "house," to one that recognizes "the reign of God anywhere and at any time." Hertig, "Dynamics in Hellenism," 80.

19. Flemming, *Contextualization in the New Testament*, 33.

20. Though commentators of this narrative have often focused on Cornelius and his conversion, the story is as much if not more about the reorientation and "conversion" of Peter as that of Cornelius. Van Engen, "Peter's Conversion," 136.

from those people and things that were "unclean." Through his vision and subsequent meeting with Cornelius, Peter begins to understand that it is not Gentiles and their lack of circumcision that makes the community "unclean."[21] Though Peter appears to understand this for the first time, this theme follows Jesus' example in Luke of including into the disciple community those traditionally deemed unclean.[22]

In this instance, the text shows that adherence to the Law potentially constrains the ability of the disciple community to embrace the ecclesial identity to which God is calling it. Though Peter responds positively, and the "word of God grows" as a result of the new ecclesial identity that the community begins to embrace (Acts 12:24), the Jewish disciple community continues to harbor questions and confusion regarding the role of the Law for their identity. In addition, they do not yet address the way in which they and Gentiles should relate to each other as members of the same family of God.[23]

In the third section of Acts (13:1–19:20) this issue is more directly addressed and resolved, particularly in the narrative of the Jerusalem council (Acts 15). In this passage the disciple community more widely affirms a redefinition of holiness and relativizes the significance of the Law. It does so by addressing the issue of whether or not circumcision should be required of Gentile followers of Christ.[24] As Paul, Barnabas and others come to Jerusalem, the believing Pharisees push forward this issue, declaring that the Gentile believers need to be circumcised and

21. Ibid.

22. In Luke's Gospel, for example, Jesus deliberately abandons conventions that maintain holiness, such as dining with "unclean" people, and thereby critiques an understanding of holiness that Pharisees have used to protect and defend special status and identity. Wells, *God's Holy People*, 234. When talking about the proper behavior and outlook of his disciples, Jesus talks more about mercy than holiness (e.g. Luke 6:36). Jesus also demonstrates this orientation in his ministry when, rather than separating himself from those that are "unclean," he freely associates with them. In this Jesus demonstrates that holiness is to be understood not as separation from uncleanness but rather as the "power to overcome uncleanness." Toews, "Be Merciful as God is Merciful," 23.

23. Thompson, *Keeping the Church in its Place*, 159.

24. The heritage of the Maccabean revolt caused Jews to view any attempt to define Jewish identity in terms other than circumcision "as opposition to God and grounds for exclusion from the covenant community." Robinson and Wall, *Called to be Church*, 169; Strong, "The Jerusalem Council," 198. Because of this it was clear to Jews that Gentiles who wanted to be a part of the covenant community needed to be circumcised.

keep the Law of Moses.[25] In addition, the Pharisees are concerned about the corrosive effect that Gentiles could have on the worship and identity of the community as well as on the covenant relationship with God.

Peter, Barnabas and Paul provide the council with testimonies and argue that Gentiles should be accepted into God's new people in all their Gentile-ness and should be free to worship God with that identity intact.[26] James then takes these experiences seriously and uses them as a "hermeneutical key" through which to understand the work of God in Scripture.[27] He affirms what Peter, Paul and Barnabas have testified to and affirms Peter's basic premise, saying that God has accepted the Gentiles as a part of his people.[28]

This affirmation of the Gentiles' inclusion into God's "tent" or community marks a significant change in cultural belief, with important structural implications. Though James does not devalue the importance that circumcision may hold for the Jewish community, he relativizes its importance as a requirement for salvation and for regulating structural connections between Gentile and Jewish followers of Christ. Uncircumcision did not make Gentiles "unclean," and was therefore not a criteria for inclusion or exclusion.

Following this, however, James continues by suggesting that the Gentiles be asked to observe four requirements. The four requirements or prohibitions have been the cause of much debate among biblical scholars. Though there are various possibilities, I agree with Witherington and others' view that the prohibitions are not primarily asking Gentiles to adhere to a part of Jewish law, since such an interpretation does not fully address the perplexing question of why one law practice (circumcision) is replaced by four law practices based on Leviticus 17–18. Rather,

---

25. The motivation behind this was not necessarily vindictive, but rather reflected a desire for a halakhic interpretation of the law, or a "legal definition of those religious practices required of repentant gentiles." Robinson and Wall, *Called to be Church*, 171. Such would help define the way in which Jews and Gentiles relate to each other as part of the same community.

26. Flemming, *Contextualization in the New Testament*, 45.

27. Ibid., 46.

28. Specifically, James says that God has taken from the Gentiles "a people for his name" (15:14). Up to this point in the Acts text, the word "people" (laos) has been used only to refer to Jewish people as the people of God. Here, however, is the first time it is used to refer and include Gentiles into God's people. God's promise is thus fulfilled when the Gentiles are included among God's people resulting in the creation of a single *laos* of both Jews and Gentiles together worshipping God.

I contend that the prohibitions are meant to address associations that Gentiles may have had with pagan cults and polytheism.[29] Because Gentiles often had backgrounds involving these practices, the council advised them to abstain from foods and other practices directly associated with idol worship, and thus keep strong their allegiance to God.

Though the prohibitions primarily address the issue of idolatry, however, the Jerusalem council is also aware of the way certain idolatrous practices could harm the Gentiles believers' witness among Jews, as well as the table fellowship between Gentile and Jewish believers. In this regard, the prohibitions serve a second purpose, helping the Gentiles to "maintain a good testimony before the watching Jewish world, consisting of both believers and unbelievers."[30] Gentiles would thus preserve their allegiance to God, as well as enhance their witness to others and relationships with the Jewish disciple community.

In summary, Acts 15 addresses idolatrous practices as well as witness and table fellowship. In addressing the question of circumcision, the disciple community re-interpreted and relativized the salvific role of the law. Importantly, the council does not negate the importance that the Law may have for the Jewish disciple community themselves. In this, the Law continues to enable them to associate structurally with the wider Jewish community. Also, the Law continues to be a resource for avoiding corrosive influences, such as idol worship. However, the Law no longer holds the same soteriological significance, and in fact is found to potentially constrain the identity of the Gentile disciple community.

The Jewish disciple community's ecclesial identity is thus broadened and redefined in significant ways in the second and third sections of Acts, particularly as it relates to the relative importance of their tradition and Law for forming that identity. In the final section of Acts (19:21–28:31), two important references give further insight into the way the Jewish disciple community related to its tradition, and particularly to the cultural and structural manifestations of it in their context. The first regards Paul's use of the word *airesis* (sect) in his interaction with Roman authorities (24:5, 14; 28:22). Though the disciple community's detractors use the word, the text interestingly accepts and applies it to

---

29. Gaventa, *The Acts of the Apostles*, 222–23; Gill, "Acts and Roman Religion, 92; Witherington III, *The Acts of the Apostles*, 460–65. This admittedly requires an interpretation of *porneia* that is less-than-common, but one that Witherington has shown to be possible. Witherington, *The Acts of the Apostles*, 463.

30. Strong, "The Jerusalem Council," 204.

the disciple community. Greek philosophical schools as well as various schools of Jewish thought of the time, such as the Pharisees, Sadducees, and Essenes, were all referred to as *airesis*. Because of this, the text characterizes the disciple community as an *airesis* in order to portray them "as a respectable school of thought or legitimate, perhaps even influential, expression of Judaism."[31] The label thus implies that the Jewish disciple community retained and fostered structural and cultural ties to the wider Jewish context, particularly as a "legitimate expression of Israel living faithfully in accordance with the Law."[32]

A second reference to the Jewish disciple community regards its short but significant role in Acts 21. In this narrative the Jerusalem church welcomes Paul to Jerusalem and gives him instruction on how to relate to the Jewish community, only to fade from the narrative scene following Paul's arrest. What should be made of the silence of the church throughout Paul's ordeal?

Though the references to the Jerusalem church are brief, some textual markers indicate that they were silent, if not silently complicit with the injustice of the Jewish and Roman authorities. In 21:20, the text says that the Jerusalem believers are "zealous for the law," contrasting Paul's later testimony that he himself "is zealous for God" (22:3). In addition, their zealotry for the law, together with the rumors they circulated regarding Paul indicates that their zealotry caused many of them to disagree with and disassociate themselves from Paul's Gentile mission and its reinterpretation of the role of the law.[33] The text thus indicates that, in this instance, the Jerusalem disciple community's embrace of the Jewish law allowed them to associate with the Jewish authority structures, but also led them to be complicit in Paul's persecution. Reflecting the actions of the disciples towards Jesus, the Jerusalem believers progressively isolate Paul, leaving him to face the Jewish and Roman leaders alone.[34]

The above discussion regarding the ecclesial identity of the Jewish disciple community presents various positive and negative vignettes. On the one hand, the Jewish practices and traditions allowed it to associate with the Jewish community structure and to demonstrate their own continuity with the historic work of God through Israel. However, there

---

31. Twelftree, *People of the Spirit*, 59.

32. Ibid., 61.

33. Rapske, "Opposition to the Plan of God and Persecution," 255.

34. Green, "Interview," 2009.

were aspects of the tradition which began to conflict with the developing theology of the disciple community. When they asserted these distinctions and critiqued the Jewish tradition, as did Stephen in Acts 7, the disciple community came into conflict with the Jewish community and their structural relationship became disrupted. Positively, some of the community relativized the particular aspects of their identity and embraced a new understanding and the morphogenesis that this entailed for their identity as God's disciple community. However, when others in the Jewish disciple community refused to relativize aspects of its identity, such as its observance of the law, it found itself silently complicit with the injustices that its own Jewish community perpetuated against other followers of Christ.

The Christocentric Shaping of Traditions

The Acts text thus identifies how the Jewish disciple community identified, and perhaps over-identified, with Jewish structural and cultural systems. In addition, however, the text suggests that the disciple community also at times develops Christocentric distinctives in its beliefs and identity. Though it identified with the traditions of its context, the disciple community was nonetheless called to be a community whose practices clearly and distinctly reflected the behaviors and teachings of Jesus.

Integral to this is the celebration of the exalted Lord Jesus and formation of a distinctive worshipping community with Jesus at its center.[35] For example, in the first section of Acts the speech practices of the disciple community proclaimed Jesus' "elevated status" and called people to respond to his status and work through repentance and baptism.[36] In addition, the worship practices of the community, such as those in 2:42–47 and 4:32–35, were shaped in response to their commitment to the Lordship of Jesus. An important part of this is the sharing that the community displayed which " . . . was clearly a practical expression of the new relationship experienced together through a common faith in Christ."[37] These passages show that conversion to Christ creates a new

35. Peterson, "The Worship of the New Community," 387–88.

36. The disciples proclaim Jesus' exalted status in various speeches, such as 1:16–22; 2:14–36, 38–39; 3:12–26; 4:8–12, 19–20; 5:29–32. Green, "Salvation to the End of the Earth, 84n1. This is done through references to Jesus as "Lord and Christ" (2:36) and "prince and Savior" (5:31), and by attributing his works as those attested by God (2:22).

37. Peterson, "The Worship of the New Community," 391.

community, and that this disciple community helps to embody and nurture that commitment.[38]

Though the Jewish disciple community has some conflict with the Jewish authorities in the first section of Acts, it is in the second and third sections of Acts that the Christocentric orientation of the community causes significant conflict with the Jewish structures. This begins in a dramatic way in the narrative of Stephen's speech and martyrdom. In addition, the new cultural understanding of salvation "through the grace of our Lord Jesus" (15:11) further relativizes the role of the Law for salvation, which caused a morphogenesis in the relationship between Jewish and Gentile structures.

The final section of Acts displays what was perhaps a lack of consensus among the Jewish disciple community regarding the ways in which it should express its Jewish identity and solidarity with Jewish structures. This was seen in particular through its silent complicity in the face of Paul's persecution. However, the text nuances this view of the overall disciple community, including the Jewish disciple community, through its introduction and use of the phrase "the Way" (18:26; 19:9, 23; 22:4; 24:14, 22). This phrase refers to a self-ascription that some of the Jewish disciple communities had apparently begun to use for themselves.[39] In 24:14 Paul relates this to the word *latreo* (worship, serve) which recalls the words of Zechariah in Luke 1:74. In that narrative Zechariah declares that the Messiah will come and rescue his people in order to "enable us to serve (*latreo*) him without fear in holiness and righteousness before him all our days." Paul thus claims that the "way" in which to worship and serve God is through Jesus, and that this is in continuity with the Law and the Prophets.[40] Thus, the Christ-following disciple community is portrayed as not only as a "sect" of faithful Jews, but also as the distinctive "true and faithful expression of Israel."[41] The Christocentric shaping of the tradition thus gives the disciple community further contours that distinguish it from its Jewish counterparts.

---

38. Robinson and Wall, *Called to be Church,* 80.

39. Twelftree, *People of the Spirit,* 60.

40. Peterson, "The Worship of the New Community," 387.

41. Twelftree, *People of the Spirit,* 61.

Critical Correlation with the Yeshu satsangs

The *Yeshu satsangs* have embraced aspects of their Hindu and Sikh tradition, particularly through the use of *bhakti* practices and invoking some of that tradition's emphasis on reverent and personal devotion. In what ways does the Acts text critically correlate with the *Yeshu satsangs'* use of the *bhakti* tradition as a marker in its ecclesial identity?[42]

One correlation regards the Jewish disciple community's incorporation and use of its Jewish tradition, and the way this facilitated association with the Jewish cultural and structural systems. Regarding 1:1–6:7, for example, I discussed how the Jewish tradition provided the disciple community with important understanding regarding its own continuity with the historic work of God as revealed through the prophets. In addition, however, and related to the *Yeshu satsangs'* structural associations through *bhakti*, the Jerusalem church's continuity with Israel also had important structural implications. The disciple community expresses this by meeting with other Jews for Jewish festivals (2:1) and meeting together in the temple (2:46). They use worship practices drawn from their "toolbox" of Jewish traditions, and even meet together as a house synagogue. In later sections, though the Law is relativized, it is still valued by the Jewish disciple community. As well, the community view themselves as a sect that is "a legitimate and perhaps even influential expression of Judaism."[43]

This identity, as I indicated, enables the Jewish disciple community to associate theologically and structurally with the wider Jewish community. However, the text also indicates that at times this identity constrains the disciple community's ability to be faithful to the Christ-oriented aspect of their identity. This was seen in the community's reticence to move beyond Jerusalem in 1:1—6:7, and their silent complicity with the Jewish community's condemnation of Paul in Acts 21.

There are also instances in Acts 10, 11 and 15 where their love for the Law—a core component in their Jewish identity—could constrain their ability to understand and embrace the wider work that God is initiating among the Gentiles. However, in these cases the Jewish disciple

42. It is important to state that I am not attempting to equate Judaism and Hinduism theologically. I acknowledge that, from a theological perspective, Israel represents a case of special revelation whereas within Hinduism there are at best aspects of God's general revelation. Because of this, the critical correlations that I make in this section emphasize the practices and identities, or social structures, which are fostered by religious traditions.

43. Twelftree, *People of the Spirit*, 59.

community successfully embraces a new understanding of the Law's relative role in relation to Christ, and undergoes a morphogenetic shift in their identity. For example, in Acts 15, James uses Amos to show how God is "rebuilding" David's tent, and affirms that they should not make it difficult for Gentiles to enter it by requiring circumcision (11:16–19). This structure or tent would traditionally have been entered through the Jewish identity marker of circumcision. However, James asserts that the new structure would have different markers not based on circumcision. James' pronouncement thus allows Jews and Gentiles to retain a level of continuity with their own structural and cultural context, while not reducing the identity of the new "tent" to either.

The Acts text would thus suggest that the cultural and structural traditions of a context could provide helpful resources for a disciple community's identity. In terms of the *Yeshu satsangs'* embrace of the *bhakti* traditions of their context, the *Yeshu satsang* leaders have adopted various practices that provide both cultural and structural resources. The cultural resources are found in the tradition's overall emphasis on personal and reverent devotion to Christ. Though these practices are being reshaped Christologically, they also provide a particular emphasis formed by beliefs regarding the appropriate ways in which to approach God. Structurally, the Hindu and Sikh *bhakti* tradition provides the *Yeshu satsangs* practices through which they can share an association with the Hindu and Sikh structures.

However, in addition to providing helpful resources, this reading of Acts would also warn against the ways in which these traditions could constrain *Yeshu satsangs'* identities and prevent them from being faithful to behaviors and practices which Scripture may call them to. Just as the Jerusalem disciple community did not initially obey Jesus' call to move beyond Jerusalem to the Samaritans and Gentiles, so the *Yeshu satsangs* could be tempted to stay within the structures with which they seek to relate and not associate with others beyond them. In addition, the Jerusalem disciple community was reticent to identify with Paul and the Gentile disciple communities with whom their wider Jewish structure disagreed. In a similar way, the *Yeshu satsangs* could be tempted to not associate with the wider Indian Christian community with whom their own Hindu and Sikh communities look down on because of their caste and religious Otherness. The text would thus critique any manner in which a community's tradition may constrain its ability to identify with the wider body of Christ.

This same constraint would perhaps also relate to the Christian church in northwest India, and elsewhere. As I discussed in Chapter 1, the Christian church in various places has placed a high level of emphasis on baptism as a marker and entry point into the church community. In response, some critics have questioned whether the level of emphasis, and the meaning that baptism holds for the wider non-Christian community, are biblical and appropriate. The *Yeshu satsangs* have responded by retaining the practice but adapting it to in some ways minimize its structural significance. The Acts texts regarding the importance of circumcision to the Jewish disciple community may speak to some Christian churches and, similar to Acts 15, call the church to re-examine the meaning of this for ecclesial identity.[44]

In addition to the ways in which a tradition can be critically embraced, the Acts text also shows the way in which a tradition can be reshaped with a Christocentric focus. Instances of the Christocentric shaping of the Jewish tradition is seen throughout Acts, including speech practices proclaiming the exalted Christ, and worship practices that reflected the behaviors modeled by Jesus. A Christocentric focus also shaped various critiques that the disciple community made of its own tradition, including that of Stephen in Acts 7. In addition, the disciple community grappled with and largely understood the ways in which the Christocentric emphasis of their new faith relativized and re-interpreted aspects of their tradition, as seen in Act 10, 11, and 15. As I showed above, these narratives show that traditions can be valued, but should be shaped, and sometimes countered, by devotion to Christ.

The ways in which the disciple community's ecclesial identity can reflect continuity and discontinuity with its traditions thus correlates with the dynamics that the *Yeshu satsangs* face as they seek a level of continuity with the Hindu or Sikh *bhakti* traditions of their context while also establishing clear Christological foci for their communities. As I mentioned in Chapter 1, some critics of Hindu followers of Christ have sometimes critiqued the supposed disconnect that such people may have

---

44. I am not suggesting that circumcision and baptism are theologically the same, and would contend that every disciple community should practice some ritual that functions as baptism for the community. Rather, I am suggesting that baptism, as it is currently practiced in the Indian Christian church, carries strong sociological meaning that may in some ways correlate with the function of circumcision for the Jewish church.

with other believers and churches.[45] This concern, framed in this way, resonates with what the Acts text presents. That is, the new disciple communities should recognize and value the continuity they have with the wider and historic work of God, first through Israel, and then continuing through other churches in history. In addition, though they should seek to express their faith in Christ through practices familiar to them and their social community, they should not privilege their identity as part of that community over their identification with other churches.

Yeshu satsangs, in their desire to separate from regional churches in their area, could perhaps fall subject to this critique. However, two factors suggest that such a critique needs to be qualified in the case of the particular *Yeshu satsangs* of this study.

First, it should be recognized that many churches and church traditions have in various ways shunned or downplayed their relationship and association with other Christian churches, whether because of doctrinal differences, social differences, or other misunderstandings. In this way, the critique and concern that *Yeshu satsangs* may seek to disassociate from other Christian churches locally, globally, or historically should perhaps be framed more widely as it could apply to any number of church traditions.

Secondly, the *Yeshu satsangs* of this study in actuality exhibit a number of traits and engage in practices and celebrations that help them to relate to the wider Christian community, even if not to those in their immediate vicinity. For example, as I discussed above, all observe and celebrate Easter and Christmas, in various ways network and relate to other pastors, and in other ways relate to the wider Christian community. In addition, the *Yeshu satsangs* have retained a number of Christian practices and key Christological and soteriological teachings that closely relate to historic traditions of Christianity.

The Hindu and Sikh *bhakti* identities are not without problems. The *satsangis* continually deliberate about the practices that could help them relate to Hindu and Sikh cultures and structures, and those that should characterize their distinctiveness, particularly in regards to culture. It is a deliberation, however, which very much reflects that of the Acts text.

---

45. Tennent, "The Challenge of Churchless Christianity."

YESHU SATSANG MARKER 2: THE EXPERIENCE OF GOD'S BLESSING AND MIRACULOUS POWER

The second ecclesial identity marker of *Yeshu satsangs* emphasized the importance of God's miraculous power and blessing in their lives. The *Yeshu satsang* leaders and *satsangis* emphasized this in various ways, through the prayers and testimonies given regarding God's power and healing. In the following I will discuss various narratives in Acts as they relate to God's blessing and miraculous power, and the ways in which these critically correlate with the *Yeshu satsangs'* experience and practices.

Ecclesial Identities and God's Blessing and Miraculous Power in Acts

How, according to the Acts text, does God's blessing and miraculous power help to form ecclesial identities? There are three particular characteristics that the text highlights regarding God's miraculous power.

THE CHRISTOCENTRIC FOCUS OF POWER

One characteristic of the blessing and miraculous power of God in the Acts text is its Christocentric focus. Ultimately, the miraculous and extraordinary work of God is credited to Jesus.[46] Two narratives emphasize the importance of a Christocentric focus of power, particularly in relation to other potential sources of miraculous power. The first is Acts 8:9–25 which narrates Philip and Peter's interaction with Simon the sorcerer. This is the first instance in the text where the work and message of God has the potential of being syncretized with another belief system.[47] The text first describes how Simon "believed and was baptized" (8:13) and continued to be "astonished" by Philip's miracles. However, though he has done this, he offers Peter money for a similar ability thus demonstrating that he has not fully understood the power behind these miracles.[48] Though Simon may have had a certain understanding of Christ and demonstrated this in some way to Philip, it is apparent that he still did

---

46. This includes narratives such as the Day of Pentecost (2:33), the lame beggar at the temple (3:6), prayers for signs and wonders (4:30), Philip in Samaria (8:5), the turning of Saul to Jesus (9:17–18), and healings through Peter (9:34). In many of these the text forefronts the presence and work of the Holy Spirit, but has also explained the Holy Spirit as the one who was sent by Jesus (Acts 2:33).

47. Flemming, *Contextualization in the New Testament*, 34.

48. Hertig, "The Magical Mystery Tour," 105.

not have a full understanding of the nature of this power.[49] The text thus uses this narrative to clearly assert the importance of a Christocentric understanding of God's power.

A second narrative regarding the Christocentric nature of God's power is 19:1–20, which narrates an example of how Gentile practices of magic and idolatry were found to be in conflict with God's purposes, and were thus discarded. The narrative begins by describing Paul's "extraordinary miracles" that were no doubt known throughout the city. In response, seven sons of Sceva tried to emulate Paul and "use the name of the Lord Jesus over those with evil spirits" (19:13). Though their prayers focused on the name of Jesus, their understanding of Jesus and his role in blessing and miraculous power was impoverished. After they were humiliated, many existing believers confessed their magic practices and burned their magic books, which had been shown to contrast the Christocentric power exhibited by Paul. As a result, the name of the Lord Jesus "was held in high honor" (19:17) and the word of the Lord consequently "grew widely and spread in power" (19:21).

Thus, while magic in Ephesus was used by people to command and manipulate powers (19:13), Paul's miracles are done with a clear understanding of Jesus and are controlled by God.[50] The ecclesial identity of the disciple community is shaped by miraculous power, and its Christocentric nature is asserted and affirmed particularly in the context of other Greco-Roman religious sources of power.

A related issue raised by the above narratives is that the experiences of miracles do not generally correspond with any particular form of prayer or worship. The text in these places models against understandings of prayer that devalue the central place of Christ and that tries to coerce God and his power. The text is clear that miracles and blessings should be understood through a strong Christology, and it does not model more specifically the types of prayers or speech practices that people like Philip used when invoking God's power.[51]

---

49. I disagree with Hertig on this point, who interprets Peter's rebuke to mean that "Simon does not embrace authentic Christian faith," (ibid., 107). I would suggest that Simon's faith could have been authentic, but incomplete or deficient.

50. See Witherington, *The Acts of the Apostles*, 578.

51. Although, even in this, Acts 19:11–12 narrates how "God did extraordinary miracles through Paul" and how handkerchiefs that had "touched him" brought healing to the sick. In this God gave particular favor to Paul, and to certain forms, for healing.

POWER AND THE DISCIPLE COMMUNITY

A second characteristic of the blessing and miraculous power of God in the Acts text regards the way in which God's power is often brought through and adds to the witness of the disciple community and its representatives. Inherent in this is a high emphasis on the disciple community as that which extends and continues to perform the miracles of Jesus.

Examples of this emphasis are seen throughout the text. One prominent place is in Acts 2. Following the coming of the Holy Spirit upon the disciple community, Peter explains this event to his audience via the prophet Joel. In doing so Peter uses the word "signs" (Joel 2:30; Acts 2:19) to argue that the present power of the Holy Spirit is a sign of the presence of God's Spirit with his people.[52] The text continues in the following summary statement by stating that such "signs" continued to be performed by the apostles (v. 43) and describes this in the midst of the practices and formation of the disciple community. In this way the "signs" of God's power were an extension and continuation of what Jesus had done during his earthly ministry, now expressed through his disciple community. Thus, though the power and Spirit of God empowered his people for witness it was also, as Turner contends, " . . . for the benefit of those in the Church, not merely to empower her to draw outsiders into her ranks."[53] In this way the Spirit was understood as the "charismatic power of Israel's restoration."[54] The power of God thus displayed the blessing and restoration of his people, now expressed through the disciple community.

THE BLESSING OF THE MARGINALIZED

A third characteristic of God's blessing and power in Acts is that such events often involve and benefit the marginalized. God is the one who, as Mary proclaimed in Luke 1, "has lifted up the humble" and "has filled the hungry with good things" (Luke 1:52–53). Likewise, as Zechariah proclaimed shortly afterwards, God has come to "rescue us from the hand of our enemies" (1:74). In this way the blessing and miraculous power of God is understood as part of God's overall work to bless the marginalized through Jesus. Though the Jews saw themselves in many ways as those marginalized by the power of the Roman "enemies," Jesus soon demonstrated that, from God's perspective, the marginalized were those

52. Twelftree, *People of the Spirit*, 82.

53. Turner, "The 'Spirit of Prophecy,'" 342.

54. Ibid., 343.

who were not only socially or economically disadvantaged, but also those on the margins of the Jewish social structure, including Samaritans and Gentiles. As Jesus and his disciple community brought blessing to those on the margins, he changed the definition of social marginality such that those who had been on the margins moved firmly into the midst of God's people by receiving Jesus' forgiveness and healing, and reorienting themselves towards him.

One example of this is seen in Acts 3:1–11, which narrates the healing of the lame beggar and includes the details of how Peter looks intently at him, touches him, and allows him to cling to him in the sight of the gathering temple crowd. Details such as this recall the way Jesus not only physically healed socially marginalized people, but also restored their social dignity (e.g. Luke 8:43–48).

Philip's ministry in Samaria in Acts 8 and Peter's interaction with Cornelius in Acts 10 serve as additional examples for how God often miraculously and powerfully blessed the marginalized. Importantly, in both instances the text gives details of how the disciple community had to grapple with the implications of God's work. For example, when the apostles in Jerusalem heard that Samaria "accepted the word of God" in Acts 8:14–25, they sent Peter and John to them. Some readers could interpret this as an expression of the Jerusalem church's need and desire to "endorse" the work of Philip. More likely, however, Peter and John themselves need this experience as much as the Samaritans, "since they had to overcome their own prejudices by witnessing the Spirit's work beyond regional boundaries."[55] They needed to see how God was blessing those at the margins of Jewish and Jerusalem society. Similarly, in Acts 10 and 11, after the Holy Spirit falls on Cornelius and his household causing them to speak in tongues and praise God, Peter returns to Jerusalem to report to the disciple community what had happened. The latter took special note of the fact that the Holy Spirit had come with power "as he had come on us at the beginning" (11:15), and accepted this as an important

---

55. Hertig, "The Magical Mystery Tour, " 111. As Hertig shows, Peter and John "lay hands" on the Samaritans and, by actually touching them, give a sign of fellowship as well as a message of healing for the "generations of hostility between Jews and Samaritans," (ibid.). In addition, as Peter and John go from that place back to Jerusalem they do so "announcing the good news" to many villages of the Samaritans" (v. 25). Though the text does not say what Peter and John's original opinion and attitudes towards the Samaritan ministry were, they appear to be inspired by the work started through Philip's preaching and they emulate the same as they return to Jerusalem.

endorsement of how God was extending his blessing to those beyond the Jewish community, including Gentiles like Cornelius.

Critical Correlation with the Yeshu satsangs

The *Yeshu satsangs* leaders have all received teaching in and have been influenced by various Christian pentecostal churches and organizations, and most leaders have retained an emphasis on the miraculous power and blessing of God. The way in which the Acts text shapes the disciple community thus critically correlates with the *Yeshu satsangs* in a number of ways.

First, the *Yeshu satsang* leaders would resonate with the Christocentric focus of power given by the Acts text. In this they are clear in their prayers to focus on Jesus and pray in his name. However, one important issue regards whether and to what degree the *satsangis* themselves view the power of Jesus as something distinct or whether, like Simon in Acts 8, they view it as a power that can be manipulated in ways similar to how shamans in their area may use rituals to manipulate sicknesses or placate smaller deities. Some interviews with *satsangis*, particularly those who were very new to the *satsang*, indicated that they may still view their healing or the power of God in Jesus as a power similar to other powers in their area.[56]

However, the *Yeshu satsang* leaders are also aware of this and actively move people towards faith in Jesus. In this, the *Yeshu satsangs'* emphasis on healing and blessing correlate closely with the second marker described from Acts: the ways in which the miraculous power of God is often brought through and adds to the witness of the disciple community and its representatives. Particularly for Dinesh and Manpreet, for whom healing is especially prominent and important, the miraculous power of God is clearly an opportunity to draw people to the *satsang* and to faith in Christ. Similar to the Acts text, the power of God blesses people and also draws their attention to the community through whom they will gain further understanding regarding the importance of Christ.

One area in which the text may correct or guide the *Yeshu satsangs*, as well as pentecostal churches of the area, regards ritualistic, and almost

---

56. One of the prime indications of this was the lack of deep reflection on Jesus or for coming to the *Yeshu satsang*. Some of Dinesh's *satsangis* who had recently begun attending, for example, came because of the healing they were experiencing and because they had a positive relationship with Dinesh or someone in the *satsang*. They as yet did not reflect deeply on the nature and person of Jesus.

magical forms of prayer. Acts 17 described a ritualistic use of prayer that was devoid of Christocentric understanding and that brought harm to those trying to use it. Thus, the text would critique any tendency to devalue the place of Christ and to emphasize the form of prayer or the person through whom the prayer is made. Though the *Yeshu satsangs* would most likely deny using prayer in this way, they could be careful not to adopt some of the more ritualistic ways in which Hindus, Sikhs, and even Christians in their area use prayer to manipulate spiritual powers.

The other correlation drawn from the Acts text regards the blessing that such miraculous work brings to the marginalized. Who are the marginalized in relation to the *Yeshu satsangs*? There are probably various groups that would be on the margins of different *satsangs*, depending on their social situation. Padman certainly identifies the Dalits as those who have been historically marginalized by his high-caste community and, in his discourses, regularly talks about his desire to work with the marginalized to help them receive justice.[57]

In addition, however, the discourses of some of the leaders suggest that they have felt marginalized by the Christian churches and church leaders. In this, they suggest that some of the Christian discourse regarding the demonic nature of the Hindu or Sikh communities, or the work that they do with *satsangs*, seeks to elevate the church and minimize the value of their communities. Seen in this light, God's miracles among their community, through their Christ-focused *satsang*, is an indicator that God also works beyond the confines of the established Christian churches of the area. One correlation with the Acts text would thus suggest that, just as the Jewish disciple community's identity and understanding was expanded by seeing God's work among the marginalized, so the Christian church's understanding and identity can or should be expanded by seeing God's work through the *Yeshu satsangs*.

YESHU SATSANG MARKER 3: THE DISCERNMENT OF EVIL

Many of the *Yeshu satsangs* share the marker of recognizing and addressing evil spirits and power, as well as critiquing the way the Christian church sometimes ascribes this to Hindu/Sikh structures. In the following I will discuss the ways in which the Acts text addresses the various

---

57. Padman shares, for example, that one of the reasons that he changed careers from medicine to law was to help those like the Dalits who often find it hard to receive just representation in the courts.

manifestations of evil, and the critical correlation that this has with the *Yeshu satsangs.*

Ecclesial Identities and the Discernment of Evil in Acts

The Acts text recognizes the presence of evil in various ways. One way in which evil is manifested is through personal, demonic beings. In addition, the text also reveals the ways in which structures sometimes set themselves against the people of God and the way in which the disciple community should resist such pressure non-violently. I will discuss these two themes in turn and then critically correlate these with the *Yeshu satsangs.*

Demonic Beings and Evil Power

As mentioned above, the texts in Acts 8 and 19 directly address shaman and magic power and assert the power that Christ has over such powers. There was, in these cases, a clear understanding that demonic power was present and prevalent, and that this could and should be overcome by the power of Jesus. This was in direct continuity with the work of Jesus, who modeled a similar interaction with demonic powers (e.g. Luke 9:1, 2; 10:17–20; 11:14–20).

In what ways, however, did the demonic powers depicted in Acts relate to Gentile religious beliefs? In various instances the text clearly asserts the centrality of Christ over Gentile beliefs. However, the text does not frame such beliefs as evil Others.[58] Two prominent examples of this can be seen from Paul's speeches to Gentile audiences.

In Acts 14:15–17, for example, Paul and Barnabas make a dramatic appeal for the crowd to not misidentify and offer sacrifices to them as gods. However, in making his appeal, Paul does not say, "you cannot offer sacrifices to us because this is prohibited by our law and religion . . . ." Rather, as Hinkle has shown, Paul draws their story into God's story

---

58. In fact, Bartchy has shown that Paul's main difficulty in addressing Greco-Roman religions was not polytheism or "renouncing the Many for the One," but rather helping them move beyond the individualistic orientation of their gods. Bartchy, "Divine Power," 90. The concept of god "did not bring to Gentile minds the practice of 'fellowship,' 'community,' or 'close personal relationship' (Greek, *koinonia*; Latin, *communitas* or *societas*)." Ibid., 60. Because of this Paul communicated the Jewish belief that God seeks to create a community "characterized by interpersonal righteousness and social justice" and to persuade non-Jewish converts to have an "understanding of God as a community-forming and community-sustaining power." Ibid., 90–91.

beginning with creation, thereby arguing "that (Paul and Barnabas') story is the Lycaonians' story too, even if it sounds at first like new information to them."[59] Paul thus does not frame the Gentile beliefs as foreign, Other or evil, but instead invites the Gentiles to understand God in a way consistent with Jewish tradition and that they can relate to, "as the Creator of all things, witnessed to you by the simple things of life such as the rain on your fields and the joy in your hearts (cf. 14:17)."[60]

As another example, in Acts 17:16–34 Paul again addresses a group of Gentiles, though quite different from that in Lystra. Here in Athens Paul interacts with the Stoic philosophers of the day, utilizing the Athenian's religious categories while also challenging them. After referencing the "unknown god" and stating his intention to make this god known to them, Paul begins with a starting point similar to that of his speech in Lystra. He speaks about God as the creator of everything including the "one" from which all nations came. Paul explains further that one of God's purposes was to create within people the desire to search, grope, and find him, since he is "not far from each one of us" (v. 27). This seeking should not be done among gods of silver or stone, as such searching will be judged faulty by "a man whom he has appointed," whom God has affirmed by "raising him from the dead."

In communicating this Paul draws on Jewish tradition. However, as Losie has shown, Paul also draws in part on the outline of classic speeches from Stoic philosophy. The Old Testament tradition, Losie says, "would certainly have been formative for Paul's thinking and also for Luke's. But . . . the way these concepts are phrased in the speech draws on the language of the Greco-Roman philosophical world, particularly the world of Stoicism."[61] The use of Stoic forms of communication allows Paul to bridge the history of God's revelation through Israel with certain concepts in the Greek's own tradition. In addition, it allows him to redirect the trajectory of those concepts towards Jesus, further redefining the relationship between God and creation.

59. Hinkle, "Preaching for Mission," 96.

60. Ibid., 99. Hinkle explains that Paul and Barnabas have not bypassed or ignored the work of God in Israel, but that "the tradition is exactly where the apostles turn for help as they run into the streets to stop people from offering sacrifices to them." Ibid., 96. In so doing they draw on Old Testament images for creation (Exodus 20:11 and Psalm 146:6) and against idolatry (Psalm 96).

61. Losie, "Paul's Speech on the Areopagus," 230–32.

Paul's speech practices among Gentiles in this section thus seek to draw Gentiles into a story different from but related to their own. In this the Old Testament scriptures provide Paul with the "interpretive frame," inviting Gentiles to inhabit the story of God and, relatedly, his people.[62] In this, however, Paul refrained from making the peoples' beliefs or religion into an evil Other. Rather, Paul sought to include them and their history into the historic work of God that climaxed with the resurrection of Jesus.

EVIL OR UNJUST STRUCTURES

The Acts text highlights another aspect of evil that the disciple community often confronted. This regards the evil power, wielded by authorities and their structures, which stood against the growth of "God's word" and community, and the ways in which the disciple community confronted these non-violently.

At various points throughout Acts the disciple community conflicts with the authority claims of various power structures. For example, the community challenges the supremacy of Roman imperial authority by applying the word *sotair* (savior) for Jesus in Luke 2:11, Acts 5:31, and Acts 13:23.[63] In addition, the use of the word *kurios* (Lord), and particularly "Lord Jesus," often indicates a critique and challenge to others who would be called "Lord," particularly the imperial powers. As a final example, the text has depicted numerous instances where the believers came into conflict with the Jewish authorities, prompting Peter to declare at one point that "we must obey God rather than men" (5:29).

As the disciple community came into these conflicts, however, it is important to note that they did so non-violently. A prominent example of this is seen in 19:21—28:31, where the text spends six chapters on the events surrounding Paul's arrival in Jerusalem and his detention by Roman authorities in Jerusalem and Caesarea (21:17—26:32). As in other instances, Paul resists the authority of the Jewish and Roman structures non-violently. Of course, readers do not necessarily expect a violent response from Paul or the other disciples, since this would not follow after the example of Jesus whom the new people of God follow and name as their Lord, nor that of the disciple community as depicted throughout Acts. Because such a response would be so out of line with the character

---

62. Hinkle, "Preaching for Mission," 96.
63. Gilbert, "Roman Propaganda," 242.

of the disciple community, it would be easy to miss the fact that such a response was not at all out of line with other movements of the time. As Witherington shows, violent movements were common, and the Roman authorities were quite aware of and concerned over any leader or movement that might violently rebel against their rule.[64] The comment of the soldier to Paul in 21:38 shows that the altercation observed and stopped by the Romans was beginning to resemble a violent one. As such the Romans were sensitized towards demonstrations and movements that could turn violent and seditious.[65]

Ironically, and similarly to Jesus' crucifixion, it is the Jewish people who bring the demonstration to such a point. The continuity of Paul's non-violent witness with that of Jesus further highlights the non-violent nature of the new disciple community. This form of evil, though not taking the form of demonic personalities, is one that the disciple community discerns and counters non-violently.

Critical Correlation with the Yeshu satsangs

In their desire to be devoted to Jesus, the *Yeshu satsangs* practice and demonstrate in their ecclesial identity the discernment of evil. Such an emphasis critically correlates with the Acts text in a number of ways. First, the *Yeshu satsangs* give attention to the realities of demonic power, idol worship, and other practices that could keep *satsangis* from truly worshipping Jesus. The leaders practice exorcism and regularly pray against Satan in order to separate him and his powers from the *satsang* and *satsangis*.

However, the *Yeshu satsang* leaders also seek to counter certain Christian church teachings that seek to separate and shield people from the "evil" of Hinduism and Sikhism. In this regard they have developed an emphasis similar to Luke-Acts, exploring the ways in which the gospel calls them to engage the Hindu and Sikh religious traditions. Rather than

---

64. Witherington, *The Acts of the Apostles*, 661.

65. In addition, in his speech before Festus in 25:8–12 Paul highlights that, in addition to the accusations leveled against him by the Jewish authorities, he knows that the Roman authorities are concerned over the more serious crime (in their eyes) of sedition. Robinson and Wall, *Called to be Church*, 250. Paul asserts in response that he has done nothing "against Caesar" (25:8) and is willing to die if he is guilty of this. Paul's clarification regarding sedition highlights the fact that, throughout Acts and up to Paul's arrival into Jerusalem, there has been no indication that the church community entertained the option of resisting authority structures through violent means.

characterizing these traditions and structures as evil Others, the leaders in some ways see their community as entering God's overall story of bringing them to Christ. For example, Padman, who as we saw has received criticism from local pastors and has been told that his *satsang* is the "devil's workshop" particularly relates to Paul's speech in Acts 17. Rather than combating the peoples' faith, Padman believes that they need care and guidance to more clearly understand the "unknown god" which they have in some ways already been worshipping. Rather than criticizing their beliefs as demonic, Padman wants to frame their beliefs as part of a trajectory that will, if they so accept it, lead them to full understanding and salvation in and through Jesus.

Also, and related to the above discussion regarding the perceptions of holiness in Acts, the *Yeshu satsangs* contend that *Yeshu satsangis* can engage some (though not all) Hindu and Sikh practices in faith. As they do so, they seek to in some ways touch those practices that were deemed "unclean" and endeavor to make them "holy." Thus, the *Yeshu satsang* leaders are initiating a discourse that counters some of the supposed power of demons to "infect" people, particularly followers of Christ. Rather than being fearful of how a practice may contaminate a follower of Christ, the *Yeshu satsangs* contend that followers of Christ can engage some of these through faith, not be impacted by demonic power, and instead be an agent and witness for Christ. However, and related to Acts 15, the *Yeshu satsangs* also recognize that certain practices, such as idol worship, may be inappropriate, and could impact the believer's allegiance to Christ and their witness. These practices, though, are more carefully engaged and discussed, and the label of "demonic" is applied more carefully.

Second, in terms of the Acts text discussion of evil and unjust structures, the Christian church in northwest India would on the whole understand what it means to be an alternative community that contrasts "evil" structures. It is a minority community in religion, and largely a disadvantaged community in terms of caste. Because the halls and avenues of power have often been monopolized by the higher-caste Hindus and Sikhs, the Christian community is sometimes subject to unjust discrimination, and even persecution. It is thus not a difficulty for Dalit Christians to counter the power and influence of the "world." Such power has, in essence, never been available to them in either of their identities, much less in its combination. The Dalit Christian church has been an "alternative" community from the majority Hindu and Sikh structures, often not by its own choice.[66]

In this regard the *Yeshu satsangs* forge an intriguing path that accepts a level of identity as an alternative community, but also seeks to redefine what it is that makes it alternative. To understand the ways in which they are seeking to contrast society, it is again helpful to look at the way in which *bhakti* has functioned in the Hindu context.

Many *bhakti* movements in India arose as movements presenting an alternative social vision to that of the existing majority. These, as Juergensmeyer has discussed, challenged normative social orders with an "alternative framework of understanding."[67] In the northwest, the *nirguni bhakti* movements, or those that emphasized worship of a divine being without attributes, has been particularly influential in resisting the ideologies of privileged classes of Hindus.[68] Yet, these *bhakti* sects also draw from the Hindu ideologies and practices of their context. As such, and as Juergensmeyer summarizes, such *bhakti* sects have often been "counter-structures that exist in symbiotic relation to the religious culture of the dominant societies around them."[69]

Though in many ways very young and incipient, the *Yeshu satsangs* are drawing on the *bhakti* tradition and presenting an alternative social vision. Some, such as Dinesh, consciously include caste as a factor of his *satsangs* ecclesial identity, and desire to champion the cause of low-caste Dalit and "Other Backward Castes" (OBCs) through a *satsang* of spiritually-renewed followers of Christ. Others make caste less of a defining feature and, similar to some *bhakti* ideologies, desire *satsangs* that are inclusive of all castes. Common to these, though, is the desire to counter both Hindu or Sikh, and Christian, versions of normative social order and to form an alternative. Of course, these groups need to develop much further organizationally and numerically, and to mature over the course of many more years and decades. However, if they do so, and if they continue to create groups or a movement that stands separate from

---

66. Chad M. Bauman has suggested that Christianity in India has historically functioned as an alternative social order and has provided a cultural critique of society. When converting to Christianity, people both dissented from the hegemony of a particular order as well as assented to a new social vision. Bauman, *Christian Identity and Dalit Religion*, 96–97.

67. Juergensmeyer, *Religion as Social Vision*, 279.

68. Lorenzen, "Introduction: The Historical Vicissitudes of Bhakti Religion," 13.

69. Juergensmeyer, "The Social Significance of Radha Soami," 69.

churches and distinct from Hindu and Sikh beliefs, they may succeed in creating an alternative social vision that carefully discerns the evils of existing structures.

YESHU SATSANG MARKER 4: WITNESS

The final, and most often articulated ecclesial identity marker of the *Yeshu satsangs* was their desire to be a witness to their Hindu and Sikh communities. The theme of witness is, of course, also a major theme in Acts. I will discuss the ways in which the Acts text highlights important aspects of witness, and the ways this critically correlates with aspects of the *Yeshu satsangs'* witness.

Ecclesial Identities and Witness in Acts

Witness is a prominent ecclesial identity marker in the Book of Acts and is developed in a number of ways that correlate with the experience and ecclesial identity of the *Yeshu satsangs*.[70] In particular, the Acts text shows how the witness of the disciple community not only brought individuals to faith in Jesus, but also added to and created disciple communities that were a part of God's people. I will discuss several aspects of the disciple community's witness, and how these helped to form disciple communities that reflected local socio-cultural practices and traditions, but that also displayed unique, Christocentric identities that contrasted local communities.

WITNESS THROUGH PROCLAMATION

One of the ways in which witness is practiced in Acts is through proclamation. In particular, the disciple community proclaimed the death, resurrection and ascension of Jesus (e.g. 1:16–22; 2:14–36, 38–39; 3:12–26; 4:8–12, 19–20; 5:29–32), including Jesus' elevated status as "Lord and Christ" (2:36) and "prince and Savior" (5:31).[71] In addition, in the midst of these proclamations the disciple community call people to respond

---

70. In Acts 1:8 Jesus identifies his disciples as "witnesses," a designation that is almost exclusive to Luke-Acts in the New Testament and that forms an integral part of the disciples,' and the church's, identity. Though individuals are involved in proclaiming the gospel, the church as whole functions as a "restored Israel" that witnesses to the nations. Turner, "The 'Spirit of Prophecy,'" 347.

71. Green, "Salvation to the End of the Earth," 84n1.

through repentance and baptism, indicative of peoples' changed or deepened allegiance to God and commitment to community practices.[72]

In the second section of Acts (6:8–12:25), the witness and proclamation of the disciple community begins to spread to the Samaritan and God-fearer communities. As it does so, the disciple community begins to re-orient itself to those on the Jewish margins.[73] Philip leads the move to the periphery in the city of Samaria and with the Ethiopian eunuch.[74] In Samaria "all of them, from the least to the greatest" (v. 6) listen to Philip eagerly. The text uses the word *euangelizo* ("announce the good news") prominently in this passage, emphasizing the action of the disciples in proclaiming good news.[75] The same word is used again in 8:26–40 when Philip announces *euangelizo* to the Ethiopian eunuch. Though the text is not clear about whether or not the Ethiopian is Jewish or not,[76] it is nonetheless clear on his identity as a eunuch. This physical deformity causes him to be "impure" according to OT law and bars him from ac-

72. Green, "Doing Repentance," 7.

73. Following Stephen's speech Jerusalem is depicted as having rejected the word and people of God and functions less and less as a central motif. Instead, the "center" of God's work now turns to those who are socially and geographically on the periphery.

74. The contrast with the prior importance of the temple for Jews highlights the sense that "Philip's initiatives to the Samaritans and Ethiopian eunuch chart new territory among people who could not participate in the Temple at Jerusalem." Hertig, "The Magical Mystery Tour," 109.

75. Luke-Acts uses the verb *euangelizo* twenty-four times, fifteen of which are in Acts (5:42; 8:4, 12, 25, 35, 40; 10:36; 11:20; 13:32; 14:7, 15, 21; 15:35; 16:10; 17:18). It is unique among the gospels in its use (except for once in Matthew 11:5) and, in contrast, only uses the noun *euangelon* twice (Acts 15:7; 20:24). In this passage, for example, the scattered disciples, including Philip, go about "preaching the good news of the word" (v. 4) and the people of Samaria believe after hearing Philip "proclaiming the good news about the kingdom of God and the name of Jesus" (v. 12). Thus, while other Gospels present the "good news" as a noun, Acts shows it as a practice connected to the witness of the disciple community.

76. There has been much discussion and diverse opinion regarding whether the Ethiopian was a Gentile god-fearer or a Jew. Some contend that he was a Gentile God-fearer, making him the first Gentile convert in Acts. See Flemming, *Contextualization in the New Testament,* 35. Others argue that he does not fit the profile of a Gentile and that, in any case, the level of attention given to the story of Cornelius in Acts 10–11 is meant to emphasize that Cornelius was the first Gentile convert. See Reeves, "The Ethiopian Eunuch"; Seccombe, "The New People of God," 360. I contend that scholars seem to be more concerned over Jewish/Gentile identity and "firsts" than the text itself is. For example, whether the eunuch was a Gentile and therefore the first Gentile convert, Cornelius still stands-out as the first Gentile convert that the Jerusalem church *knew about,* and with whose situation they had to come to terms.

cess to the temple at Jerusalem (Deuteronomy 23:1). Exclusion from the temple also indicates and reminds the eunuch that he cannot enjoy full inclusion into the people of God. Philip, however, announces that the scripture the Ethiopian is reading applies to him through Jesus, and he responds positively.

Philip's encounter with the Samaritans and Ethiopian eunuch indicates that the Spirit of God is calling his people to go to and announce good news to those whom Judaism had "forgotten."[77] Acts 8 thus shows how God pushes the church to go across boundaries into places where it did not plan to go so that it may "call and create a new community."[78]

God further pushes the disciple-community to go and announce the good news in the story of Cornelius in Acts 10 and 11. Perhaps to help Cornelius function as a bridge figure that introduces the Jerusalem church to this new work of God, the text portrays Cornelius as an atypical Gentile who is devout and God-fearing, giving alms generously, and praying constantly to God.[79] Cornelius is thus not fully pagan in the eyes of the Jews, but neither is he a circumcised proselyte.[80] Though the text endows Cornelius with characteristics that help Peter to eventually approach and interact with him, there is nonetheless an ethnic barrier that has to be crossed. The narrative shows with great detail some of the barriers that Peter crosses, finally crossing the threshold of Cornelius' house, sharing the gospel, and witnessing the endorsement of God's Spirit on Cornelius and his household into the people of God. Throughout this section, the text emphasizes the role of the disciple community in proclaiming the good news to those on the cultural periphery, inviting them to join his people.

In the third section of Acts (13:1–19:20) the witness of the disciple community, and particularly that of Paul and his colleagues spreads continually further among non-God-fearing Gentiles. It is in this section that Paul proclaims the good news in relation to those practicing Greco-Roman religions. This, as discussed above, takes into consideration the

77. Robinson and Wall, *Called to be Church*, 126.

78. Ibid., 127.

79. The uniqueness of Cornelius is also indicated in Peter's sermon within which he contextualizes his message for a Gentile audience while also emphasizing Jesus' Jewishness. Whereas this shows continuity between Jesus and God's saving plan as begun through Israel, such Jewish connections could have been important for a synagogue God-fearer. Flemming, *Contextualization in the New Testament*, 41.

80. Ibid., 36.

Gentile's history and religious and philosophical thought, but does not accept it as the determining framework for understanding the gospel. Rather, Paul acknowledges and begins to re-interpret Greek history and religion in light of God's scriptures and revelation through Jesus. Though the content of his speeches are short, it is apparent that Paul is inviting people to believe in God's work through Jesus, not just in individualistic terms, but as that which forms and sustains communities.[81]

As a final point regarding proclamation, the text in this section shows that the witness of the disciple community not only proclaims the supremacy of Christ, but also redirects people from false understandings of God. Among Gentiles at Lystra, Paul and Barnabas critique the desire of some to offer sacrifices to them and redirected them to "turn from these worthless things to the living God" (14:15). In Athens Paul gently but clearly redirected the focus of the Epicurean and Stoic philosophers from the various objects of worship to making the "unknown God" known to them (17:23). Finally, as mentioned above, the Jerusalem council gives four requirements to the Gentile believers representing practices associated with idol worship. In these various ways, the text models the need for Gentiles to separate from certain practices of their context, particularly if and when they undermine the centrality of devotion to Jesus.

Witness through Service

In addition to their proclamation, the disciple community also bore witness to Jesus through practices of service. These were often directed to the marginalized, or those on the fringes of Jewish society, as well as to each other. Such practices of service followed the example of Jesus, who proclaimed that God was building a community whose behavior would reflect God's vision for a new community as prophesied through Isaiah and others.

Acts 1:1–6:7 presents two examples of this type of witness. The first, in Acts 4:32–35, demonstrates the generosity of the new community. Contrary to some interpretations, this text is not establishing a policy regarding the sharing of possessions.[82] Rather, it presents a picture of how

81. Bartchy, "Divine Power, Community Formation, and Leadership," 90–91.

82. Bartchy has argued that this text draws on the LXX of Deuteronomy 15:4–5, which talks about blessing, lack of need, and generosity, and links the disciple community with the promises and work of God as revealed in Israel. However, where the Deuteronomy text is expressed as a command, the selling and generosity in Acts is portrayed as a voluntary response to the "great grace" that was "upon them all."

the disciple community can express its life together in a way that presents a persuasive message to others.[83]

The second example provides a mixed view of the Jewish disciple community's servant witness. This occurs in Acts 6:1–6, where the disciples have an apparent misunderstanding regarding the nature of service (*diakonia*) by dividing the service of the word from the service at the table of the widows.[84] The end result of the decision of the twelve in Acts 6:1–6 corrects the problem by once again allowing widows to be served. However, the rationale that they apply demonstrates a slowness to understand and apply Jesus' own teaching regarding the way they are to "serve" others and thus be a witness. Nonetheless, though the apostles employed a faulty understanding and dichotomy between the *diakonia* of the word and that of widows, the overall conclusion of the passage is the affirmation of a community that serves.[85]

BARRIERS TO WITNESS

In addition to its teaching and examples regarding witness, the Acts text demonstrates several characteristics of ecclesial identity that were barriers or potential barriers to the disciple community's witness. For example, and as mentioned above in 1:1–6:7, the Jerusalem disciple community engaged in practices that reflected Jewish structure and culture and accentuated its structural association with the Jerusalem community. On the positive side, the text shows how the disciple community adapted these practices to reflect their Christological emphasis, proclaiming the work of God through Jesus and embodying the example of Jesus in their community practices. Jewish religious practices thus provided, among other things, a resource for structural association.

Bartchy, "Divine Power, Community Formation, and Leadership."

83. Robinson and Wall, *Called to be Church*, 83.

84. Support for this interpretation comes from the disciples' otherwise inexplicable deviation from Jesus' instructions in Luke 22:26–27, where Jesus shows how he comes as one who serves (at the table), and encourages his disciples to also be like one who serves (at the table).

85. In addition, this is done in the midst of, and across, a language and cultural distinction that had developed within the Jerusalem church. Flemming, *Contextualization in the New Testament*, 32. However, though the text infers the presence of groupings that were differentiated by language and cultural markers, it does not indicate that the groups had an acrimonious relationship. See Hertig, "Dynamics in Hellenism and the Immigrant Congregation," 75; Gaventa, *The Acts of the Apostles*, 112.

However, this association also hindered the disciple community from witnessing to others. Even when the Jewish disciple community's witness spread among the Gentiles, not everyone quickly embraced this. Though some of their representatives, such as Peter, more quickly embraced the importance of this for their self-understanding, others were more concerned over its implications. The Jerusalem council settled a halakhic question regarding the legitimacy and inclusion of Gentiles into the disciple community, but questions continued to linger in the community. When Paul arrived in Jerusalem in Acts 21, rumors continued to circulate regarding how Paul was not instructing Gentiles to "live according to our customs" (21:22). Though the Jerusalem church's leadership appeared supportive of Paul, the church sinks into narrative silence when Paul faces accusation from and is arrested by the Jewish and Roman authorities. Though the text does not elaborate, it indicates that the Jerusalem church was perhaps ambiguous, and even conflicted, regarding its association with the wider Jewish structures and cultures. It may have been viewed as a Jewish "sect," and perhaps enjoyed a level of association and witness among Jews because of this, but this association hindered its ability to relate to the witness that they and others were to have among Gentiles.

Critical Correlation with the Yeshu satsangs

The Acts text critically correlates with the *Yeshu satsangs'* ecclesial identity of witness in several areas. First, the *Yeshu satsangs* may be challenged or guided in part through the text's emphasis on the role of community formation. In particular, though the *Yeshu satsangs* have a growing sense of their own corporate identity and witness, this is still incipient. Whether because of the young age of the *satsangs*, or because of the importance given to leaders in guru *bhakti* sects such as theirs, the leader carries a high level of responsibility for the character and witness of the group. Whereas this would not conflict with the Acts text's notion of witness, Acts would give greater emphasis to the life of the community as a whole, and not just the choices and actions of the leadership, for its witness. The gifts of everyone in the *satsang* combine together to give full expression as Christ's body in that area.

Second, similar to what was discussed from the Acts text, the *Yeshu satsangs* emphasize a Christological focal point in their proclamation, usually and primarily in the *satsang* itself. The *Yeshu satsang* leaders are in many ways continuing to work-out the ways in which to proclaim a clearly Christological witness to their Hindu and Sikh communities in ways that do not invoke the situational logics often associated with the Christian church. As discussed regarding the discernment of evil, one move the leaders make is to not directly or indirectly label the Hindu or Sikh religious structures as evil. Rather, the leaders recognize that God is at work, though in limited ways, through the scriptures and practices of these communities. There can be some truth in them, and the people themselves are often seeking or worshipping the "unknown god." What they need, however, is the fullness of revelation as given through Jesus and the Bible, and a (sometimes miraculous) demonstration that God is real and cares for them. Though they are in some ways reticent to denounce the beliefs and deities of others, they are clear in upholding their devotion to Jesus and to teaching on his life, death and resurrection. They also call people to repent of sin so as to have blessing in this life, and eternal life with God in heaven.

Third, in addition to their proclamation, the *satsangs* also display certain marks of service, though this is more developed in some than in others. Gaurav, for example, regularly conducts medical camps and youth educational camps in partnership with the international NGO that he represents. In addition, his *satsang* regularly hosts *langars*, or common meals, similar to the Sikh practice of hosting meals after a temple service. These are popular events that often draw people who are not able to attend the *satsang* on a regular basis. For Gaurav, these practices help to show care for those in the *satsang* community, as well as outside of it.

Fourth, the *Yeshu satsang* leaders highly value God's blessing and miraculous power as a part of their witness. In Acts, as people, and particularly the marginalized, experience God's blessing and power, they often become followers of Christ. In addition, the miracles of the disciple community showed that God's favor was on the disciple community, lending authority to their speech and community-building practices. As a correlation, the *Yeshu satsang* leaders have experienced in various ways the importance of God's miraculous power for witness. In their own lives most of the leaders can point to a miraculous event that was decisive in the overall journey towards Christ. In addition, in many of their ministries prayer and answers to prayer continue to be one of the main ways in which new people are brought to faith in Jesus and fellowship in the *Yeshu satsang*. Such miracles provide people with the same types of decisive moments that the leaders themselves experienced, and also provide a level of authority to their work, words and ministry.

Fifth, the Acts text raises numerous opportunities and tensions for witness when closely engaging structural relationships. Among the *Yeshu satsangs*, the current emphasis is on re-engaging their association with Hindu and Sikh social structures, and thereby enhancing their witness to these communities. The *bhakti* tradition provides them with a toolkit of practices and resources from which to draw, and which provide helpful cultural and structural connections. It is important to note, however, that structural associations such as those made through the *bhakti* tradition can constrain the disciple community in its wider identification and witness. In this regard none of the *Yeshu satsangs*, as per the data that I gathered in this study, have yet encountered an Acts 21 situation where association with their Hindu or Sikh context has conflicted with association and support for the Christian church. Some situations, however, hint that their responses may be diverse and dependent on the situation.

For example, in February 2010 a Hindu group displayed an offensive poster of Jesus in one Punjabi town, prompting Christian protests and riots for the next few days. Christians continued to unite across the region in solidarity against the offense.[86] When one pastor contacted Gaurav, he indicated that he would not join the protest marches, nor encourage his *satsangis* to go since, for him, the offense was trivial. If, however, a Christian were attacked, he said, he might join with others in protest. Jagdeep and Manpreet were also upset about the poster and empathized with the Christian community, though they did not themselves join in the protests.

If and when deeper conflicts arise between Christian and Hindu or Sikh communities, the *Yeshu satsangs* will perhaps have to more deeply grapple with the implications of their dual association, what such conflict means for their ecclesial identity, and what non-violent responses might be appropriate. Though association and witness through the Hindu/Sikh social structures is important, Acts would perhaps challenge the *Yeshu satsangs* to not be silent on behalf of fellow followers of Christ.

---

86. Whereas the Christian leaders did not encourage a violent response, neither did they condemn the violent responses of some Christian youth. One Christian friend of mine in fact justified some of the violence, saying that a strong reaction was needed so that the Hindus and Sikhs know that they cannot oppress the Christians.

CHAPTER SUMMARY

How does a theological understanding of ecclesial identities based on the Book of Acts critically correlate with the ecclesial identities of the *Yeshu satsangs*? First, regarding the *Yeshu satsangs'* incorporation of the Hindu and Sikh *bhakti* tradition, Acts would suggest that the socio-structural traditions of a context, including aspects of the Hindu and Sikh traditions, could provide helpful resources for a disciple community's identity. In this Acts would affirm the way the *Yeshu satsang* leaders seek to incorporate and modify practices from their traditions. Such practices, and the structural association that this provides, can help form and express the disciple community's worship, and are important aspect of the disciple community's witness.

However, while a tradition may provide helpful resources for the community's worship and witness, Acts would also warn against the ways in which these traditions could constrain *Yeshu satsangs'* identities and prevent them from being faithful to behaviors and practices to which Scripture may call them. In particular, Acts would caution groups such as *Yeshu satsangs* from devaluing their relationships and associations with other Christians and churches when these conflict with their own community and community identity.

In addition, the disciple community's identity, though informed by and related to their particular tradition and community, is ultimately broadened and redefined by their devotion to Christ. For example, the Jewish disciple community's embrace and understanding of the Law as an ecclesial identity marker was ultimately relativized. Likewise, the *Yeshu satsangs* may find that they need to relativize certain practices in sensitivity to other communities,[87] and the Christian church in India may re-examine the practices of baptism in light of its sociological significance for Hindu and Sikh communities. In sum, the Christocentric nature of the disciple community will lead it to have both continuity and discontinuity with its local traditions.

Second, in relation to their experience of God's blessing and power, Acts would affirm the value the *Yeshu satsangs* place on healings, miracles, and other manifestations of God's power. It would, however, firmly emphasize that such manifestations be interpreted Christologically, giving

---

87. Gaurav, as I discussed above, in many ways exemplifies this. Recognizing that not all Sikhs would appreciate Hindu symbols for communion, for example, he relativizes the importance of these by alternating between different symbols when celebrating communion.

emphasis to the role and importance of Christ. In addition, Acts would confirm that God displays his power particularly in order to bless the marginalized and to draw peoples' attention to the community through whom they will see the example of Christ. For their part the *Yeshu satsangs* would agree with the Christocentric emphasis to God's power and its role in drawing people to the *Yeshu satsang*. However, they would perhaps need caution against exalting the guru or leader through whom the power is displayed over-and-against Christ.

Third, in their desire to carefully discern evil, the Acts text would in various ways affirm the *Yeshu satsangs'* reticence to label the Hindu and Sikh religious beliefs as evil or demonic. Instead, Acts would promote a re-interpretation of holiness as first espoused by Jesus. Instead of trying to maintain holiness through separation, Acts would advocate spreading holiness through touch and interaction. This would relate to the *Yeshu satsang's* emphasis on engaging the Hindu and Sikh structures and seeking to share Christ among them, rather than separating from them for fear of spiritual contamination. This is not to say, however, that all practices are helpful to the disciple community. Rather, Acts would counsel the *Yeshu satsangs* to be very clear about maintaining a strong emphasis on Christ and, as seen in Acts 15, refraining from practices that could hinder the community's witness and devotion to Christ.

Another aspect of discerning evil that Acts emphasizes is the need for the disciple community to resist and stand apart from certain structures that may be unjust. In this Acts would affirm the general way many *bhakti* movements have sought to present an alternative social vision in terms of caste and social structure. Some of the *Yeshu satsangs* display the beginnings of caste critique in their teaching and community, and Acts would affirm and encourage the further development of this.

Finally, Acts would shape the witness of the *Yeshu satsangs* in a number of ways. First, Acts would emphasize the importance of community formation as an outcome of witness. True witness, Acts would say, does not leave followers of Christ isolated from each other. This is a critique that, as I discussed in Chapter 1, would be shared by some critics of Hoefer and the individual *Yeshu Bhakta* of Churchless Christianity. For their part the *Yeshu satsangs* would agree with this point from Acts, as seen in their desire to form *satsang* communities.

Another aspect of witness that Acts emphasizes is the centrality of Christ, and grappling with the tensions that this may create for community identity. The *Yeshu satsangs* would resonate with the tension between their desire to minimize structural barriers and the need to differentiate between and resist practices that would undermine their allegiance and witness to Christ. Finally, Acts would counsel the *Yeshu satsangs* to not privilege their association with the Hindu and Sikh communities over their identification with other Christian churches, even if such association is meant for witness. Just as some in the Jewish disciple community under-valued God's work beyond them, so also it would be possible for the *Yeshu satsangs* to give too high of a focus to their own communities, and thus miss the way they are supposed to be witnesses to other communities.

In this chapter I have examined the ways in which the Acts text develops ecclesial identities, with particular attention on those that correlate to the ecclesial identity markers that the *Yeshu satsangs* are developing. I have shown how the Acts text addresses these, and resonates with many of the concerns and emphases of the *Yeshu satsangs*. The Acts text also points to areas of identity that the *Yeshu satsangs* could continue to develop, and areas that could, if they are not careful, constrain the *satsangs'* allegiance and witness to Christ. Having found and discussed these various points of critical correlation, I will now consider some final conclusions and recommendations as it regards ecclesial identities, *Yeshu satsangs*, and their related ministries.

CHAPTER 11

Conclusion and Recommendations

THE PURPOSE OF THIS study has been to understand the nature and emergence of the ecclesial identities and the markers of the *Yeshu satsangs*. My central argument has been that an Emergentist theory of identity formation and an analysis based on the Book of Acts will help me to identify and analyze the ecclesial identities of six *Yeshu satsangs* in northwest India. This focus was motivated in part by a lack of attention and clarity in studies of Hindu insider movements regarding the types of ecclesial identities and practices that may be helpful for leaders who want to establish such groups. The following is a summary of my findings and contributions to academic knowledge, leading to my final recommendations.

SUMMARY OF FINDINGS

In terms of academic theory the goal of this study has been to articulate a theory of ecclesial identity appropriate for Hindu and Sikh insider movements that takes into account the way identities are formed, and a biblical theology that critically correlates with this. I will review the different theoretical components and how they contributed to this study, and then discuss the contributions these make to academic scholarship.

Ecclesial Identity Formation: An Emergentist Theory of Identity Formation

To gain greater understanding of the *Yeshu satsangs* and their ecclesial identity formation I developed a theory I call an Emergentist theory of identity formation. This is comprised of four components; an Emergentist theory of agency, Analytical Dualism, the Morphogenetic process, and Retroduction. I employed these various components through a two-part process: an inductive analysis of the *Yeshu satsangs'* current ecclesial identities and markers via their practices; followed by a retroductive analysis of the leaders' past interactions and how these helped to shape these identities.

THE PRACTICES AND ECCLESIAL IDENTITY MARKERS

In the first step of this process I considered the question: How do *Yeshu satsang* leaders in northwest India use, modify and resist various practices to shape their ecclesial identities? Based on an Emergentist theory of identity formation I discussed how leaders were incorporating various Hindu and Sikh practices. These practices, I found, provided the *satsangis* with structural associations that they valued, as well as positive feelings regarding the ways in which to worship and approach God. The *Yeshu satsang* leaders sought to incorporate these while also infusing new cultural meanings based on the Bible and their faith in Jesus. In addition, the leaders also retained various Christian practices that they deemed central to their faith and, in general, sought to minimize various structural associations that these held with the Christian church.

After analyzing the various practices and the various reasons why leaders used these practices I then asked: What are the ecclesial identity markers of six Hindu and Sikh *Yeshu satsangs* in northwest India? Through an analysis of the *Yeshu satsang* practices and leaders' and *satsangis'* explanations of them I was able to identify four ecclesial identity "markers," or theological themes, that express important aspects of the *Yeshu satsangs'* ecclesial identities. These were (1) a *bhakti*-influenced devotion to Jesus, (2) experience of God's blessing and miraculous power, (3) the desire to carefully discern evil, and (4) the desire to be a witness to the Hindu and Sikh communities. All of the *Yeshu satsang* practices discussed contribute to one or more of these markers and help to give them expression in the life of the *Yeshu satsang*.

Thus, Chapters 5 through 8 demonstrate that in order to analyze the markers and "projects" of the *Yeshu satsang* leaders, it is important to have a clear theory regarding peoples' agency. In addition, these chapters show the ways in which Analytical Dualism helps conceptualize the type of properties with which leaders are interacting. Thus, the *Yeshu satsang* leaders, by exercising their agency, choose practices from their "toolkits" that help them form an identity, or *modus vivendi*, that gives expression to their Hindu and Sikh identities. It also helps them relate to those communities, and expresses and develops their devotion to Jesus.

THE EMERGENCE OF YESHU SATSANG ECCLESIAL IDENTITIES

After analyzing the present markers of ecclesial identity, I then considered the cultural, structural and agential processes and interactions that occurred to help form and shape these markers. This addressed my research question: How did the *Yeshu satsang* leaders' Hindu and Sikh backgrounds and interaction with Christian churches help shape the ecclesial identity markers of their *Yeshu satsangs*?

Again using an Emergentist theory of identity formation I used a retroductive method to consider the histories of the *Yeshu satsang* leaders and the ways in which their interaction with their own contexts and with the Christian churches of their areas helped form the particular identities of the *Yeshu satsangs*. Through an analysis of their testimonies I identified and discussed the influence of competitive contradictions, but also the nuance that *habitus* brings to the practices of the *Yeshu satsang* leaders. In this I found that, though in many ways they are seeking to change the identities of their groups, they are also influenced by both acting on a *habitus* informed by their Hindu or Sikh practices and belief in healing, as well as pentecostal practices of healing.

The main contributions of this section regard the importance of understanding antecedent processes, or morphogenesis, that help to shape existing identities. Though, as I assert through Emergentist theory, these antecedents do not determine the actions and identities that *Yeshu satsang* leaders pursue, they nonetheless constrain and enable these. In addition, the leaders' *habitus*, or "pre-logical logic, may actually work to counter or supersede some of the other goals the leaders have for their *satsangs*.[1] I was thus able to give further insight into the way in which the four ecclesial identity markers had been formed and why they were important to the leaders. This was seen in terms of the leaders' own immediate experiences as well as the wider historical and sociological interactions between the Christian churches and other communities in the region.

---

1. Bourdieu, *The Logic of Practice*, 19.

Critical Correlation of Yeshu satsang Ecclesial Identity Markers with the Book of Acts

My final research question asked: How does a theological understanding of ecclesial identities based on the Book of Acts critically correlate with the ecclesial identities of the *Yeshu satsangs*? In this I identified areas where biblical theology gave added insight and guidance to the *Yeshu satsangs'* ecclesial identity markers. One particularly important theme regarded the ways in which the Jewish disciple community's socio-cultural associations both enabled and constrained its growth in identity. I also identified points of tension between a disciple community's socio-cultural identification and its association with other disciple communities.

SUMMARY OF CONTRIBUTIONS TO THEORY

In formulating a theory appropriate for understanding ecclesial identities of the *Yeshu satsangs* I have attempted to expand upon the scholarship of various social theorists. I will summarize three contributions that I believe the development and application of this ecclesial identity theory offer to academic scholarship.

Development and Use of an Emergentist Theory of Agency

In Chapter 2, I built on the theory of Elder-Vass to articulate an Emergentist theory of identity formation. In this, Elder-Vass postulated that agency and *habitus* together co-determine the actions of people. That is, that any given situation will involve a combination of reflexive agency and *habitus* to make and implement a decision. However, Elder-Vass did not further conceptualize the relationship between these or what may cause one to dominate over the other. In response I contended that agency and *habitus* could be conceptualized as a continuum, and that the movement across "fields" was one factor that could move people along the continuum to become more conscious and reflexive in their decision-making.

In Chapter 9 I further described this process after finding and describing the occurrences of crises in the lives of *satsang* leaders. The accounts of crisis and their resolution highlighted the reflexivity that these leaders engaged as they began to, as Archer says, resurvey their sets of concerns. There was also evidence of what Bourdieu called the "hysteresis effect," where *habitus* responses did not change immediately, adding to the sense of crisis. However, as the leaders resurveyed concerns and responses, they reflexively embraced new sets of responses, including prayer from Christian pastors. As prayers were answered and the crises resolved, they joined Christian churches and learned new ways in which to worship God and appropriate his blessing and miraculous power. Some of these practices reflected aspects of previous healing practices while others were shaped by south Indian and other pentecostal-style churches. As they learned these practices, new *habitus'* were created. Thus, the interview data regarding peoples' faith journeys and practices in the *Yeshu satsangs* indicates that people move along a continuum of agency and *habitus*, drawing on one or both in combination depending on the nature of their context and situation. Attention to the *habitus-agency continuum* is thus an important area for investigation for those seeking to analyze group identity formation, including for those leaders seeking to change or influence the ecclesial identities of their churches or *satsangs*.

Analytical Dualism and Ethnographic Research

Archer formulated her theory of Analytical Dualism against the backdrop of sociology and macro studies of society and its structures and cultures. Though she has spent much time in describing micro processes, such as the "internal conversation" of people and their agency and how these theoretically contribute to social elaboration, her concept of Analytical Dualism has not, to my knowledge, been actively applied to an in-depth ethnographic study. Seeing potential in her conceptions of structure and culture for understanding "religion," I sought to analyze the *Yeshu satsangs* through her analytical grid. In doing so I identified some limitations as well as benefits.

The limitations that I continually struggled with regarded Archer's separation and definitions of structure and culture. Anthropologists often conceive of social structures as a product, or an aspect of, culture. Archer critiques this as a type of conflation and argues that researchers can benefit from separating the two. While I agree with this and with Archer's theoretical rationale, this framework is more easily applied on a macro versus a micro level. I found this to be the case when analyzing the history of the Christian church in northwest India in Chapter 4. In this case Analytical Dualism, together with the morphogenetic process, provided a helpful framework for conceptualizing the tensions that had developed between the Christian church and the wider society.

On the micro level, it became necessary to supplement Archer's definition of culture. Doing so, as described in Chapter 2, allowed me to more effectively apply Analytical Dualism in my ethnographic research. In light of this, I proposed that the concepts of the "cultural toolkit" help to better frame culture through Swidler's view, "symbols, stories, rituals and worldviews, which people may use in varying configurations to solve different kinds of problems."[2] I found that more carefully defining culture in this way aided the use of Analytical Dualism for an ethnographic context and helped to alleviate some of its weaknesses. Analytical Dualism proved a helpful way to understand the ways in which cultural ideas interact with family and other social structures, particularly in cultures where there is a high level of social cohesion, such as those often found in India.

Emergentist Theory and Biblical Interpretation

In Chapter 10, I applied Analytical Dualism and Morphogenesis to aspects of identity formation in the Book of Acts. In particular, these concepts helped me better understand the structures with which the Jewish disciple community sought to associate, as well as the way this association was strained or redefined by their cultural understandings of the gospel. Thus I found aspects of the early church's identity formation were highlighted and given further clarity when read through Emergentist theory. I suggest that biblical interpretation could be enriched through further applications of Emergentist theory.

SUMMARY OF CONTRIBUTIONS TO YESHU SATSANG RESEARCH

In addition to social and biblical theory, this study also makes contributions to *Yeshu satsang* or *Yeshu Bhakta* research. I will summarize three areas of contribution.

Ecclesial Identity: Hindu/Sikh, Christian, or Other?

The first contribution this study makes is to bring greater clarity regarding the types of identity that this particular group of *Yeshu satsangs* is forming. In Chapter 1, I discussed some of the literature pertaining to Hindu insider movements, or *Yeshu Bhaktas*. Out of this I determined

2. Swidler, "Culture in Action," 273.

that further theory was needed to help explain the ecclesial identity of insider groups, such as the *Yeshu satsangs*. Through my research I found that these particular *Yeshu satsangs* are creating an alternative ecclesial identity that is not fully related to or "inside" the Hindu, Sikh or Christian communities. I will discuss each of these in turn.

First, the *Yeshu satsangs* are related to but not fully a part of the Hindu or Sikh communities. This is seen in the *satsangs* as well as in the responses of *satsangis'* communities and families. The *Yeshu satsangs* utilize modified Hindu or Sikh practices, and *satsangis* and their Hindu or Sikh family members associate these with the Hindu or Sikh communities. However, *satsangis'* family members also sometimes indicate that, though the *Yeshu satsang* and practices are associated with the Hindu or Sikh communities, the *Yeshu satsangs* are not fully a part of those communities. One of the reasons for this, as leaders and their own *satsangis* attest, is their Christocentric focus as seen through their devotion to and worship of Jesus. Another factor that distinguishes them is their use of certain practices that are associated with the Christian community. Some—such as the use of the Bible, communion, and baptism—are retained though modified in some cases to reduce structural associations. Others are retained because of their association with God's miraculous power.

Second, though the *Yeshu satsangs* are not fully Hindu or Sikh, neither are they fully a part of the Christian community. In this the *Yeshu satsangs* are reacting against and trying to provide an alternative to the unhelpful aspects of Christian church identity and the barriers and contradictions that exist between the Christian and the Hindu or Sikh communities. The alternative, the *Yeshu satsang* leaders hope, will increase the association with and witness to the Hindu and Sikh communities. The leaders attempt this by minimizing practices that associate them with Christian structures, although they also readily accept certain practices that, for them, are integral to their allegiance to Jesus and the Bible, and that give them a connection to God's power.

The *Yeshu satsangs* thus occupy an alternative space between the Hindu and Sikh, and Christian communities. In light of this, what might the *Yeshu satsangs* look like in the future? What type of identities and community associations might they develop? The full answer to this will only be known in the future as the *Yeshu satsang* leaders persevere with their current project. However, some leaders seem to envision an extension and development of this alternative identity. Gaurav, for example, envisions that his, and *Yeshu satsangs* like his, will follow the example of the numerous *bhakti* deras and sects of the region, such as the Radha Soami. Groups like this have managed to develop a distinct identity that is neither fully Hindu nor Sikh, but that is accepted in varying degrees by those communities. It is acceptable, for example, for a Sikh to remain Sikh but be wholly devoted to and a member in the Radha Soami sect. In this way, Gaurav hopes and anticipates that, over time, the *Yeshu satsangs* will become their own sect that allow Hindus and Sikhs to remain in their communities but calls them to be wholly devoted to Jesus and a member of the *Yeshu satsang*.

Though it will take many years before it is possible to assess whether the *Yeshu satsangs* will develop in the ways of other *bhakti* sects, the four markers of their ecclesial identity, and the ways in which they are being formed, would seem to be potentially important elements for the new theological and social space the leaders envision. These, as I have suggested above, have incorporated elements of the Hindu and Sikh traditions, and also critiqued and nuanced certain teachings from the Christian churches to formulate an alternative way of following Jesus in the midst of a Hindu and Sikh context.

The hybrid identities and markers that the *Yeshu satsang* leaders are attempting to form in many ways parallel the experience and formation of the Jewish disciple community in Acts. This community adapted and retained a Jewish identity through their Jewish practices, but also adapted these practices to reflect a Christocentric focus. By the end of Acts the Jewish disciple community was both a "Jewish sect" as well as a distinct group called "the Way." As a group with a hybrid identity, they grappled with the meaning of this for their relationships with the different communities, particularly when those communities came into conflict. At times this Jewish ecclesial identity allowed them to witness to and within their community, but at other times constrained them from embracing the wider work that God was doing, and from identifying with believers of other communities. If the *Yeshu satsangs* continue to develop as Christ-following communities that relate to but are distinct from the Hindu, Sikh and Christian communities, they would very likely grapple with the same constraints and tensions as did the Jewish disciple community.

Yeshu satsangs and Their Growth

A second contribution that this study offers regards the type of "church" that *Yeshu satsangs* are forming, and how these might grow and create further "movements." As my review of precedent literature in Chapter 1 revealed, discussions among missiologists regarding Hindu "insider movements" have largely focused on individuals and families accepting and spreading the gospel through their homogenous community networks. The hope and theory is that Christ-centered movements among Hindus and Sikhs will most effectively and extensively spread through people and groups who remain situated within their socio-religious structures. However, these discussions and theories have not always been clear about what "church" may look like within such a movement. This study, and the example of the particular *Yeshu satsangs* upon which I focus, offer further clarity regarding the type of church and growth that such groups could have.

Among the *Yeshu satsangs*, there is of course hope that families will begin following Jesus and together worship Jesus as a structural unit, and perhaps provide a core part of the emerging disciple community. Indeed, this is what Padman is endeavoring to do with his Arya Samaji family as he develops his *Yeshu satsang* and its practices for them. However, as the study of Acts shows, it can become problematic if and when the disciple community's ecclesial identity is equated too closely with, and reduced to the family or community structural unit. As the Acts study has shown, the disciple community is quickly challenged to understand itself as part of a wider and multi-ethnic community, whether or not it is multi-ethnic itself.

Interestingly, this reading of Acts also resonates with what I found and discussed regarding aspects of the *bhakti* tradition embraced by the *Yeshu satsangs*. As Gaurav indicated, many of the *bhakti* movements of the northwest have been multi-caste and multi-religious communities, and yet have grown substantially. Indeed, most of the *Yeshu satsangs* of this study, with the exception of Padman's *satsang*, fit this same profile with their inclusion of people from different caste and religious backgrounds. Though they have not yet grown in significant numbers, the leaders argue that the pattern that they are following is highly indigenous to their region and will bear numerical fruit after some time.

Ecclesial Identity Markers and the Development of "Vernacular" or Contextual Ecclesiology

The ecclesial identity markers of the *Yeshu satsangs* provide helpful input for the ongoing development of a more developed contextual ecclesiology. Simon Chan, in reflecting on the need to develop more evangelical theology in Asia, suggests that this does not need to only encompass "critical reflection," which is the dominant way that theology is done in the West. Rather Chan argues that theologians should first look to the vernacular or "primary" theology that is already occurring in the "stories, testimonies, and songs coming from ordinary Christians" in their ecclesial communities.[3] These vernacular theologies provide an important and vital resource for further theological reflection. As Chan says, "It is in the systematic reflection on the ongoing primary theology of the church and making it explicit that Asian evangelicalism is likely to make a distinct contribution to the larger church."[4]

The *Yeshu satsangs* are, of course, just one expression of God's disciple community in India. They are also new and unique. However, the practices that have been analyzed here and the themes that have been highlighted—a *bhakti* personal and reverent devotion, experience of God's blessing and miraculous power, carefully discerning evil, and their unique approach to witness—can provide helpful material for further "systematic reflection." I have offered the beginning of such reflections by critically correlating these themes with a biblical theology. This process revealed rich possibilities for developing the theology of these themes, and for expanding the ways in which the biblical text could be read and interpreted. An ethnographic study of local, vernacular theology and its practices can reveal important theological themes for further reflection.

Beyond Theories of Contextualization

I have in this study focused on the Emergent processes at work as leaders shape practices in ways that fit their hoped-for ecclesial identities. Whereas the concepts and discussions of contextualization and indigenization have been and are immensely helpful, I have in this study shifted the focus of this discussion to the Emergentist interaction between *Yeshu satsangs* and their cultural and structural contexts. Whereas "contextualization"

3. Chan, "Evangelical Theology in Asian Contexts," 231.
4. Ibid., 234.

often implies a high level of control on behalf of one introducing and implementing contextual practices and ideas, an Emergentist theory of identity formation recognizes that a continual dialogue is occurring between systems and people. Because of this the intentions and "projects" of people are at best only partially realized. Unintentional influences and unaccounted for *habitus* impact the process. In addition, whereas "contextualization" often focuses on outside agents seeking to impact various cultural and structural systems, the emphasis of the present framework is on those who are "inside" the systems in varying degrees, and the ongoing processes they engage in as they re-read their cultural context in light of the gospel in a morphogenetic interaction.[5]

For example, Christianity as it has come to be understood and practiced in northwest India was found to be quite influential among the *Yeshu satsangs* of this study. Some missionaries or leaders who advocate a contextual "inside" approach may envision starting a fresh movement that takes pains to stay separate from Christian associations and influence in order to remain inside the Hindu and Sikh structures, and to more purely contextualize the gospel to those structures. However, in a setting such as northwest India, the history and ongoing influence of Christianity cannot be ignored. Any group that seeks to follow Jesus will be responding to, drawing from, or resisting expressions that have been already established by other followers of Christ in the area. An Emergentist theory of identity formation suggests that these will invariably enter the group's morphogenetic process, impacting the elaboration of their theology and ecclesial identities.

RECOMMENDATIONS

In light of this study I present several recommendations: first of all for those involved in the Hindu and Sikh "insider" discussion; second, for persons and organizations involved in working with *Yeshu satsang*-type ministry; and third, for further study.

---

5. In this I agree with R. Daniel Shaw who argues for a "new missional perspective" that moves "beyond contextualization." Based on an inferential understanding of cognition and on relevance theory he contends, "It is necessary to move beyond contextualization, as previously conceived, to recognition of God's presence in the midst of people everywhere and to recognition of the ways that presence enables people to 'know God.'" Shaw, "Beyond Contextualization," 212.

Recommendations for Persons and Organizations Working with Yeshu satsangs

In recent years more and more people and organizations have taken an interest in new ways of developing churches or *Yeshu satsangs* in India. I have several recommendations designed to help these people and organizations in their continued pursuit.

SATSANG-AS-IDENTITY VS. SATSANG-AS-OUTREACH

The first regards the emphasis and focus given to evangelism strategy versus the formation of an ecclesial identity. Many people who advocate a *Yeshu satsang* approach, including many of the leaders of this study, place outreach as the prime reason for the practices and style that they have adopted. This emphasis on outreach can have strengths and weaknesses attached to it. The strength is that it focuses efforts on adapting practices in a way that will minimize the Otherness of following Jesus and will hopefully be appealing to Hindus and Sikhs. In this we can and should applaud efforts for effective witness that will encourage Hindus and Sikhs to become followers of Jesus and to worship and live-out their devotion to Jesus in ways that appeals to their extended family and community.

However, the emphasis on outreach easily reduces *Yeshu satsang* practices to tools for evangelism. In such cases the move towards being "Hindu" is much less about identity than it is about presenting a witness. When used as tools such practices can sometimes be used inconsistently, and perhaps in ways that do not appear authentic. Though they desire to reach out to their people, the *satsang* style can be seen simply as a means of outreach, not an expression of identity.

Though the *Satsang*-as-outreach is an important motivation and discussion, I suggest that further discussion, attention, and teaching be given to *Satsang*-as-identity, or the legitimacy of *Yeshu satsangs* as an expression of God's disciple community. This views the ecclesial identity that the *Yeshu satsangs* are attempting to forge not only as an evangelism strategy, but an expression of one's own identity, or as Dayanand Bharati calls it, one's "birthright."[6]

---

6. Bharati, *Living Water and Indian Bowl*, 33.

TEACHING AND EMPHASIS ON GOD'S MIRACULOUS POWER

Many of the *Yeshu satsangis*, and leaders themselves, were initially at-tracted to Jesus through their first-hand experience of God's power, whether through dreams, healings, or deliverances. If these testimonies represent a more generalized experience among others who have come to Christ through miracles, it is hard to ignore the impact of the miraculous in the life and growth of a disciple community. In light of this it is little wonder then that *Yeshu satsang* leaders, who desire their *satsangs* to grow, would draw on prayer practices that have helped elicit healing and other miracles. However, though they modify the practices slightly to reduce their Otherness, the practices are not fully understood as a part of Hindu and Sikh experiences.

Discussions on "contextualization" in the Hindu and Sikh contexts, such as those in Chapter 1, have perhaps not grappled deeply enough with the role of miracles in drawing people to Christ, and the impact such experiences have on a *satsangi* and the shape of a *satsang*. Future *satsang* work could perhaps benefit from further discussions on how to embrace the power of God while remaining socially close to Hindu and Sikh communities and if, or what, Hindu or Sikh healing practices could be shaped Christologically.

Recommendations for the Hindu and Sikh "Insider" and "Indigenous Church" Discussions

Based on this study, I put forward two recommendations for those in-volved in discussions regarding "insider movements" in India. The first is for scholars to give greater attention and clarity to ecclesiological frame-works and definitions. The second is to more fully explore the reality of what I call hybrid religious identities.

DEFINITIONAL AND CONCEPTUAL CLARITY REGARDING "CHURCH"

First, and as my review of literature in Chapter 1 presented, this study points to the need for clarity regarding ecclesiology and the church when discussing Hindu and Sikh insider movements or groups. Many scholars generally have similar Christologies, agree on the centrality of Christ, the need to eschew idol worship and devotion to other gods, and the need to call Hindus and Sikhs to receive salvation and become followers of Jesus. However, ecclesiological issues—particularly those regarding the identity that the church pursues in relation to its socio-cultural context—are often contentious and the source of much tension between people with varying viewpoints.

Part of the difficulty is imprecision regarding what is meant by being outside of "the church," what makes a church "Indian," "indigenous," and so on. Though scholars such as Roger Hedlund have done much to raise awareness of new churches with indigenous origins, I recommend that scholars discussing issues related to *Yeshu satsangs* or Indian churches give careful reflection regarding what constitutes "Indian" ecclesial identities, and clarify these concepts in their discussions.

Affirming Hybrid Identities

Another issue regarding insider movements and church identities regards some of the bounded, or "inside" and "outside" language that some scholars have adopted when categorizing churches or *Yeshu Bhaktas* and *satsangs*. In response, I have shown through an Emergentist framework that identities are often fluid and drawing on a variety of structural and cultural resources. I have also shown how the *Yeshu satsangs* of this study are seeking to move back "inside" the Hindu and Sikh communities in some ways, but how they are also comfortable with distance from them in other ways. Some of this distance derives from the leaders' Christological focus, their experiences in Christian churches, and some of the practices that they continue.

Some who argue for clearer identifications "inside" the Hindu and Sikh communities may argue that future leaders should seek to establish *Yeshu satsangs* that are "inside" the Hindu and Sikh communities from the start, rather than ones that transition from Christian house churches. However, the experience of these *satsangs* indicates that the "internal" changes of the heart will quickly lead to choices, particularly in the public realm, that will begin to form distinctions between them and those around them. Even if the *satsangis* refuse to demonize the beliefs of their family, for example, their allegiance to Jesus begins to call them to make distinctions in some public practices. In addition, the wider Hindu and Sikh communities will view *Yeshu satsang* gatherings as distinctive and perhaps at best a variation of a Hindu or Sikh dera, even if they use Hindu and Sikh symbols and styles.

In light of this, more consideration should be given to the possibilities of alternative ecclesial identities and how these can or should be developed. Some of this can be derived from, as I will describe below, studies on existing Hindu *bhakti* sects and the ways these have developed. In addition, understanding how ecclesial identities are formed through a mix of influences, including *habitus*, reflexive deliberation, and cultural and structural influences, can encourage training of *Yeshu satsang* leaders that incorporates reflection on such influences.

Recommendations for Further Research

There are several areas that I suggest would be helpful for further research. First, further research needs to be conducted on the different *bhakti* movements, including the ways in which they have grown and developed alternative, unique identities that also associate with the Hindu and Sikh communities. Such a study could consider the ways in which *Yeshu satsangs* could similarly develop leadership and frame its practices and identities in ways that relate to their families and communities, while also presenting a unique and appealing identity.

Second, this study focused on qualitative interviews to determine the identities of particular *Yeshu satsangs*. However, further quantitative research can be conducted regarding the number of people that become followers of Christ in pentecostal churches and in *Yeshu satsangs*, and the reasons that they do so, including the occurrence of miracles. Such a study could provide important indicators regarding the areas of growth in disciple communities, the castes and communities in which the growth is occurring, and the various reasons for this. Such a study could also begin to offer comparisons and contrasts between the types of growth occurring in *Yeshu satsangs* and different types of churches.

Third, this study focuses on ecclesiology and ecclesial identities of *Yeshu satsangs*. Further studies focusing on areas of Christology, soteriology, and other theological themes within the *Yeshu satsangs* would be rich additions that would help to give further resources for theological reflection. Beyond the *Yeshu satsangs*, in recent years some Indian theologians, particularly within more ecumenical circles and with a liberation orientation, have been developing new Indian theologies. Further work can and should be done, however, by Indian evangelical theologians on ecclesiology, ecclesial identities, Christology, and other themes. In particular, further work is needed to probe the theologies of the growing independent pentecostal churches, as well as the impact and response of ecclesiology in the face of urbanization and globalization.

Finally, it would be helpful and important to continue the analysis of the *Yeshu satsangs* and their ecclesial identity formation over time. Such analysis will give further clarity regarding which hopes and "projects" of the *Yeshu satsang* leaders are emerging in the ways that they hope, which unintended results are emerging, and why. For example, it may be that the *Yeshu satsang* will grow, have a wider impact in their regions, and counter the existing situational logics. However, it will also probably be the case that new, unintended consequences will occur which they will need to address. Further research over time would be needed to further understand the ways in which the *Yeshu satsang* leaders are allowed to interact with their communities, which practices they can effectively incorporate, and the amount of influence and agency they can exert on the ongoing morphogenesis.

CLOSING THOUGHTS

The *Yeshu satsangs* have begun the exciting but challenging task of shaping new Christ-centered communities that challenge conventional models of "church" and "church-planting." The path they have chosen, as the leaders themselves testify, is not always easy and is often misunderstood, particularly by Christian leaders. However, their contextual approach is bearing fruit, as seen in the lives of the *satsangis* who are discovering the joys of following and worshipping Christ in ways familiar to them and their communities. As they move forward, the *Yeshu satsangs* will encounter new challenges and situational logics, as happens in any morphogenetic process. However, as I hope this study has demonstrated, it is important for those of us who desire to see Hindus and Sikhs become followers of Jesus to understand and learn from the *Yeshu satsangs*. If Christ-centered communities are to flourish among the Hindus and Sikhs of India, more disciple communities whose practices and identities challenge the church's Otherness will be vital. The *Yeshu satsangs* are one such initiative that, with the power and guidance of God, can continue to shape a new movement and expression of disciple community in India.

APPENDIX A

Delimiting Region Versus Religion

My INITIAL FOCUS IN this project was upon *Yeshu satsangs* among Hindu communities that are using primarily Hindu practices and that were spread across various regions. However, several factors soon indicated that a regional versus a religious focus would be most helpful for this study, and that it would be helpful to analyze Hindu and Sikh *Yeshu satsangs* together.

The first reason for this regards the religious, cultures, structures and histories that are unique to northwest India. Though Hindu and Sikh religious communities differentiate themselves from each other, these distinctions are relatively recent, developing in part through the impact of British colonial practices, the work of elites and leaders of religious communities, and the politicization of religious identities. As Harjot Oberoi, Indian historian and sociologist has observed, up until the nineteenth century the Sikh and Hindu communities showed much overlap and lacked the distinct identities implied by religious identifiers such as "Hinduism" and "Sikhism."[1]

---

1. Oberoi, *The Construction of Religious Boundaries,"* 13. Oberoi's thesis states, "Religion, as a systematized sociological unit claiming unbridled loyalty from its adherents and opposing an amorphous religious imagination, is a relatively recent development in the history of the Indian peoples. Once such a tidy cultural construct surfaced, probably sometime in the nineteenth century, it rapidly evolved, gained wide support, and became reified in history. Out of this reification it easily turned into something separate, distinct and concrete: what we now recognize as Hinduism, Buddhism and Sikhism" (ibid., 17). Oberoi's point, and the nature of religious identities prior to colonization is still strongly debated. Several scholars contend that the British and their policies, including the practice of census-taking, which categorized

In addition, despite the work of religious leaders and elites to strengthen the identities and contours of their religious traditions and communities, a high level of fluidity continues to exist between these groups, and there continues to be a wide range of definition as to what makes a person a "Hindu" or "Sikh." Regarding the Sikh community, for example, Ron Geaves has stated:

> The late twentieth century saw a polarisation and increasingly rigid compartmentalisation of both (Hindu and Sikh) communities but there remain tens of thousands of Sikhs, especially in rural Punjab, who are indistinguishable from Hindus except for their claim to be Sikhs. Their homes contain Hindu images, they acknowledge caste distinctions and observe purity and pollution rules.[2]

Similarly, as seen at various times in this study, testimonies from and participant observation of *Yeshu satsangi*s from Hindu and Sikh families confirm that people in their respective communities have very diverse experiences in religious practices. People from Hindu families regularly visit Sikh gurdwaras and Muslim shrines, and many Sikhs have some practices that overlap with Hindus.[3]

The historic and current diversity and fluidity of practices between religious groups expresses a religious plurality that, while certainly evident throughout India, is nonetheless particularly strong in northwest India. One of the common expressions of this plurality are the large number of *sant* or *bhakti* (devotional) sects with *deras* (religious centers) focused

---

people into religious communities, essentially created religious communities that did not exist before. See Oddie, *Imagined Hinduism*; Dalmia, *The Nationalization of Hindu Traditions*; Frykenberg, "The Construction of Hinduism as a 'Public' Religion"; van der Veer, *Religious Nationalism*. Others, however, contend that such identities existed before colonization. See Lorenzen, *Who Invented Hinduism?* Though this is debated, there exists a level of consensus that, whether or not the policies and forces of colonization (including missionary work) *created* categories and "religions" such as Hindus and Muslims, these influences nonetheless significantly strengthened such identities. Such identities have been further strengthened in recent decades through both Hindu and Sikh fundamentalist movements that, while not unanimously accepted by all in their respective communities, have succeeded in further defining and creating boundaries between themselves and other religious groups, at least at an elite religio-political level.

2. Geaves, "Sikhism, Relationship with Hinduism," 793–94.

3. Some Sikhs, for example, had Hindu gods in their homes and went to the graves of Muslim "pirs," or holy men who's spirits are now believed to have powers over people and need to be placated.

on the personality and teaching of a particular guru. Many, such as the Radha Soami, Nirankaris, and Dera Sacha Sauda, have formed within the last fifty to 150 years, and are thus relatively recent movements.[4] Though *deras* have distinct foci, they commonly attract people from both Hindu and Sikh communities and employ devotional and music practices that relate to a mix of communities. Those attending *deras*, though becoming devoted to the guru and his teachings, often also continue relating to their Hindu and Sikh families, practices, and identities.[5] The *dera* culture of the northwest thus highlights the ability of many to continue identifying with Hindu or Sikh religious structures, such as castes and families, while sharing practices and beliefs with others in the context of *bhakti* devotional groups. This has important implications for the formation of new religious groups in the northwest, including *Yeshu satsangs*.

Though some recent movements, such as *bhakti deras*, have challenged religious categories, other movements have sought to redefine and specify Hindu and Sikh religious traditions, thus pluralizing these identities in a different way. Even within the *Yeshu satsangs*, for example, some have been a part of the Hindu Arya Samaj, a group that rejects all idol worship, and who do not use many of the symbols of traditional *Sanatan* Hindus.[6] Some have come from high-caste Hindu families who practiced "orthodox" Hindu rituals linked to idols, temples and rituals, while others from low-caste or village communities related more to local family Hindu deities and the spirits of Muslim and Sikh saints. Still others associated with the Hindu Ravidas tradition, a movement that has challenged high-caste hegemony and reshaped Hindu practices and community in favor of low-caste Dalits. The northwest region, similar to other regions, offers a plurality of "Hinduisms" and "Sikhisms."

4. Geaves, "Baba Balaknath"; Juergensmeyer, *Radhasoami Reality*.

5. Such identity retention is not new or unique to these *deras*. A similar mix of identities was also a part of the early formation of the *bhakti* sect that came to be known as Sikhism. One story that illustrates this regards the death of the founding leader, Guru Nanak, in 1596. As a traditional account presents it, as his death approached Guru Nanak's followers argued about the method of his burial. Those from Muslim families wanted to bury his body, while those from Hindu families wanted to cremate it. Through a miraculous event in which Nanak's body vanished, the followers decided to divide the cloth that had covered Nanak's body so that Muslims could bury one part and the Hindus burn the other. McLeod, *Guru Nanak and the Sikh Religion*, 50–51. Thus new religious movements, particularly in the northwest, have often attracted people from diverse community backgrounds and who, at least initially, had to negotiate between the community rituals and identities of these various backgrounds.

6. Llewellyn, "Arya Samaj," 44.

As the above indicates, the plurality that exists among religious groups and in the various *bhakti deras* of the region is sometimes found within the *Yeshu satsangs* themselves. Within *Yeshu satsangs*, particularly in more urban settings, it is common to have a mix of people from various Hindu and Sikh backgrounds, as well as mixed marriages between Hindu, Sikh and Christians.[7] These *satsangs* thus display a confluence of influences and communities similar to some of the *deras* in the region. In addition, the leaders of predominately Hindu *Yeshu satsangs* often differentiated the Hindu practices and beliefs of their community and region from that of other parts of India.

A final reason that led me to mix Hindu and Sikh *Yeshu satsangs* in this study regards my focus on the emergent processes and shaping of ecclesial identity. It became apparent that, though the Hindu and Sikh *Yeshu satsangs* have some unique practices and beliefs, they are nonetheless responding to common concerns regarding the Christian ecclesial identity as it has come to exist in northwest India, and reflecting the broader *bhakti* tradition in their response. In addition, the *Yeshu satsang* leaders are essentially engaging in similar processes as they seek to establish new and contrasting ecclesial identities to those that exist.

---

7. I encountered no one in any of the *satsangs* from a Muslim background, the other main religious group of the area.

APPENDIX B

Summary of *Yeshu Satsangis* and Leaders

Name[A]	Age	Caste	Education	Gender	How Long A Believer	How Long At Present Satsang	Occupation
Dinesh *Satsang*							
Dinesh	50–59	Hindu Dalit	11–12	Male	11+ years	6–10 years	Full-time Ministry
D-1	50–59	Hindu Dalit	7–10	Female	1–3 years	1–3 years	Housewife
D-2	30–39	Hindu Dalit	None	Female	1–6 months	0–12 months	Housewife
D-3	20–29	Hindu Dalit	11–12	Female	7–12 months	0–12 months	Housewife
D-4	40–49	Hindu FC	?	Female	6–10 years	1–3 years	Business Owner
D-5	20–29	Hindu Dalit	Bachelors	Female	1–3 years	1–3 years	Housewife
D-6	30–39	Hindu Dalit	7–10	Male	1–3 years	1–3 years	Business Employee
D-7	20–29	Hindu Dalit	11–12	Female	1–6 months	0–12 months	Teacher
D-8	40–49	Hindu Dalit	7–10	Female	4–5 years	4–5 years	Small Vendor

Appendix B

Name[A]	Age	Caste	Education	Gender	How Long A Believer	How Long At Present Satsang	Occupation
Gaurav *Satsang*							
Gaurav	40–49	Hindu FC	Bachelors	Male	11+ years	6–10 years	Free To Serve
G-1	20–29	Hindu FC	7–10	Female	1–3 years	1–3 years	Housewife
G-2	40–49	Tribal	None	Male	6–10 years	6–10 years	Small Vendor
G-3	20–29	Nepali Tribal	1–6	Female	4–5 years	4–5 years	NGO
G-4	20–29	Nepali Tribal	7–10	Male	11+ years	6–10 years	NGO
G-5	20–29	OBC	Bachelors	Female	4–5 years	4–5 years	Student
G-6	20–29	Hindu FC	7–10	Male	4–5 years	1–3 years	Gov Worker
G-7	20–29	Hindu FC	11–12	Male	6–10 years	?	Student
G-8	40–49	Nepali Tribal	1–6	Male	6–10 years	1–3 years	Factory
G-9	30–39	Hindu Dalit	1–6	Male	1–3 years	?	Service Sector
G-10	20–29	Hindu FC	Bachelors	Male	1–3 years	0–12 months	Business Employee
G-11	40–49	Hindu FC	11–12	Male	4–5 years	0–12 months	Business Owner
G-12	30–39	Hindu FC	11–12	Female	11+ years	6–10 years	NGO
G-13	30–39	Nepali Tribal	7–10	Male	11+ years	11+ years	NGO

Name[A]	Age	Caste	Education	Gender	How Long A Believer	How Long At Present Satsang	Occupation
G-14	30–39	Hindu FC	Bachelors	Male	6–10 years	6–10 years	?
G-15	30–39	Tribal	None	Female	11+ years	6–10 years	Housewife
G-16	30–39	Dalit	7 10	Male	4–5 years	4–5 years	Factory Worker
Jagdeep/Manpreet *Satsang*							
Jagdeep	50–59	Sikh Dalit	Bachelors	Male	11+ years	4–5 years	Gov Worker
Manpreet	40–49	Sikh Dalit	Bachelors	Female	11+ years	4–5 years	Gov Worker
J-1	50–59	sikh Dalit?	?	Female	4–5 years	4–5 years	Housewife
J-2	40–49	Sikh Dalit	7–10	Female	11+ years	1–3 years	Housewife
J-3	30–39	FC	1–6	Female	6–10 years	1–3 years	Housewife
Navdeep/Naveen *Satsang*							
Navdeep	40–49	Sikh Dalit	Bachelors	Male	11+ years	1–3 years	Full-time Ministry
Naveen	40–49	Sikh Dalit	7–10	Male	11+ years	6–10 years	Full-time Ministry
N-1	20–29	Hindu Dalit	Masters	Female	1–3 years	1–3 years	Teacher
N-2	20–29	Sikh FC	11–12	Female	6–10 years	6–10 years	Housewife
N-3	40–49	Sikh Dalit	None	Male	1–3 years	1–3 years	Daily Wages
N-4	30–39	Sikh FC	7–10	Male	4–5 years	4–5 years	Farmer
N-5	40–49	Sikh Dalit	7–10	Male	4–5 years	1–3 years	Daily Wages

Name[A]	Age	Caste	Education	Gender	How Long A Believer	How Long At Present Satsang	Occupation
N-6	20–29	Sikh Dalit	1–6	Male	1–6 months	0–12 months	Tractor/ Truck Driver
N-7	30–39	Sikh Dalit	1–6	Female	1–3 years	1–3 years	Daily Wages
N-8	60–69	Sikh Dalit	None	Male	1–3 years	1–3 years	Daily Wages
N-9	50–59	Sikh Dalit	None	Male	1–6 months	0–12 months	Daily Wages
N-10	60–69	Sikh Dalit	None	Male	1–6 months	0–12 months	Daily Wages
Padman *Satsang*							
Padman	40–49	Hindu FC	Masters	Male	6–10 years	1–3 years	Professional
Padman *Satsang*i 1	30–39	Hindu FC	Masters	Female	6–10 years	1–3 years	Housewife
Padman *Satsang*i 2			?				
Ravi *Satsang*							
Ravi	20–29	Hindu OBC	11–12	Male	6–10 years	4–5 years	Full-time Ministry
Ravi *Satsang*i 1	20–29	Hindu OBC	Bachelors	Male	Not Applicable	0–12 months	Student
Ravi *Satsang*i 2	20–29	Hindu OBC	11–12	Male	1–6 months	0–12 months	Student
Ravi *Satsang*i 3	20–29	Hindu OBC	7–10	Male	1–6 months	0–12 months	Service Sector
Consultants & Relatives/Friends							

Name[A]	Age	Caste	Education	Gender	How Long A Believer	How Long At Present Satsang	Occupation
Ruth	60–69	Hindu/ Christian Dalit	Bachelors	Female	11+ years	Not applicable	Professional
Jasbir	20–29	Sikh FC	Bachelors	Male	11+ years	Not applicable	Full-time Ministry
Nandita	20–29	Sikh FC	Masters	Female	4–5 years	Not applicable	Full-time Ministry
Nandita father	40–49	Sikh FC	7–10	Male	4–5 years	Not applicable	Farmer
Nandita mother	40–49	Sikh FC	7–10	Female	4–5 years	Not applicable	Housewife
Jasbir friend 1	40–49	Sikh FC	?	Male	Not Applicable	Not applicable	Business Owner
Jasbir friend 2	Unassigned	Sikh FC	?	Male	Unassigned	Not Applicable	Business Owner

A. Names of all *Yeshu satsang* leaders and members have been changed to pseudonyms in this study for confidentiality purposes.

APPENDIX C

Leadership Questionnaire

1. Please share your testimony.

2. What was your belief before following Jesus?

3. Before you were a follower of Jesus to whom or what was your family devoted? Where did you attend, and how often? How did this devotion impact family decisions and relationships?

4. Had you heard about Jesus growing up? What did you think about Jesus at that time? Of Christians? Of Christian churches?

5. When did you first hear about Jesus? What or who influenced you to become a follower of Jesus?

6. What did your family (parents, uncles, brothers/sisters) think and say when you began following Jesus?

7. How did your pastor counsel you regarding Hinduism/Sikhism? What became your attitude and actions towards it?

8. What was the process for changing your attitude towards your Hindu community?

9. How do you describe your beliefs now? How do people greet you? Do you want to be known as a "Christian?"

10. What is your opinion of Hindu *prasad*? Have you taken *prasad* recently? How do you counsel your people in this regard?

11. Do you eat non-veg? Why or why not?

12. Do you go to temple or gurdwara? What do you teach on this?

13. What were your hopes for the *satsang* when you started?

14. How has your approach to the *satsang* changed over the years? Why?

15. What are your hopes for the *satsang* in the future? How do you hope for it, or the people in it, to relate to the Hindu/Sikh communities?

16. Please describe your understanding of baptism. How do you describe and practice it?

17. How do you give communion?

18. Is there anything else that you would like to share?

APPENDIX D

Satsangi Questionnaire

Particulars:

Name: Age: Gender: Married? To whom? Number and Names of children: Education: Occupation: Caste:

1. Please share your testimony with me. What was your life like before following Jesus, and how did you come to follow Jesus? (Allow them to start where they would like. After they stop, prompt for any of the following information that was not covered):

2. Before you were a follower of Jesus to whom or what was your family devoted? Where did you attend, and how often? How did this devotion impact family decisions and relationships?

3. Had you heard about Jesus growing up? What did you think about Jesus at that time? Of Christians? Of Christian churches?

4. When did you first hear about Jesus? What or who influenced you to become a follower of Jesus?

5. What did your family (parents, uncles, brothers/sisters) think and say when you began following Jesus? What did they see you do, or hear you say, that made them say this?

6. Some believers believe that its okay to take *prasad*, others do not. What do you think? Have you, or do you take *prasad* at Hindu events?

7. Do you eat non-veg? Why or why not?

8. Do you go to temple or gurdwara? Why or why not?

9. What was your belief before following Jesus? How do you call yourself now?

10. Do you want to be known as a vishwasi, Masihi, Christian, or something else?

11. What do your non-believing friends and family call you? How do they greet you?

12. Have you heard about *jal diksha*? *Jal sanskar*? *Naam Daan*? Baptism? What do they mean? How are they different?

13. Have you taken baptism (or *jal diksha*)? If not, do you want to? Why or why not?

14. What changes have you seen occur in your life since following Jesus?

15. People call their worship gatherings by different names. How do you usually call your gathering?

16. When did you begin attending the *satsang*? Why?

17. Of the various things that happen in a *satsang*, which are your favorites? Can you recall a particular instance or example of this?

18. (If person has been in *satsang* for a long time): How has the *satsang* worship service changed over the years?

19. Have you been to other churches? Other *satsang*s? Which ones? What was your experience in those places?

20. (If *satsang* uses Hindu symbols) how did you feel when you first saw the Hindu symbols? How do you feel about these now?

21. How does the *satsang* celebrate the Lord's Supper?

22. Is there anything else that you would like to share?

APPENDIX E

Summary of *Yeshu Satsang* Leaders by Community

Satsang Leader	Parents' religious and caste affiliation	Current Work	Current Location	Region in NW	Size of *satsang(s)**
Hindu *Yeshu Satsang* Leader					
Gaurav	Hindu, Forward Caste	Directing local Christian NGO	Hindu and Sikh city	Eastern Punjab	4 satsangs, app. 80–100 people total
Dinesh	Hindu Ravidas, Scheduled Caste	Small business	Hindu Town	West Himachal Pradesh	2 satsangs, 50–60 people total
Ravi	Hindu, Other Backward Caste (Ramgharia)	Staff of Christian mission org	Hindu city	north Haryana	1 satsang, 30–40 people

Satsang Leader	Parents' religious and caste affiliation	Current Work	Current Location	Region in NW	Size of satsang(s)*
Hindu Arya Samaj *Yeshu Satsang* Leader					
Padman	Hindu Arya Samaj, Forward Caste	Lawyer	Hindu Village	north Haryana	1 satsang, 10 family members
Sikh *Yeshu Satsangs* Leaders					
Jagdeep	Sikh, Scheduled Caste (Majhabi)	Government worker	Sikh and Hindu town	Eastern Punjab	1 satsang, 10–20 people
Manpreet (wife of Jagdeep)	Sikh, Scheduled Caste (Majhabi)	Government-Teacher	Sikh and Hindu town	Eastern Punjab	Same as above
Navdeep	Sikh, Scheduled Caste (Majhabi)	Satsang leader	Sikh Villages	Western Punjab	2 satsangs, 50–60 people total
Naveen (co-leader with Navdeep)	Sikh, Scheduled Caste (Majhabi)	Satsang song-leader	Sikh Villages	Western Punjab	Same as above
Potential Sikh *Yeshu Satsang* Leaders (Consultants)					
Jasbir	Sikh, Forward Caste (Jatt)	Church pastor	Sikh Village	Western Punjab	
Nandita	Sikh, Forward Caste (Jatt)	House church leader	Sikh Village	Western Punjab	

* Most *satsangs* do not have formalized membership and people affiliate with the *satsangs* to varying degrees over time. Numbers of people involved in each *satsang* thus approximate those who attend somewhat regularly.

APPENDIX F

The Use of *Bhajans* by *Yeshu Satsangs*

THE ORIGINS OF HINDU *bhajans* as a genre can be traced to the *bhakti* sant-poets from as early as the eighth century, but more prominently in the works of poets such as Sur Das and Mira Bai from the sixteenth century onwards. Etymologically, *bhajan* is related to *bhakti*, which is usually translated "devotion" and describes a branch of Hinduism emphasizing a deep relationship to God and to others who share a similar devotion.[8] *Bhajan*, in traditional Sanskrit, is the action noun of *bhakti* and therefore, as Hawley describes, "implies the doing of *bhakti*."[9] This "doing" of devotion through *bhajan*, however, has taken on a musical connotation, such that *bhajan* music and *bhakti* devotion are inextricably linked.[10] Because of this background, the definition of a *bhajan* is first and foremost understood as a music expressing devotion to God, and only secondarily as a style of music. The *Yeshu satsangis* similarly emphasized the devotional nature of *bhajans* and rarely reflected on the style of a *bhajan*.

However, a closer look at the structure of certain *bhajans* and their use reveals that there are certain musical characteristics that distinguish them from other church song styles. For example, most *bhajans* normally consist of a *tek*, or two-line unit that is repeated like a refrain, and several verses.[11] In *Yeshu satsangs* such *bhajans* often last six-to-eight minutes. By contrast, many of the worship songs popular in northwest churches

---

8. Hawley, "The Music in Faith and Morality," 244.

9. Ibid.

10. See also Dicran, "Hindi Christian Bhajans; Ranade, *Music Contexts.*

11. Ranade, *Music Contexts,* 76.

have only one or two verses and last for three-to-four minutes on average. The *bhajan* refrains, and sometimes the verses, often have a responsorial structure, with the leader singing a line and the *satsangi*s repeating it back. This feature has traditionally aided non-literate communities to learn *bhajan*s without the aid of written material.[12] In addition, when leading a slow *bhajan*, leaders often repeat the final refrain several times at increasing tempos and volume, which also increases the urgency and excitement of the *bhajan*.

Historically certain segments of the Indian Church have developed *bhajan* traditions. However, these have largely been concentrated in southern (Andhra Pradesh and Tamil Nadu) and central (Maharastra) India. By contrast, much of the music of the Hindi-speaking north has drawn from western-oriented forms. Musician and lay-researcher C. H. Dicran confirmed this general characteristic in his 1999 survey of churches and composers throughout north India, and noted that this trend would probably continue since "Young Protestant Christian musicians have found their niche in the increasing demand for quality Western music in India."[13] Nonetheless, and as Dicran found, there have been and continue to be some who compose music in a *bhajan* style.

R. C. Das was an early pioneer in this, and some Catholic leaders and churches continue to promote the composition and use of *Yeshu bhajan*s (also known as *Krist bhajan*s) for the purposes of indigenization and evangelism. Protestant churches throughout north India have adopted some of these compositions and a small number of composers, such as Anil Kant, have begun writing and performing Christian songs in a *bhajan* style. Commenting on some of the *bhajan*s that his *Yeshu satsang* shares with Christian churches, Gaurav says, "Christians all sing those songs. Those are common *bhajan* songs. The point is that some of the *bhajan*s came up [and] the church also took [them]. . . . Anything [that] comes in the name of Christ, anybody's free to take it" [E].[14]

In addition, and more recently, Hindi speaking *Yeshu satsang*s in various parts of north India, particularly in and around Varanasi, have written *Yeshu bhajan*s and compiled these into song books that are popular among the Hindi-speaking *Yeshu satsang*s around the country, including in the northwest. Some *satsangi*s also write their own songs, or

---

12. See Myers, *Music of Hindu Trinidad*, 303.

13. Dicran, "Hindi Christian Bhajans," 114.

14. Interview with Gaurav, Mar 6, 2010.

adapt the Hindu devotional songs of popular Bollywood movies to reflect devotion to Jesus.

While the *Yeshu satsangs* primarily use *bhajan*s, some also use *geets* or songs that have been written in a more Western-Christian style. These *geets* tend to be shorter and use words typical in the Christian community, such as "Hallelujah" and "*Yeshu Masih.*" In instances where a song has such a word or phrase in the refrain, the *Yeshu satsang* leaders sometimes introduce an alternative word or refrain. For example, the song leader in Ravi's *satsang* one time led a *geet* singing "Hallelujah" in the refrain, but substituting the words "*Jai, jai ho Yeshu*" (Victory to Jesus) the next time the refrain was repeated.

Glossary

Aarti: Hindu worship ritual

Aarti bhajan: Popular Hindu devotional song

Akal Purkh: Sikh term for God, literally "eternal being"

Amritdhari: An initiate into the orthodox Sikh khalsa

Ardas: Sikh term for prayer

Arya Samaj: A Hindu reform movement founded by Swami Dayananda in 1875

Ashram: Spiritual retreat center or hermitage

Bandagi: A Christian prayer meeting

Bani: Sikh term for written scripture

Bhagwan: Sanskrit term for God

Bhajans: Devotional songs

Bhakta: Devotee or worshipper of God

Bhakti: Practices of worship or devotion to a deity

Bhakti Marga: Way of devotion that leads to moksha, or salvation

Bindi: Beauty sign on a woman's forehead; can refer to the existence and well-being of the husband

Dalit: "Crushed, Oppressed"; A marginalized person in India whose caste community is outside of the caste system.

Dera: Literally "camp" or "settlement." The location where a guru resides and leads worship.

Dhan Satguru Yeshu: Blessed master-guru Jesus

Dharma: Caste duty; righteous act

Diksha: Hindu ordination or initiation

Diya: Hindu oil lamp

Geets: A song of praise; sometimes denoting a short, popular song

Grahastha: (also grihastha) The "householder," or second phase of life where a person maintains a household and family

Gurdwara: Sikh temple

Guru: Spiritual master

Habitus: (Latin) Used by sociologist Pierre Bourdieu to refer to peoples' unconscious dispositions and actions

Halwa Prasad: Sweet food distributed during or after Hindu and Sikh worship. Same as kadah prasad

Havan: Worship ceremony using fire

Havan Kund: Bowl in which to make fire for havan

Havan Samagri: Spice mix for use during a havan

Isai: Urdu word for Christian

Jaati: Another word for "caste"

Jadugar: Shaman

Jai masih ki/jai masih di: (Hindi/Punjabi) Christian greeting meaning "Praise to the Messiah"

Jal Diksha: Water initiation

Jal Sanskar: Water initiation

Jyoshi: Shaman or practitioner of astrology

Kadah Prasad: Sweet food distributed during or after Hindu and Sikh worship. Same as halwa prasad

Kalash: Small pot used in Hindu worship

Kamma: Caste of landowners in south India

Khuda hai: Praise the Lord

Kirtan: Devotional songs; Sikh devotional songs

Ladoo: A sweet food

Majhabi: Common name for various Dalit castes in northwest India.

Mandala/mandala: A community of disciples

Mandir: Hindu temple

Masihi: Christian

Moksha: Hindu concept of salvation; freedom from the birth cycle

Muktee: Power

Naam daan: "Take the name"; initiation

Nariyal: Coconut

Om: Hindu chant; sound related to the creation of the universe

Pandit: Hindu scholar

Paramatma: Great Spirit/God

Parmeshwar: God, Supreme Lord

Pavithra: Holy

Pir: Muslim saint; also referring to the saint's grave

Prabhu: Lord

Prabhu Bhoj: General Hindi/Punjabi Christian term for the Lord's Supper

Prasad: Hindu food offering

Puja: Devotional Ritual

Rehal: Wooden bookstand

Roti: Flat bread

Sadhana dharma: Literally "spiritual duties." Described by Brahmaband-hav Upadhyay as one of two components of Hinduism

Samaj dharma: Literally "social duties." Described by Brahmabandhav Upadhyay as one of two components of Hinduism.

Sanskrit: Ancient language of India

Sannyasi: One who has renounced worldly or material pursuits

Sat Sri Akal: God is the ultimate truth; Sikh greeting

Satbachan: True word; So be it

Satguru: Supreme master

Satguru Yeshu: Jesus the Supreme Guru

Satsang: Truth-gathering; Religious fellowship

Shankh: Shell-horn used in Hindu worship

Svaha: Hail; So be it

Tatasthu: So be it

Vedas: Primary Hindu scriptures

Vishwasi: Literally "believer;" commonly used by Christians

Waheguru: Wonderful Guru/God

Yeshu: Jesus

Yeshu Bhakta: Devotee of Jesus

Yeshu Darbar: Literally the "court of King Jesus." The name of a large church in Allahabad, Uttar Pradesh

Bibliography

Adams, Matthew. "Hybridizing *Habitus* and Reflexivity: Towards an Understanding of Contemporary Identity?" *Sociology* 40, no. 3 (2006) 511–28.

Airan, C. D. *Kalagara Subba Rao*. Vijayawada, India: n.p., 1965.

Alcoff, Linda Martin. "Who's Afraid of Identity Politics." In *Reclaiming Identity: Realist Theory and the Predicament of Postmodernism*, edited by Paula M. L. Moya and Michael R. Hames-Garcia, 312–44. Berkeley, CA: University of California Press, 2000.

Aleaz, K. P. *Christian Thought through Advaita Vedanta*, Contextual Theological Education Series. Delhi: ISPCK, 1996.

Alphonse, Martin. "The Gospel and Hindu *Bhakti*: Indian Christian Responses from 1900 to 1985. A Study in Contextual Communication." PhD diss., Fuller Theological Seminary, 1990.

Anderson, Benedict. *Imagined Communities: Reflections on the Origin and Spread of Nationalism*. Rev. and extended ed. New York: Verso, 1991.

Animananda, B. *The Blade: Life and Work of Brahmabandhab Upadhyaya*. Calcutta: Roy & Son, 1945.

Appasamy, A. J. *Christianity as Bhakti Marga: A Study of the Johannine Doctrine of Love*. Madras: Christian Literature Society, 1930.

Archer, Margaret Scotford. *Being Human: The Problem of Agency*. New York: Cambridge University Press, 2000.

———. *Culture and Agency: The Place of Culture in Social Theory*. Rev. ed. New York: Cambridge University Press, 1996.

———. *Realist Social Theory: The Morphogenetic Approach*. New York: Cambridge University Press, 1995.

———. *Structure, Agency, and the Internal Conversation*. New York: Cambridge University Press, 2003.

Baago, Kaj. *The Movement around Subba Rao: A Study of the Hindu-Christian Movement around K. Subba Rao in Andhra Pradesh*. Bangalore: The Christian Institute for the Study of Religion and Society, 1968.

———. "The Post-Colonial Crisis of Missions." *International Review of Missions* 55 (1966) 322–32.

Bartchy, S. Scott. "Divine Power, Community Formation, and Leadership in the Acts of the Apostles." In *Community Formation in the Early Church and in the Church Today*, edited by Richard N. Longenecker, 89–104. Peabody, MA: Hendrickson, 2002.

Bauman, Chad M. *Christian Identity and Dalit Religion in Hindu India, 1868–1947.* Grand Rapids: Eerdmans, 2008.

Bernard, H. Russell. *Research Methods in Anthropology: Qualitative and Quantitative Methods.* 4th ed. Oxford: AltaMira, 2006.

———. *Social Research Methods: Qualitative and Quantitative Approaches.* Thousand Oaks, CA: Sage, 2000.

Berner, Ulrich. "Synkretismus Und Inkulturation." In *Suchbewegungen—Kulturelle Identitat Und Kirchliches Bekenntnis,* edited by Siller, 130–44. Darmstadt: Wissenschaftliches Buchgesellschaft, 1991.

Bharati, Dayanand. *Living Water and Indian Bowl: An Analysis of Christian Failings in Communicating Christ to Hindus, with Suggestions toward Improvements.* Pasadena, CA: William Carey Library, 2004.

Bhaskar, Roy. *The Possibility of Naturalism: A Philosophical Critique of the Contemporary Human Sciences.* 3rd ed. New York: Routledge, 1998.

Blue, Bradley. "Acts and the House Church." In *The Book of Acts in Its Graeco-Roman Setting,* edited by David W. J. Gill and Conrad Gempf, 119–222. Grand Rapids: Eerdmans, 1994.

Blundel, Richard. "Critical Realism: A Suitable Vehicle for Entrepreneurship Research?" In *Handbook of Qualitative Research Methods in Entrepreneurship,* edited by Helle Neergaard and John Parm Ulhoi, 49–74. Northampton, MA: Edward Elgar, 2007.

Bottero, Wendy. "Intersubjectivity and Bourdieusian Approaches to 'Identity.'" *Cultural Sociology* 4, no. 1 (2010) 3–22.

Bourdieu, Pierre. *Language and Symbolic Power.* Translated by Richard Nice. Cambridge, MA: Harvard University Press, 1991.

———. *The Logic of Practice.* Translated by Richard Nice. Oxford: Polity, 1990.

———. *Outline of a Theory of Practice.* Translated by Richard Nice. New York: Cambridge University Press, 1977.

———. *The Social Structures of the Economy.* Translated by Chris Turner. Malden, MA: Polity, 2005.

Boyd, Robin H. S. *An Introduction to Indian Christian Theology.* Delhi: ISPCK, 1975.

Census Commissioner of India. "Census of India." No pages. Online: http://www.censusindia.gov.in/Tables_Published/Basic_Data_Sheet.aspx.

Chan, Simon. "Evangelical Theology in Asian Contexts." In *The Cambridge Companion to Evangelical Theology,* edited by Timothy Larsen and Daniel J. Treier, 225–40. Cambridge: Cambridge University Press, 2007.

Chase, Susan E. "Narrative Inquiry: Multiple Lenses, Approaches, Voices." In *The Sage Handbook of Qualitative Research,* edited by Norman K. Denzin and Yvonna S. Lincoln, 651–79. Thousand Oaks: Sage, 2005.

Cornell, Stephen E, and Douglas Hartmann. *Ethnicity and Race: Making Identities in a Changing World.* Thousand Oaks, CA: Pine Forge, 1998.

Davey, Cyril James. *The Story of Sadhu Sundar Singh.* Chicago: Moody, 1950.

Dev, Anil. *Deep Jale:* Aradhna Music, 2000.

Devasahyam, D. M., and A. N. Sunarisanam, eds. *Rethinking Christianity in India.* Madras: Hogarth, 1938.

Elder-Vass, Dave. "Reconciling Archer and Bourdieu in an Emergentist Theory of Action." *Sociological Theory* 24, no. 4 (2007) 325–46.

Elliston, Edgar J. *Introduction to Missiological Research.* Unpublished Manuscript, 2008.

Farquhar, J. N. *The Crown of Hinduism.* London: Oxford University Press, 1913.

Fernando, Leonard, and G. Gispert-Sauch. *Christianity in India: Two Thousand Years of Faith*. New Delhi: Penguin, 2004.

Flach, Sabine, Daniel Margulies, and Jan Söffner, eds. *Habitus in Habitat I: Emotion and Motion*. New York: Peter Lang, 2010.

Flemming, Dean E. *Contextualization in the New Testament: Patterns for Theology and Mission*. Downers Grove, IL: InterVarsity, 2005.

Franzosi, Roberto. "Narrative Analysis—or Why (and How) Sociologists Should Be Interested in Narrative." *Annual Review of Sociology* 24 (1998) 517–54.

Freitag, Sandria B. "Contesting in Public: Colonial Legacies and Contemporary Communalism." In *Making India Hindu: Religion, Community, and the Politics of Democracy in India*, edited by David E. Ludden, 211–34. Delhi: Oxford University Press, 1997.

Fuller, C. J. *The Camphor Flame: Popular Hinduism and Society in India*. Princeton: Princeton University Press, 1992.

Gaventa, Beverly Roberts. *The Acts of the Apostles*. Abingdon New Testament Commentaries. Nashville: Abingdon, 2003.

Gibbs, Graham R. *Analyzing Qualitative Data*. Los Angeles: Sage, 2007.

Gilbert, Gary. "Roman Propaganda and Christian Identity in the Worldview of Luke-Acts." In *Contextualizing Acts: Lukan Narrative and Greco-Roman Discourse*, edited by Todd Penner and Caroline Vander Stichele, 233–56. Atlanta: Society of Biblical Literature, 2003.

Gill, David W.J. "Acts and Roman Religion: Religion in a Local Setting." In *The Book of Acts in Its Graeco-Roman Setting*, edited by David W.J. Gill and Conrad Gempf, 80–92. Grand Rapids: Eerdmans, 1994.

Gottschalk, Peter. *Beyond Hindu and Muslim: Multiple Identity in Narratives from Village India*. New York: Oxford University Press, 2000.

Green, Joel B. *The Acts of the Apostles*. New International Commentary on the New Testament. Grand Rapids: Eerdmans, forthcoming.

———. "The Challenge of Hearing the New Testament." In *Hearing the New Testament: Strategies for Interpretation*, edited by Joel B. Green, 1–9. Grand Rapids: Eerdmans, 1995.

———. "Doing Repentance: The Formation of Disciples in the Acts of the Apostles." *Ex Auditu* 18 (2002) 1–23.

———. *The Gospel of Luke*. The New International Commentary on the New Testament. Grand Rapids: Eerdmans, 1997.

———. "Interview." March 5, 2009.

———. "Learning Theological Interpretation from Luke." In *Reading Luke: Interpretation, Reflection, Formation*, edited by Craig G. Bartholomew, Joel B. Green and Anthony C. Thiselton, 55–78. Grand Rapids: Zondervan, 2005.

———. "Living as Exiles: The Church in the Diaspora in 1 Peter." In *Holiness and Ecclesiology in the New Testament*, edited by Kent E. Brower and Andy Johnson, 311–25. Grand Rapids: Eerdmans, 2007.

———. "Salvation to the End of the Earth: God as the Savior in the Acts of the Apostles." In *Witness to the Gospel: The Theology of Acts*, edited by I. Howard Marshall and David Peterson, 83–106. Grand Rapids: Eerdmans, 1998.

Griswold, Wendy. *Cultures and Societies in a Changing World*. Thousand Oaks, CA: Pine Forge, 2008.

Gunn, David M. "Narrative Criticism." In *To Each Its Own Meaning*, edited by Steven L. McKenzie and Stephen R. Haynes, 201–29. Louisville, KY: Westminster John Knox, 1999.

Hardgrave, Robert L., and Stanley A. Kochanek. *India: Government and Politics in a Developing Nation*. Boston, MA: Thomson Higher Education, 2008.

Harding, Christopher. *Religious Transformation in South Asia: The Meanings of Conversion in Colonial Punjab*. New York: Oxford University Press, 2008.

Hedlund, Roger. "Introduction: Indigenous Christianity as a Field for Academic Research." In *Christianity Is Indian: The Emergence of an Indigenous Community*, edited by Roger E. Hedlund. Delhi: ISPCK, 2004.

———. "Present-Day Independent Christian Movements: A South Asian Perspective." In *Christian Movements in Southeast Asia: A Theological Exploration*, edited by Michael NaiChiu Poon, 39–58. Singapore: Genesis Books, 2010.

———. *Quest for Identity: India's Churches of Indigenous Origin—the 'Little Tradition' in Indian Christianity*. Delhi: ISPCK, 2000.

———. "The Witness of New Christian Movements in India." Unpublished Paper for the IAMS Assembly in Malaysia, 2004.

Hegde, Rajaram, Esther Bloch, and Marianne Keppens. *Rethinking Religion in India: The Colonial Construction of Hinduism*. London: Routledge, 2010.

Hertig, Paul. "Dynamics in Hellenism and the Immigrant Congregation." In *Mission in Acts: Ancient Narratives in Contemporary Context*, edited by Robert L. Gallagher and Paul Hertig, 73–86. Maryknoll, NY: Orbis, 2004.

———. "The Magical Mystery Tour: Philip Encounters Magic and Materialism in Samaria." In *Mission in Acts: Ancient Narratives in Contemporary Context*, edited by Robert L. Gallagher and Paul Hertig, 103–13. Maryknoll, NY: Orbis, 2004.

Hiebert, Paul G. *Missiological Implications of Epistemological Shifts*. Harrisburg, PA: Trinity, 1999.

Hiebert, Paul G., R. Daniel Shaw, and Tite Tienou. *Understanding Folk Religion*. Grand Rapids: Baker, 1999.

Higgins, Kevin. "The Key to Insider Movements: The "Devoted of Acts."" *International Journal of Frontier Missions* 21, no. 4 (2004) 155–65.

Hinkle, Mary E. "Preaching for Mission: Ancient Speeches and Postmodern Sermons." In *Mission in Acts: Ancient Narratives in Contemporary Context*, edited by Robert L. Gallagher and Paul Hertig, 87–102. Maryknoll, NY: Orbis, 2004.

Hoefer, Herbert. *Churchless Christianity*. Pasadena, CA: William Carey Library, 2001.

———. "An Introductory Paper on the Relationship of the Church to Non-Baptized Believers in Christ." In *Debate on Mission*, edited by Herbert Hoefer, 353–65. Chennai, India: Gurukul Lutheran Theological College and Research Institute, 1979.

Hunsberger, George. "Conversion and Community: Revisiting the Lesslie Newbigin-M. M. Thomas Debate." *The International Bulletin of Missionary Research* 22, no. 3 (1998) 112–17.

Hymes, Dell. *Foundations in Sociolinguistics: An Ethnographic Approach*. Philadelphia, PA: University of Pennsylvania Press, 1974.

———. "Models of the Interaction of Language and Social Life." In *The Ethnography of Communication*, edited by John Gumperz and Dell Hymes, 35–71. New York: Blackwell, 1972.

Ikegami, Eiko. "A Sociological Theory of Publics: Identity and Culture as Emergent Properties in Networks." *Social Research* 67, no. 4 (2000) 989–1029.

Ilaiah, Kancha. *Why I Am Not a Hindu: A Sudra Critique of Hindutva Philosophy, Culture, and Political Economy*. Calcutta: Samya, 1996.

Inden, Ronald B. *Imagining India*. Oxford; Cambridge: Basil Blackwell, 1990.

Jacobsen, Douglas. *Thinking in the Spirit: Theologies of the Early Pentecostal Movement*. Bloomington, IN: Indiana University Press, 2003.

Jeyaraj, Dasan. *Followers of Christ Outside the Church in Chennai, India: A Socio-Historical Study of a Non-Church Movement*. Zoetermeer: Boekencentrum Academic, 2009.

Jorgensen, Danny L. *Participant Observation: A Methodology for Human Studies*. Newbury Park: Sage, 1989.

Jorgensen, Jonas Adelin. *Jesus Imandars and Christ Bhaktas: Two Case Studies of Interreligious Hermeneutics and Identity in Global Christianity*. New Yord: Peter Lang, 2008.

Juergensmeyer, Mark. *Radhasoami Reality: The Logic of a Modern Faith*. Princeton: Princeton University Press, 1991.

———. *Religion as Social Vision: The Movement against Untouchability in 20th Century Punjab*. Berkley: University of California, 1982.

———. "The Social Significance of Radha Soami." In *Bhakti Religion in North India*, edited by David N. Lorenzen, 67–93. Albany, NY: State University of New York Press, 1995.

Kakar, Sudhir. *Shamans, Mystics, and Doctors: A Psychological Inquiry into India and Its Healing Traditions*. Chicago: University of Chicago Press, 1982.

Kaplan, Steven. "Introduction." In *Indigenous Responses to Western Christianity*, edited by Steven Kaplan, 1–8. New York: New York University Press, 1995.

Kärkkäinen, Veli-Matti. *Introduction to Ecclesiology*. Downers Grove, IL: InterVarsity, 2002.

Kathettu, Sabu Mathai. *The Sikh Community and the Gospel: An Assessment of Christian Ministry in Punjab*. Delhi: ISPCK, 2009.

Krishan, Gopal. "Demography of the Punjab (1849–1947)." *Journal of Punjab Studies* 11, no. 1 (2004) 77–92.

Lewis, Rebecca. "Insider Movements: Honoring God-Given Identity and Community." *International Journal of Frontier Missiology* 26, no. 1 (2009) 16–19.

Lieblich, Amia, Rivka Tuval-Machiach, and Tamar Zilber. *Narrative Research: Reading, Analysis, and Interpretation*. Thousand Oaks: Sage, 1998.

Lipner, Julius. *Hindus: Their Religious Beliefs and Practices*. New York: Routledge, 1994.

Lorenzen, David N. "Introduction: The Historical Vicissitudes of *Bhakti* Religion." In *Bhakti Religion in North India*, edited by David N. Lorenzen, 1–32. Albany, NY: State University of New York Press, 1995.

———. *Who Invented Hinduism? Essays on Religion in History*. New Delhi: Yoda, 2006.

Losie, Lynn Allan. "Paul's Speech on the Areopagus: A Model of Cross-Cultural Evangelism." In *Mission in Acts: Ancient Narratives in Contemporary Context*, edited by Robert L. Gallagher and Paul Hertig, 221–38. Maryknoll, NY: Orbis, 2004.

Ludden, David E. "Introduction." In *Making India Hindu: Religion, Community, and the Politics of Democracy in India*, edited by David E. Ludden, 1–23. Delhi: Oxford University Press, 1997.

Marriott, McKim. "Little Communities in an Indigenous Civilization." In *Village India: Studies in the Little Community*, edited by McKim Marriott, 171–222. Chicago: University of Chicago Press, 1955.

Marshall, Howard I. "How Does One Write on the Theology of Acts." In *Witness to the Gospel: The Theology of Acts*, edited by I. Howard Marshall and David Peterson, 3–16. Grand Rapids: Eerdmans, 1998.

McGavran, Donald Anderson. *Understanding Church Growth*. 3rd ed. Grand Rapids: Eerdmans, 1990.

McKnight, Edgar V. "Reader-Response Criticism." In *To Each Its Own Meaning*, edited by Steven L. McKenzie and Stephen R. Haynes, 230–52. Louisville, KY: Westminster John Knox, 1999.

Mesny, Anne. "A View on Bourdieu's Legacy: Sens Pratique V. Hysteresis." *Canadian Journal of Sociology* 27, no. 1 (2002) 59–67.

Newbigin, Lesslie. "The Finality of Christ." In *The Lyman Beecher Lectures, Yale University Divinity School*, edited by Lesslie Newbigin. London: SCM, 1966.

———. "Review of Salvation and Humanisation." *Religion and Society* 18, no. 1 (1971) 71–80.

O'Mahoney, Joe. "Constructing *Habitus*: The Negotiation of Moral Encounters at Telekom." *Work, Employment and Society* 21, no. 3 (2007) 479–96.

Oberoi, Harjot. *The Construction of Religious Boundaries: Culture, Identity and Diversity in the Sikh Tradition*. Chicago: University of Chicago Press, 1994.

Pernau, Margrit. "Multiple Identities and Communities: Re-Contextualizing Religion." In *Religious Pluralism in South Asia and Europe*, edited by Jamal Malik and Helmut Reifeld, 147–69. New Delhi: Oxford, 2005.

Peterson, David. "The Worship of the New Community." In *Witness to the Gospel: The Theology of Acts*, edited by I. Howard Marshall and David Peterson, 373–95. Grand Rapids: Eerdmans, 1998.

Philip, T. M. "A History of Baptismal Practices and Theologies." In *Debate on Mission*, edited by Herbert Hoefer, 315–22. Chennai, India: Gurukul Lutheran Theological College and Research Institute, 1979.

Pickett, J.W. *Christian Mass Movements in India*. New York: Abingdon, 1933.

Polhill, John B. *Acts*, New American Commentary. Nashville, TN: B&H, 1992.

Polkinghorne, Donald E. "Narrative Configuration in Qualitative Analysis." In *Life History and Narrative*, edited by J.A. Hatch and R. Wisniewski, 5–24. Bristol, PA: Falmer, 1995.

Raj, Solomon. *A Christian Folk-Religion in India. A Study of the Small Church Movements in Andhra Pradesh, with a Special Reference to the Bible Mission of M. Devadas*. Bangalore: Centre for Contemporary Christianity, 2004.

Rajashekar, J. Paul. "The Question of Unbaptized Believers in the History of Mission in India." In *Debate on Mission*, edited by Herbert Hoefer, 323–41. Chennai, India: Gurukul Lutheran Theological College and Research Institute, 1979.

Rao, Kalagara Subba. *Retreat, Padri!* Machilipatnam, India: n.p., 1958.

Rapske, Brian. "Opposition to the Plan of God and Persecution." In *Witness to the Gospel: The Theology of Acts*, edited by I. Howard Marshall and David Peterson, 235–56. Grand Rapids: Eerdmans, 1998.

Redfield, Robert. *Peasant Society and Culture*. Chicago: The University of Chicago Press, 1956.

Reeves, Keith H. "The Ethiopian Eunuch: A Key Transition Form Hellenist to Gentile Mission." In *Mission in Acts: Ancient Narratives in Contemporary Context*, edited by Robert L. Gallagher and Paul Hertig, 114–22. Maryknoll, NY: Orbis, 2004.

"Rethinking Forum Purpose." No pages. Online: http://www.rethinkingforum.com/rf/.

Richard, H. L. "Community Dynamics in India and the Praxis of 'Church.'" *International Journal of Frontier Missiology* 24, no. 4 (2007) 185–94.

———. *Exploring the Depths of the Mystery of Christ: K. Subba Rao's Eclectic Praxis of Hindu Discipleship to Jesus*. Bangalore: Centre for Contemporary Christianity, 2005.

———. *Following Jesus in the Hindu Context: The Intriguing Implications of N. V. Tilak's Life and Thought*. Pasadena, CA: William Carey Library, 1998.

———. *Hinduism: A Brief Look at Theology, History, Scriptures, and Social System with Comments on the Gospel in India*. Pasadena, CA: William Carey Library, 2007.

———. "Correspondence," June 20, 2011.

———. "Religious Movements in Hindu Social Contexts: A Study of Paradigms for Contextual "Church" Development." *International Journal of Frontier Missiology* 24, no. 3 (2007) 139–45.

———. "A Response to Timothy C. Tennent." *International Journal of Frontier Missiology* 24, no. 4 (2007) 196–97.

Richard, L. C. *The Theology of Dr. Savarirayan Jesudasan*. Madras: CLS, 1989.

Riessman, Catherine Kohler. *Narrative Analysis*. Edited by Catherine Kohler Riessman. Newbury Park, CA: Sage, 1993.

Riggins, Stephen Harold. "The Rhetoric of Othering." In *The Language and Politics of Exclusion*, edited by Stephen Harold Riggins, 1–30. Thousand Oaks, CA: Sage, 1997.

Riley, Sarah C.E., Wendy Sims-Schouten, and Carla Willig. "Critical Realism in Discourse Analysis: A Presentation of a Systematic Method of Analysis Using Women's Talk of Motherhood, Childcare and Female Employment as an Example." *Theory and Psychology* 17, no. 1 (2007) 101–24.

Robinson, Anthony B., and Robert W. Wall. *Called to Be Church: The Book of Acts for a New Day*. Grand Rapids: Eerdmans, 2006.

Robinson, Rowena. "Introduction." In *Sociology of Religion in India*, edited by Rowena Robinson, 15–33. New Delhi: Sage, 2004.

Rosner, Brian S. "The Progress of the Word." In *Witness to the Gospel: The Theology of Acts*, edited by I. Howard Marshall and David Peterson, 215–33. Grand Rapids: Eerdmans, 1998.

"Sat Sri Akal." No pages. Online: http://www.sikhiwiki.org/index.php/Sat_Sri_Akal.

Sayer, Andrew. *Method in Social Science: A Realist Approach*. 2nd ed. New York: Routledge, 1992.

Sayer, R. Andrew. *Realism and Social Science*. Thousand Oaks, CA: Sage, 2000.

Seccombe, David. "The New People of God." In *Witness to the Gospel: The Theology of Acts*, edited by I. Howard Marshall and David Peterson, 349–72. Grand Rapids: Eerdmans, 1998.

Selvanayagam, Israel. "Waters of Life and Indian Cups: Protestant Attempts at Theologizing in India." In *Christian Theology in Asia*, edited by Sebastian C.H. Kim, 41–70. Cambridge: Cambridge University Press, 2008.

Shaw, R. Daniel. "Beyond Contextualization: Toward a Twenty-First-Century Model for Enabling Mission." *International Bulletin of Missionary Research* 34, no. 4 (2010) 208–15.

Singer, Milton. *When a Great Tradition Modernizes: An Anthropological Approach to Indian Civilizations.* New York: Praeger, 1972.

Singh, Yogendra. *Modernization of Indian Tradition.* New Delhi: Rawat, 1996.

Smith, James K. A. *Thinking in Tongues: Pentecostal Contributions to Christian Philosophy.* Grand Rapids: Eerdmans, 2010.

Snyder, C. Arnold. *From Anabaptist Seed: The Historical Core of Anabaptist-Related Identity.* Kitchener, ON: Pandora, 1999.

Spradley, James P. *The Ethnographic Interview.* New York: Holt, Rinehart and Winston, 1979.

———. *Participant Observation.* San Diego: Harcourt Brace, 1980.

Srinivas, M. N. *The Remembered Village.* Berkeley: University of California Press, 1976.

Staffner, Hans. *Jesus Christ and the Hindu Community: Is a Synthesis of Hinduism and Christianity Possible?* Anand, India: Gujarat Sahitya Prakash, 1988.

Strong, David K. "The Jerusalem Council: Some Implications for Contextualization." In *Mission in Acts: Ancient Narratives in Contemporary Context,* edited by Robert L. Gallagher and Paul Hertig, 196–208. Maryknoll, NY: Orbis, 2004.

Swidler, Ann. "Culture in Action: Symbols and Strategies." *American Sociological Review* 51, no. Apr (1986) 273–86.

———. *Talk of Love: How Culture Matters.* Chicago: University of Chicago Press, 2001.

Tennent, Timothy. *Building Christianity on Indian Foundations: The Legacy of Brahmabāndhav Upādhyāy.* New Delhi: ISPCK, 2000.

———. "The Challenge of Churchless Christianity: An Evangelical Assessment." *International Bulletin of Missionary Research* 29, no. 4 (2005) 171–77.

———. "A Response to H. L. Richard's Community Dynamics and the Praxis of 'Church.'" *International Journal of Frontier Missiology* 24, no. 4 (2007) 195–96.

Thomas, M. M. *Salvation and Humanisation: Some Crucial Issues of the Theology of Mission in Contemporary India.* Madras: Christian Institute for the Study of Religion and Society, 1971.

———. *Some Theological Dialogues.* Madras: Christian Institute for the Study of Religion and Society, 1977.

Thomas, M. M., Lesslie Newbigin, and Alfred C. Krass. "Baptism, the Church, and Koinonia: Three Letters and a Comment." *Religion and Society* 19, no. 1 (1972) 69–90.

Thompson, Richard P. *Keeping the Church in Its Place: The Church as Narrative Character in the Book of Acts.* New York: T&T Clark, 2006.

Tippett, Alan R. *Church Growth and the Word of God.* Grand Rapids: Eerdmans, 1970.

———. *Introduction to Missiology.* Pasadena, CA: William Carey Library, 1987.

Toews, John E. "Be Merciful as God Is Merciful." In *The Power of the Lamb,* edited by John E. Toews and Gordon Nickel, 17–24. Hillsboro, KS: Kindred, 1986.

Trigg, Jonathan D. *Baptism in the Theology of Martin Luther.* Leiden: Brill, 1994.

Turner, Harold W. "Religious Movements in Primal (or Tribal) Societies." *Mission Focus* 9, no. 3 (1981) 45–55.

Turner, Max. "The 'Spirit of Prophecy' as the Power of Israel's Restoration and Witness." In *Witness to the Gospel: The Theology of Acts,* edited by I. Howard Marshall and David Peterson, 327–48. Grand Rapids: Eerdmans, 1998.

Turner, Victor. *Dramas, Fields, and Metaphors: Symbolic Action in Human Society.* Ithaca: Cornell University Press, 1994.

———. *The Forest of Symbols. Aspects of Ndembu Ritual.* New York: Cornell University Press, 1967.

———. *The Ritual Process.* New York: Walter de Gruyter, 1995.

Twelftree, Graham H. *People of the Spirit: Exploring Luke's View of the Church.* Grand Rapids: Baker Academic, 2009.

Tyson, Joseph B. *Images of Judaism in Luke-Acts.* Columbia, SC: University of South Carolina Press, 1992.

Upadhyay, B. "Conversion of India—an Appeal." *Sophia* 1, no. 10 (1894).

Van Engen, Charles E. "Peter's Conversion: A Culinary Disaster Launches the Gentile Mission." In *Mission in Acts: Ancient Narratives in Contemporary Context*, edited by Robert L. Gallagher and Paul Hertig, 133–43. Maryknoll, NY: Orbis, 2004.

Wallace, Anthony F. C. *Religion: An Anthropological View.* New York: Random House, 1966.

———. "Revitalization Movements." *American Anthropologist* 58 (1956) 264–81.

Walls, Andrew F. *The Missionary Movement in Christian History: Studies in the Transmision of Faith.* Maryknoll, NY: Orbis, 1996.

Webster, John C.B. *A Social History of Christianity: North-West India since 1800.* New Delhi: Oxford, 2007.

Wells, Jo Bailey. *God's Holy People.* Sheffield: Sheffield Academic Press, 2000.

Wilfred, Felix. *Beyond Settled Foundations: The Journey of Indian Theology.* Madras: University of Madras, 1993.

Williams, Simon J. "Theorising Class, Health and Lifestyles: Can Bourdieu Help Us?" *Sociology of Health and Illness* 17, no. 5 (1995) 577–604.

Witherington, Ben, III. *The Acts of the Apostles: A Socio-Rhetorical Commentary.* Grand Rapids: Eerdmans, 1998.

Index

Acts
  and demonic/evil power, 223–25, 238
  ecclesial identity. *See* ecclesial identity: and book of Acts
  and the marginalized, 219–20
  proclamation witness, 229–32
  service witness, 232–33
  speeches and speech practices. *See* speech practices: in book of Acts
  structure of, 199–200
  and unjust structures, 225–26
Adams, Matthew, 33
Ambedkar, B. R., 88, 125, 168
Analytical Dualism, 35–38, 73, 154, 241, 244–45
Archer, Margaret, 31–33, 35–41, 58, 60–62, 75–78, 97, 101, 135, 161, 164, 167, 173, 243–45
  and Analytical Dualism. *See* Analytical Dualism
  and Critical Realism. *See* Critical Realism
  and morphogenesis. *See* Morphogenetic Process
  and the "myth of cultural integration," 36
  emotions, 75–76
Arya Samaj, 59n23, 60–61, 259
Arya Samaji *Yeshu satsang*, 53–54, 103, 117, 124, 125, 143, 144, 147, 155–56, 158, 187, 189n46, 248

Bago, Kaj, 11–12, 11n23
bhajans, 74, 98, 272–74, 275

and affect, 75–76, 147
  in *Yeshu satsangs*, 74–79, 81, 96n60, 98, 105–6, 124, 125, 130, 147, 153, 185
bhakti
  Hindu/Sikh, 28, 74, 87, 89, movements, 20, 29, 90, 125, 155, 180, 228
  of *Yeshu satsangs,* 51–53, 99, 124, 137, 143, 146–48, 194, 200, 202, 213–16, 234, 236–38, 241, 247, 248, 249, 254, 258–60, 272, 275
Bhaskar, Roy, 161–62
bindi, 124, 143, 144, 148, 184–85, 275.
Bourdieu, Pierre, 32, 33n6, 37, 76n8,
  and *habitus*. *See habitus*

Christian ashrams, 10n19, 21
Christian baptism, 12
  See also under Yeshu satsangs
Christianity in northwest India
  Attitude towards *prasad*, 120–21, 128
  Dalit identity of, 64–66, 92, 194
  and "demonic"/evil power, 102–3, 115, 143–44, 222
  history of, 58–69
  foreign legacy, 58–64, 128
  Pentecostal, 66–69, 128
  persecution, 151
  rules for behavior, 128, 144
competitive contradictions, 40, 61, 65
  and Jewish identity in Acts, 205–6
  and northwest Indian Christianity, 61–68

289